THE BOY IN THE WINDOW

A journey through an unexpected tragedy

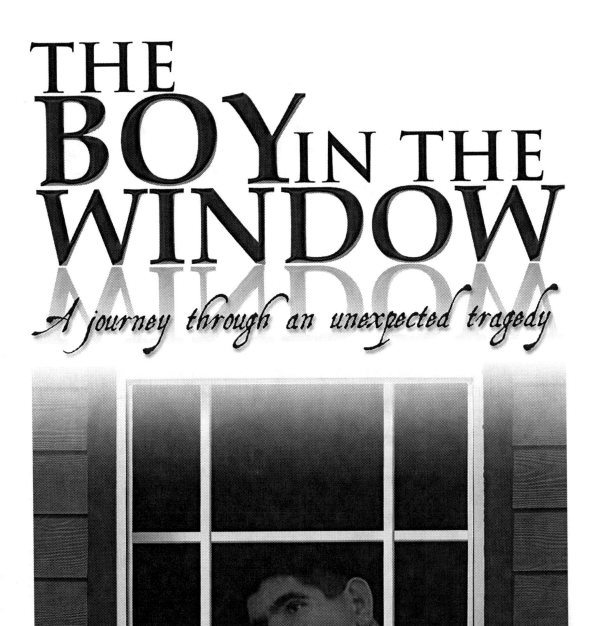

BARBARA COPPO

New York

THE BOY IN THE WINDOW

By Barbara Coppo

© 2007 All rights reserved.

ISBN: 978-1-60037-265-0 (Paperback)
ISBN: 978-1-60037-266-7 (Hardcover)

Published by:

www.morganjamespublishing.com

Morgan James Publishing, LLC
1225 Franklin Ave. Suite 325
Garden City, NY 11530-1693
800.485.4943
www.MorganJamesPublishing.com

Habitat for Humanity®
Peninsula
Building Partner

Cover & Interior Design by:

Megan Johnson
Johnson2Design
www.Johnson2Design.com
megan@Johnson2Design.com

Kenny in Window Photo by:

Audrey Usher-Alvarez
Fantazma41@yahoo.com

DEDICATION

This book is dedicated to my children and grandchildren...

To Kenny:

You have probably suffered more in your life than anyone will ever really know.
Many times you have been more courageous than I.
You are loved more than you can comprehend.

To Rhonda Baldi:

You have always been loved and never forgotten

To Jake and Mike:

You beautiful boys are my sunshine, and the loves of my life.
You give me such joy every time I see you. I love you both so much.
Someday, when you are old enough to understand, I hope you will read this book about your Uncle Kenny.

THE BOY IN THE WINDOW

the boy in the window

ACKNOWLEDGMENTS

To my husband Ken: You fought the battles for Kenny and got him into the programs I thought were best for him at the time. You have always been a hardworking man and a devoted father to both of your children. It takes great strength to live our difficult lives, and a weaker man would have walked away.

To Mary Benitez: You came into our lives and treated Kenny as your own. You and your husband Cesar have included Kenny in all of your family celebrations, and have expanded his world in doing so. You managed him at times when no one else could. You have given me comfort in all these things, and Ken and I are able to have some freedom because of you.

To my sister Nancy Razes, and my brothers Frank Jereb and John Henderson: I can't imagine my life without you Nancy, and your great sense of humor. Frank, you are the most understanding and compassionate man I know. John, you give the best advice, and Rita (John's wife), thanks for encouraging me to just keep writing. I love you all.

To my friend Diana Haney: You gave me strength in my darkest hours, and a shoulder to cry on. Throughout the years, we have both laughed and cried together many times. Thank you for being the most wonderful friend. I love you.

To Keith and Jeanne Douglas: What would Ken and I have done without your friendship, love and support? You both have been the brightest lights in our world. Your words of praise, as Kenny's parents, encouraged us, and the laughter and humor the four of us have shared when that was all we had left, sustained us. Thank you for always being there. We love you.

To George and Linda Coppo: Thank you for the wonderful sanctuary you provide when Ken and I have a chance to get away. You are both such a comfort to us. George, you have been so good for Ken, more than you know.

To all of the teachers and school aides who really did care for Kenny, and worked so diligently with him, I thank you. To all of Kenny's favorite respite girls from the past, and who did great work with him; **Kim, Malia, Vicky, Heather, and Rhonda B.** (who passed away) thank you, thank you, from the bottom of my heart!

To Mike Ursini from the North Bay Regional Center: Thank you Mike for always doing your best for Kenny and us! We appreciate you so much.

In loving memory of my mother, **Lou B. Jereb**, who will be in my heart always, my father **Frank Jereb**, my husband's parents, **George and Alba Coppo**, who will be remembered as loving grandparents, and to my nephew, **Johnny Razes**, who died way too young. I love all of you so much and I know you are in a better place.

PROLOGUE

The naked young man appeared at the top of the stairway and started shaking the banister forcefully.

The unsuspecting delivery men carrying a heavy dresser I had purchased were half way up the stairs. They stopped dead in their tracks at the bizarre sight, almost dropping the heavy load in their disbelief.

I reassured them of their safety and quickly gave my sincere apologies. Though the brave Hispanic duo nodded and smiled, I don't think they could speak or understand English very well, so I didn't try to explain the odd behavior they were witnessing.

They slowly ascended toward their destination, the room to the left and unfortunately, past the raving obstacle who was none other than my son! The men placed the new dresser in position and hastily fled the premises.

To Kenny, these men had intruded upon his domain and interrupted his evening regime, which did not leave room for visitors of any stature. Therefore, antagonistically, he stripped off his clothes and became Mr. Hyde.

Mr. Hyde is a very familiar character around here and likes to show a little muscle to intimidate, (not that he has any because he is just a six foot toothpick with hair), but there is strength beyond his own recognition.

We recently replaced the wood banister with wrought iron after it finally collapsed from too many shakings. Harboring Mr. Hyde is a very costly commodity.

Kenny had returned to his window seat to make sure the men and their truck had indeed departed.

The only visible sign left of his tantrum were the piles of clean laundry he had thrown over the open balcony.

One would think he had been in the middle of solving some world crisis to become as upset as he did. However, he was merely sitting and staring out of his favorite window that overlooks the neighborhood.

While it's true that Kenny's behaviors have been, more often than not, impossible to deal with, causing unbelievable stress, worry, anxiety, and pushing us way past our limits as parents at times, there is a part of him that is magnificent, brilliant and lovable in spite of his brain damage. He wasn't born this way and he didn't ask for the tragedy that created this preposterous lifestyle that the three of us have engaged in for some 28 years. But all he has to do is smile that infectious smile of his and nothing in the world is more beautiful to me.

Often, as I have driven up to our two story house that looks like many other homes on our court, I catch a glimpse of his shadowy figure peering out of the upstairs window and I start to wave, but he has shrunk back out of view, not wanting to acknowledge me.

The movie, *Psycho* comes to mind like the apparition in the Bates Motel window that disappears when you drive by, wondering what or who it could be. I laugh to myself and though it is no laughing matter, I know exactly who the occupant upstairs is, and I know he likes to think he is "invisible" while he focuses on his private thoughts and the comings and goings of the neighborhood, his own personal television.

I glance around at the surrounding homes, and ponder the normalcy and freedom of the families who live there, before I enter my unusual world that can feel as confining as Alcatraz at times.

It would be hard for most to imagine or even begin to fathom what goes on at 251 Devonshire Ct., Vallejo, Ca. And tucked away in my mind with fragile remembrance, is that horrible day when it all began, and changed our lives forever.

I'm not writing this book to gain therapeutic value for myself as some have surmised to be the reason, because having to go back and relive painful experiences while existing ones still monopolize our lives today, only makes me feel more exhausted.

But what this book is about, above all else, is love, tremendous hardships and the determination to unlock and unravel the mysteries of the "Boy in the Window."

TABLE OF CONTENTS

CHAPTER
ONE

THE BOY IN THE WINDOW

the boy in the window

I woke up one morning when I was 35 years old and had a very peculiar taste in my mouth that was disturbingly familiar. I flashed back to that very same taste about 15 years before when I had become pregnant with my only daughter, Rhonda. *Oh my God, could I be pregnant?*

It seemed like an eternity ago, not 15 years. I thought about how young my husband and I were when we got married. I was 19 and he was 21. I had studied cosmetology in my senior year and got a job as a hair stylist right after high school.

But my heart wasn't in my work because what I really wanted was my own baby girl. My best friend had her baby before she graduated and I could hardly wait to be married and start a family. Although Ken thought we should wait a little longer before we tied the knot, I put the pressure on him and got my way. Besides, when we first met at an after school social and although I was only 16, he told his friends that I was the girl for him.

He had a good job and worked at Mare Island Naval Shipyard where his father and grandfather both worked all their lives. I thought *why should we wait?* Both of us knew eventually we would say our "I do's."

A year later I had my baby girl. Rhonda was everything I imagined she would be and more, so much more. She was darling with the same light olive complexion like her dad, soft brown curly hair, big brown eyes and a perfect little face. I knew she would grow up to be a beauty and she did. I loved and adored her and my life revolved completely around her.

She was so smart and said her first word at seven months and then there was no stopping her. By the time she was 18 months old she could say the alphabet and sing along with the Beatles. She entertained my mom and me many an evening while Ken was at the golf course. My mother enjoyed being at our house and loved Rhonda.

She was the first baby girl in the family, though my sister Nancy had two darling boys, Johnny and Nickie. I was very close with my family and loved playing second mommy to my nephews.

Because Rhonda was so adored by my mom and sister, it made me love her even more.

When she was about four years old, I wanted to make a little spending money of my own and decided on a part time job at Sears. It was just a few days a week and I knew Rhonda would be in loving hands with my sister. Although, financially, we were getting ahead through Ken's dedication to his job and hard work, I felt the need to meet people and stimulate my mind. I enjoyed fashion and looked forward to buying clothes with my own money.

Although I knew Ken loved me, there was always some sport he was engaged in and it consumed him, making me feel so unimportant in his life. I thought having an outlet of my own would fill that emptiness. Neither of us knew how to set goals together as a husband and wife should and instead of growing closer we were growing apart. I nagged about our issues out of frustration, because he didn't want to discuss them. Soon, the years were just going by and my life had long surpassed the girlish dreams I had while watching the movie A Summer Place with Sandra Dee, my idol.

And now, after all of these years, there was a possibility I might be pregnant. I wanted to find out right away instead of waiting to get in to see the doctor at Kaiser, so I called Geri. She was my brother's wife and worked at a local hospital and assisted in the lab. I asked her if she could do the rabbit test on me to see if what I suspected might be true. The test came back positive. I was so shocked and bewildered she suggested we run the test again to be sure. There was indeed a baby on the way and I felt myself reeling from the excitement and of the unexpected results.

I wanted to feel joyous and after my doctor confirmed the pregnancy, a part of me did. But aside from everything else I had been thinking about, my mother had just died a few weeks ago, on June 9th 1977. It was hard to except the reality of both life-changing events. Although my mom had been very sick for a long time and I tried to prepare myself for her death, I never imagined how much pain and sorrow I would feel in my loss and I was in mourning. She was such a big part of my life and now she was gone, and I was going to have a baby.

Eventually, I tried to see the loss of my mother and my pregnancy as a loved one taken and another one given. Through my tears I learned to see the beauty in that.

As the reality of my new condition began to sink in, I bombarded myself with questions. I started pondering everything. *Would I have to give up my career in Real Estate that was fulfilling my sense of self worth?* I studied long and hard to obtain my license and it seemed as if I had found my niche. I felt I had finally accomplished a personal challenging goal and I was proud of myself and the person I had become.

It was a perfect time to not have a baby. My daughter was busy with her social life as teenagers are and Ken was now into racing motorcycles at a dirt bike track every chance he got. So I had plenty of time to devote to my job without the pressure of feeling guilty. Ken and I were barely communicating and when we did, it was through unkind words. Yet, strangely enough, about seven years before, during one of those rare times when we actually agreed on something, we talked about having another child. Eventually, after not conceiving, we gave it up as a lost cause.

And then while studying for my Realtor's license at Anthony's School, I met a very intense young woman named Diana, and we became good friends. From the beginning, I found I could make her laugh and enjoyed doing so.

We went to work at the same office and when she had floor duty the phone would ring off the walls. But when it was my turn the phones were silent and we laughed about that. I had to make cold calls while trying to keep a straight face because we sat across from each other. Those calls helped teach me assertiveness, something I always felt I was lacking. I loved the challenges of my job and my wonderful friend who eventually became one of Vallejo's top selling agents.

Now, I was going to have a baby and my emotions were on a roller coaster ride, experiencing the highs of a new member in the family and the lows of sacrifices that would have to be made. I was healthy and fit and could certainly manage a baby, but I couldn't handle it with the self destructive relationship Ken and I were in. I would need his full support and we would have to work on breaking the pattern of our past and become united for our future.

Rhonda had always wanted a brother or sister growing up, but now she was a teenager in high school and might possibly feel some embarrassment with my pregnancy because of her age. But I still felt she would be overjoyed and excited.

If we were to have this baby there would have to be some serious discussions between the three of us. What was I saying, "If we were to have this baby?"

Yes, I knew this was an era of pro choice and abortion could have been an option if we were not in agreement. But in my heart, I knew before the three of us had our talk, I wanted this child no matter what. The outcome of our decision was indeed unanimous.

Rhonda was exuberant and Ken promised to change, become more involved with his family and put a leash on his short temper. We all agreed that a new baby would give us a fresh new outlook.

So with a renewed sense of hope, I began to make plans for our baby and began to feel the joy of a new life growing inside of me.

I began to visualize myself with a baby and a career too. I thought I could work part time in real estate once the baby was older and work out of my home as much as possible, phone calls, paper work, etc. I have always been energetic and eager and I would just pursue both wholeheartedly. Yes, I had it all figured out and behold, the best laid plans of "mice and man" hath begun.

As with any pregnancy, a mother has all of the nagging little fears. Mine were mostly about childbirth itself. I remembered it was anything but a picnic and I wasn't looking forward to labor and delivery. But I also remembered how much I loved being a new mom when Rhonda was born. Even though I was so young, I loved everything about caring for her from sterilizing bottles of formula to washing diapers. I cherished every moment from infancy to toddler. I still have the first picture she drew in kindergarten.

I remember feeling an overwhelming love for her to the point of aching and the thought that I would die if anything were to harm her. She was my life, my own little baby girl. And now, 16 years later, I would finally be bringing her home a brother or sister to love.

During these next nine months, Ken and I grew closer than we had ever been in our entire marriage. He was softer and more considerate of my feelings. We attended the natural childbirth classes together and I believe he actually started forming a bond with our baby then.

I was determined not to have any drugs during labor or delivery and he was to "coach" me through the ordeal. Even though I secretly hoped for another girl, I thought about all of the many adventurous sports Ken would enjoy teaching and sharing with a son. He plays golf, is a deer and duck hunter, loves to go dirt bike riding on his motorcycle, and river rafts on white water and excels at each. He is also a very intelligent man and can discuss any topic with worldly knowledge. He could be the ideal father to a boy.

I was becoming eager to have this baby and waited in great anticipation. I felt wonderful and was able to work throughout my pregnancy. If my mother were here, it would have completed this special time in my life. I missed her so much. Staying busy really helped get me through my sorrow and I had continuous comfort from my friend Diana, even later as my world began to unravel.

CHAPTER TWO

THE BOY IN THE WINDOW

the boy in the window

The morning my water broke, our office was preparing to attend the weekly multiple listings, (preview of homes for sale) but they had to leave without me, and stopped by my house to wish me well before I left for the hospital. Our broker, Maurie Hair, a retired naval officer, was a man we all admired. Because of his professionalism, we had camaraderie with one another. We were not just associates working together, but friends as well. I was grateful for their support.

I tried not to think about the fear that wanted to envelope me on that day. I took deep breaths and tried to stay focused on all of the good that surrounded me. I now had a family that was communicating, a career I loved, and a baby close to being in my arms.

When Ken and I arrived at the hospital and my labor began, it was just as I had remembered. I yelled out in pain with each contraction, yet I relinquished any claim to the assorted drugs of choice that the doctor offered me to ease the misery of childbirth. I didn't want to risk anything that might cause the baby harm, so I wasn't about to give in to the pain.

Ken was by my side coaching me as each contraction wracked my body. I felt that his presence strengthened my spirit and kept me going throughout the long and painful process.

He kissed my forehead many times as I dug my nails into his arm during the pushing. In a very empathetic voice he told me he never wanted me to have to go through this again.

No worry there I thought. But I could feel the closeness we had achieved these last months and his comforting words meant so much to me. As the pain would ease between contractions, I thought about how much he had changed, what a good father he would be to our new child and how supportive he had become.

A surge of welcoming relief swept through my entire body when it was finally over and I heard my baby's first cry on the evening of Feb 1st 1978.

"It's a boy!" they said as they laid the tiny red bundle on my stomach. He turned his little face and looked right into my eyes as if to question what all the

9

fuss was about. He just kept staring right at me with his little fist in his mouth, hungry already. *Typical man* I thought.

My forehead wrinkled with worry as I asked the question every mother asks, "Is he okay?" The doctor reassured me, "Yes, he is perfect alert and beautiful." He rated high on the apgar scale, which is the means for measuring the condition of infants at birth. I smiled at the realization that every second of the pain I had endured had been worth it because I had delivered a perfect baby boy.

Ken stood by my side, staring down at his son. He was happy as he thought to himself, *here is my future hunting, motorcycle riding and rafting buddy that I've waited for all these months.* He was thrilled to have a boy, knowing he would have an active role in raising him.

In my exhausted state, I started wondering what it was going to be like having a son. I knew boys fell down a lot and got hurt and that they played baseball and other games that could be dangerous. I didn't want him to ever get hurt. Rhonda was so cautious when she was little, I don't remember her with scrapes or bruises. My mind was racing with fearful possibilities as I drifted off to sleep.

Later, when they brought him to me and I examined this precious little creation, I knew just how easy it was going to be to adore this miniature male as I felt the love genes stirring deep within my being.

I gazed into his curious dark brown eyes and I could see the reflection of my soul. I touched the soft golden brown curly hair that framed an angel's face. Except for an unexplained shiver that ran down my spine, I was joyous as I held my new son.

We brought him home from the hospital on the second day and Rhonda waited anxiously to receive her baby brother. She sat in the new maple rocker in his nursery and held him. I had painted the room a soft blue with creamy gold accents and put a border of wallpaper with little bears, trees and birds on it all around the room. His crib was dark maple with a matching dressing table. The bassinet had a beautiful gold and blue satin skirt that my sister made, with a wide trim and bow that matched the border. It was as royal looking as the little prince who would be sleeping in it.

Double glass sliding doors led out to a large shaded balcony safely enclosed with a wrought iron railing. It was going to be a great spot for Kenny to play. There was plenty of room for the three of us to sit in lounge chairs and watch our baby scooting around in a walker or toddling about surveying his new world.

Rhonda loved to rock him and I was so glad that after all of these years with no siblings, she finally had one to spoil and fuss over. He was a living doll to her and her friends as well.

Kenny was the center of attention and his first year of life was wonderful. Everyone who met him adored him. He ate well and slept sound. He was such a good baby with a great disposition. He was cute, chubby, cuddly and irresistible.

When Kenny was six months old his sister wanted to enter him into a local baby contest. She was so sweet with him and it was wonderful to see my daughter and son together. We mothers took turns on the stage parading our little darlings in diapers for audience approval through applause.

The judges gave points to the tiny contestants on their appearance, personality and response to the strange faces that were in theirs. Did they laugh, cry or were they indifferent? The tickets sold for the event went to charity. Of course, the amount sold per baby was helpful in determining the winner. My daughter and her little cousins, Bobbie Jo and Nancy, had been very busy selling tickets. Kenny won second prize out of 50 or 60 babies. To us he was the cutest baby of all!

Months were going by and Kenny was doing what babies do and adorable while doing it. His health was robust other than a few minor ear infections so common in baby boys. He was always in or surpassed the normal range of progress at his baby check ups.

At 18 months, he was a happy, healthy and curious toddler exploring his world with delight. Though he didn't have a vocabulary as early as his sister did, he said his first words before the average age. While giving him little licks from my ice cream cone at 10 months, he grabbed it out of my hand and said "more." Hey Mikey, he likes it!

I loved Kenny so much and was enjoying being a "new" mom again. Although it was a big adjustment in our lifestyle, he made it easy with his lovable demeanor.

Babies grow quickly and I was dreading the realization that it was time for his 18 months booster shots. He was almost 19 months old and I had been putting it off. His first injections had been in the months required, at two, four and six months old. I don't know why I had the apprehension, even though when he received his six month shot he had a large red swelling on his upper leg where the injection site was. It looked quite painful, but I was told that it was "normal." He also ran a temperature on and off for a few days and cried a lot, something he didn't do often. "It's to be expected." The nurse casually announced. "Just give him infant Tylenol."

Still, I just couldn't shake the foreboding. Later, I would be haunted by my inability to acknowledge the warning signs coming to me in the form of extrasensory perception, or better known as "a mother's intuition."

So, on September 6th, 1979, a day that would change all of our lives forever, I brushed aside my uneasiness and dutifully followed the tragically flawed guidelines set by the doctors to insure protection against childhood diseases, and took my baby for his last series of the d.p.t. vaccination.

I remember as if it were yesterday how beautiful Kenny looked to me on that sunny hot afternoon. What a sweet chubby little toddler he was with a complexion of olive cream, smooth and flawless, and big brown velvety eyes that could melt your heart. He was wearing his new tan colored short overalls with a brown and ivory stripe tee shirt underneath. How trusting and innocent he was as I pushed him in his stroller down the painfully long grey corridor into the injection clinic at Kaiser Hospital in Vallejo.

Never in my life could I have imagined that the baby I brought home with me that day was not the baby I had wheeled into Kaiser Hospital, nor would he ever be that baby again. He would not become the son by husband would take hunting, rafting or motorcycle riding or share in any of the typical things a father and son do together.

Moreover, I would never hear the words, "Mommy, look I drew you a picture in school today," or "I love you mommy."

The day after his vaccination, in the late afternoon, we were getting ready to visit Ken's parents. They loved to see Kenny and we saw them often. They were in their late 70s and it had been a long time since their last grandchild was a baby.

Kenny had just woken from a short nap and I was choosing between two outfits for him to wear. I decided on his yellow, tan and blue striped tee shirt with matching blue shorts. The colors accentuated his olive, tan skin. I loved buying cute little baby clothes for him. I smothered him in kisses and got him dressed.

I thought he seemed more quiet than usual. He wasn't readily responding to the word games we played, which he loved. I told him, "Kenny, say 'grandpa'." He would repeat in baby babble. I would clap and he would clap. However, on that day he just didn't seem interested or amused at all.

I sat him down on the floor to put on his little sandals. Suddenly, he fell backwards as if an invisible hand had pushed him. I yelled out to my husband who was getting ready in our bedroom. "Ken, something strange just happened! Come quickly!" I described what took place. He thought Kenny was just playing a game or acting silly. By that time, Kenny was smiling and seemed fine. I was still concerned, but Kenny was already toddling off to the door. So, we just got in the car and left.

About an hour and a half into our visit at his grandparent's house, I noticed Kenny stumble a bit. I was overcome by a terrible uneasiness and I didn't take my eyes off of him. He followed his grandpa into the kitchen with me right behind him and suddenly his legs buckled and he just collapsed onto the floor.

I screamed for my husband as I gathered him up in my arms. We got in the car and made a mad dash to the Kaiser emergency room that was just a few miles away. I was in a panicked daze. My baby who had always been healthy was now convulsing in my husband's arms as we rushed through the entrance of the hospital doors. Kenny's eyes were staring, but not seeing, and he was unresponsive.

We were whisked into a large examination room. Two doctors immediately took him from Ken and laid him on the table. They measured his vital signs while the questions flew at us. "What happened? Did he fall? Could he have ingested poison? Had he choked?"

Of course the answer was "no" to all of them. Then they asked us, "Was anything different in his routine the last few days?" "Yes!" I said, crying hysterically. "He had his d.p.t. vaccination yesterday."

There was no comment from the doctors. I stood helplessly watching my baby convulsing and nothing they were doing was helping. Continuing with the vital signs, one of the doctors told us that they must do a spinal tap, which is a very painful test, to rule out meningitis.

I was out of my mind with fear for my baby and I couldn't believe this was happening. I was crying hysterically while pacing back and forth. They didn't seem to know what was happening to him, which added to my panic. They made me leave the exam room before they did the spinal because I couldn't get a grip on myself. They said it wasn't good for my baby and that it would upset him if he could hear me.

Ken stayed in the room with Kenny and I remember other patients sitting out in the waiting room, wanting to console me. But I couldn't be consoled. "What is happening to my baby?" I cried out. I clung to the outside of the door that led to my son, trying to hear if he was crying. I wanted to barge in.

Grandpa said repeatedly, "Please God, don't take Kenny. Take me instead. I've lived my life and his has barely begun."

No one knew if this terrible "thing" Kenny was suffering from was life threatening.

My God, I thought, *he could die!* All I knew was if he was going to die, then I wanted to die too!

There are no words to describe what I was feeling or how afraid I was. I was overwhelmed with the ordeal and it took over my entire existence! I couldn't stand this unbearable suffering! I wanted to change places with anyone or anything in this awful place.

Suddenly, as if I were having an out of body experience, I was looking down and saw a crazy woman running up and down the long grim hallway screaming

"Please God, help my baby! Help my baby!" Unfortunately, that crazy woman was me!

I was begging God to save him and even though I hadn't spent much time in a church, I have always believed in Him and felt sorry I had never taken the time to really study the Bible. But from the beginning of Kenny's ordeal, I turned to God and prayer. Rarely has a day gone by that I haven't prayed for my son.

After what seemed like an eternity, but was perhaps a period of two hours, I tried to regain some composure after the doctor told me the tests were negative. He said there was no meningitis and they couldn't find anything pertinent to his convulsing and unresponsiveness.

By then Kenny, though exhausted and looking so pale and unsure of his surroundings, managed to smile at us. The doctor thought he had recovered enough to take him home. He said to keep him as quiet as possible, make him rest and watch him closely, as if someone would have to tell me that. He felt it may be just a "fluke" and to try not to worry. From that point on in my life, I became the best worrier you ever saw.

The next day, we were rushing Kenny back to Kaiser again as he started convulsing just like the day before. I felt like I was going to lose my mind with fear for my son.

Ken carried our baby through the emergency room doors once again and panic was evident in both of our faces. The doctors examined him, and it was obvious they were more than perplexed.

I was beside myself and wanted some answers from someone, anyone, but there was none to be had and much to my chagrin, they sent us home again with the doctor's words ringing in my ears as I cuddled my baby, "If he has a reoccurrence, we'll think about an anticonvulsant medication. This could be the start of epilepsy."

My God, I thought, *how could this be? Kenny is the epitome of a healthy robust toddler. There is no history of seizures on either side of our families. He never sustained a fall or injury of any magnitude and has never been sick. It just doesn't make any sense!*

We barely made it home and he started convulsing again. In a flash, we were driving back to Kaiser and we weren't going home until someone helped my baby. I was exhausted from lack of sleep and worry but I knew something terrible had happened to Kenny, and it wasn't a "fluke" as the doctor had said.

CHAPTER
THREE

THE BOY IN THE WINDOW

the boy in the window

We charged through the entry of Kaiser Hospital and Kenny was taken "stat" into the examination area and admitted immediately. The doctors took his vitals and reviewed his chart. They would not, or could not, come up with a diagnosis other than the possibility of epilepsy.

I never left his side for one moment. Later, I read in a report from Kenny's medical record that the nurse on duty during this time stated, "The mother was overreacting" along with a few other critical remarks. Yes, I'll admit, I had become a lunatic, watching my son convulsing, not knowing what was wrong with him. With each seizure, I would call out for a doctor, and I could be seen running down the hall to find one, determined to get him immediate care. I was suffering having to see Kenny go through this. I felt like I was dying over and over again.

The nurse was used to seeing sick babies or babies who were barely clinging to life. I was not. Kenny wasn't just any baby. He was my baby boy. I wasn't following her protocol of how a mother should behave in a hospital environment. Therefore, she felt I was "overreacting."

Too bad I didn't know what she had written then. I knew there were other sick babies in the ward, and there were other parents worrying and suffering too, but I don't remember them as I was wrapped up in my own grief. I didn't really care what anyone thought about my behavior, I just wanted my healthy, happy child back.

At night, the staff tried to get us to go home to sleep, but someone would have had to kill me to get me to leave my baby. I wasn't going anywhere. If he had to stay in the hospital then I would too, no matter how long it had to be.

Kenny looked so tiny in the large hospital crib. It seemed to swallow him up. And each time he fell asleep, the nurses would wake him when they checked his blood pressure, his heart and temperature. He was in and out of awareness, so exhausted from the seizures and whatever else was going on in his little body.

Kenny had nine seizures in all during the three days after his vaccination, including the two days he was hospitalized, when they started him on Phenobar-

17

bital. It was supposed to be a medication with the least side effects for babies to help control seizures.

As we were leaving the hospital on the last day, a doctor who had seen Kenny during this time, briefly confronted us and asked, "They told you Kenny's problem was from the vaccination he received didn't they?"

We shook our heads "No." He then rushed off without another word.

I thought to myself, *they didn't have to, because I had already come to that conclusion and now it had just been confirmed.* Through this whole ordeal, I felt that the doctors might be holding back information from us. I had a terrible inclination that we were going to have to fight to get answers.

Once we got home, Diana and her husband, Jimmy, who was a pastor, came to see us. They offered their much needed moral support as I was literally a basket case by that time. I felt exhausted from worry and no sleep and disillusioned in the doctors.

Diana held Kenny in her arms and gently patted his little back while she swayed back and forth to soothe him. They prayed for all of us and we were grateful. There was little more we could do at that time but love and pray for him. I felt so helpless and lost. I was his mother and supposed to protect him and I had failed him somehow.

My sister and brother came over as soon as they heard the news and tried to console me. My world had shattered before my eyes. There was nothing anyone could do to help.

Ken had to go back to work the next day. I feared being alone with Kenny, in case he started convulsing again. Rhonda had to go back to school. Everyone had to return to their daily lives, but I knew that our world would never be the same.

The following weeks were pure agony as I struggled to observe Kenny's every moment of the day and night. My weary, sleep deprived eyes searched for signs of seizures. His body struggled to adjust to the medication. He walked unsteadily and wobbly and when he fell, I was right behind him, so that I could catch him. He would get right back up and want to run like he used to, but he didn't have the coordination and would fall down.

I found myself unconsciously imitating each movement he made. If he teetered to one side, then I did too, thinking he would lose his balance. I'm sure it was a tragically funny sight. It became our own version of the Bunny Hop.

I barely slept and was exhausted as I tried to keep up with this easily agitated and unstoppable little man. He had now mastered getting around much more than he needed to, and seemed to be on a constant endless mission with no purpose. He would run to the stairs and climb them, run into a room and run back out and go down the stairs again. All with me right behind him.

Sometimes, he stopped long enough to pull toys out of his toy box and throw them, but not look at them. He ran through the kitchen opening cupboard doors and slamming them shut. I had to put locks on them. If any food or drinks had not been put away, he found them and emptied their contents on the floor. He was in a constant state of movement without direction and what seemed like no end in sight.

The doctor had said the medicine might make him drowsy, but it seemed to have the opposite effect. I would try holding and rocking him as I always had, but he no longer responded to my touch.

I would hold his face with both hands, look into his beautiful brown eyes and tell him how much I loved him. He didn't seem to want to be cuddled or held and I couldn't seem to get eye contact from him.

His smiles were not as bright and as time went by, I noticed his baby "talk" had diminished and there were only a few familiar utterances.

My eyes would well up and my tears would flow as the realization hit me that the little boy that I once knew as my son no longer existed.

Although the seizures had subsided, they seemed to be triggered with an illness or fever, which the doctor thought was a "good" sign as febrile seizures were somewhat common in small children. But I worried about the seizures and couldn't sleep at night. When I did, I learned to sleep with one eye open. Sometimes, I slept on the floor in his room, next to his crib or I would drag my tired body out of bed several times a night to reassure myself that he was okay, a habit that stayed with me. They didn't have baby monitors then.

As months went by, I was beginning to feel the medication might be holding Kenny back as he was not improving with time. He was constantly on the go and needed supervision every minute of the day. He was like a little wild animal leaving a path of destruction at every turn. I tried hard to teach him and interact with him in meaningful ways, but he couldn't seem to stay focused on one activity for any length of time.

Eye contact was almost impossible with him now, and when I picked him up to give him playful hugs and kisses, he only pushed me away. Though he could enjoy some things, it was only if it didn't require much effort from him. He could manage to stack large blocks, eventually, but was easily frustrated. He also became very obsessed with loud noises, the garbage truck, the vacuum and they sent him into an ecstatic frenzy. But usually, it was all of the naughty things he did that he enjoyed the most.

It didn't faze him in the least to rip off his messy diaper and throw it before I could change him. He loved to grab food off a table and play in it or smear it on the walls or carpet. I was continuously running after him with a wash cloth in one hand and a bottle of Mr. Clean for the walls in the other. With each "game" he thought up, it became a repetitious ritual with him.

One of his favorite pastimes was to stuff the toilet with anything he could get his hands on, and then flush it to watch it disappear. It could be makeup, toothpaste, clothes or whatever was in his reach at the moment. The number of times we had a backed up toilet and flooding was astronomical. We had our own personal plumber who discounted his visits as he felt sorry for us. Once, Kenny even tried to see if his teddy bear that was as big as he was would flush. Either that or he was trying to potty train it.

This had become my life now; coping with behaviors I couldn't control or understand. In spite of these devilish deeds, he was so darn cute and that was a good thing, because though he tried our patience every day, we couldn't get angry at him. I knew I should have named him "Damien," my first choice.

He was close to three now and it had been a while since his last seizure so we started discussing all of the pros and cons about weaning him off the seizure medication with the doctor. We were told there was a good chance he could outgrow the seizures as a lot of young children did, but there would be better seizure control by remaining on the medication if they were to return at a later time. I also had to weigh the fact that anti-convulsants can do major damage to a young growing body and I hated giving him this poison if there was a chance he wouldn't have more seizures.

I was just starting on the long journey of crucial decision making, not only about medications, but anything and everything regarding his welfare.

We decided to wean him off, with the doctor's supervision. I was so afraid that he would start convulsing again, but there was no other way to find out. I was so upset when he had another seizure and we put him back on the Phenobarbital for a year. We took him off again and didn't see any signs of seizures for at least a year, then, he had one with an illness. We rushed him back to the hospital. He had a high fever and the doctor said that brought on the seizure. The doctor thought we should put him back on the medicine, so we did. Then by 1982, he was weaned off again.

Although I didn't see a big difference in his behavior, he didn't seem quite as irritable and he looked as if he felt better, which made me feel better too.

As time passed, our lives quickly became engulfed in pandemonium as we tried so hard to comfort and communicate with Kenny in his fragmented world, while he led us down his manipulative path.

Everything we did was at a fast and furious pace and became as obsessive as his games. We had to take him for nightly drives in the car down the same streets in the same directions. Any deterrent created so much agitation in him that we just kept with the familiar routes and places. If we went to a park, it had to be the same park.

There still was no sign of new language. Yet, he did well getting what he wanted from us without any. On one of our regular follow up visits with his neurologist, he suggested getting a hearing test for Kenny to rule that out as a possible reason for his inability to talk.

So we made the appointment with the audiologist even though I didn't believe anything was wrong with his hearing. There wasn't and I wanted some answers from doctors, but couldn't get a straight one. Frustrated, worn out and filled with worry, we struggled through what should have been joyful years raising a normal, happy, healthy toddler but instead, we lived with the alternative that we came to know as Kenny.

I am eight months along. Ken and I can hardly wait to hold our new son!

Any day now, I am nine months, and doing my hair with Rhonda's help. She is so excited!

Rhonda is so proud of her baby brother!

Kenny took second place in a baby pageant at six months old.

Growing fast! Scooting around in his walker at eight months.

My happy little toddler.

Kenny is about 13 months and these are happy, easy times.

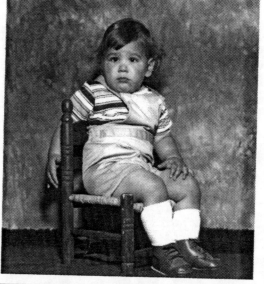

Fifteen months old.
Pouting for a picture.

23

THE BOY IN THE WINDOW
the boy in the window

CHAPTER FOUR

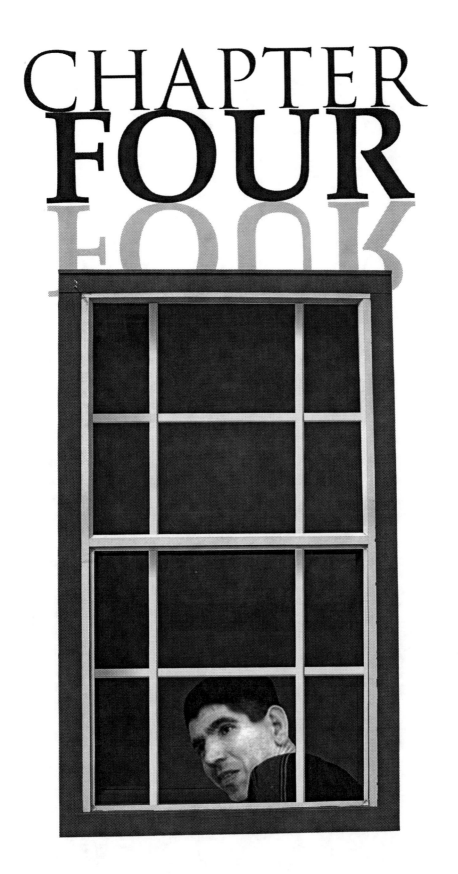

THE BOY IN THE WINDOW
the boy in the window

Someone I met told me about "special classes" for children with extreme behaviors. Instinctively, I visualized Kenny with a small group of classmates with a loving person taming his outbursts and excitability. I pondered that and was momentarily delighted until I exclaimed, "But he is only three years old!"

"Yes," she responded, "and the earlier the better to get control of his behaviors before they worsen."

Oh my God! I thought to myself, *they could worsen?* The very next day I called the school district for information. They told me a psychologist from the district had to come out first and evaluate Kenny in his home. They said it would take a few hours to observe him in his environment and it would be necessary to do assorted tests with him.

Although I felt uncomfortable having a stranger come into my home to assess Kenny, I realized I didn't have any other options. If a "special class" could help him catch up to his age level, then so be it. When the psychologist arrived and opened her suitcase full of colorful blocks, puzzles, shapes, beads and even some story books, I knew immediately he would be frustrated. They were all very similar to items I used every day in hopes of getting a positive response from him. And he definitely did not like her attaché case filled with paper work. It was as if he knew she would be there awhile taking up my time and his. She explained to me how she would utilize these things to extract the information she needed for her evaluation. She had a hard time getting Kenny to slow down before presenting her array of paraphernalia, but soon he became curious about the woman, not the toys. She tried hard to work with him and he displayed his usual lack of interest, but at times, I could see him trying, as if he wanted to please her.

Once he calmed down during the evaluation, I thought he was doing quite well, especially with the blocks. He stacked at least five big ones, more than I could get him to do. I couldn't tell what she was thinking. Her demeanor remained calm, no matter what Kenny did. She was very patient and gave Kenny every opportunity to achieve success no matter what the task was. I thought she felt he just needed extra coaxing to perform better and not a special class.

Although my husband and I knew Kenny was behind, and that his behavior was out of the ordinary, I didn't realize just how much in denial we were about Kenny, nor was I prepared when she confronted me with her shocking diagnosis upon completing her observation.

"Mrs. Coppo" she said, "Although your son is three years old, he is only functioning at about 15 to 19 months old and is retarded. I would highly recommend that he be enrolled immediately in a special education class."

That is how bluntly it was put to me. The statement that my son was retarded was so matter of fact and expressed without emotion from the psychologist. It was as if it were a common description of one's child you heard every day. Suddenly, all that I had known in my heart for months but couldn't admit to myself out loud was true. Kenny suffered not only the seizures from his 19 months old d.p.t. booster shot, but brain damage as well. *He had brain damage, seizures, and no, no, no he was not retarded, he wasn't!*

I broke down and cried my eyes out and through my tears asked this stranger in my home, "What did I do wrong? Was I being punished for all of the mistakes I had ever made in my life? Will he improve, get better? Will he be able to talk some day?" Of course, this woman had no answers for me. She quietly gathered up her things and left me alone with my agony.

I received a call from the school district about a week later. I was to take Kenny to view the classroom that they thought would be most appropriate for him. It was so hard to think of Kenny going to a school at his age and worse, he really wasn't his age.

On the day of our appointment, I told Kenny we were taking a drive to see some other children play all together in a room where everyone had lots of fun. I didn't know if he understood "school" or "class" and I didn't want to scare him. I was never sure of how much he was aware of. I didn't tell him until we were ready to leave that morning to avoid anxiety. I learned through the years that if you tell him something is going to take place, it better be now, not later or the next day.

I drove Kenny to Grant School in Vallejo which was located in an older, less desirable neighborhood in town. I held tightly to his little hand and knocked at the door to the classroom. We were greeted by a young and attractive teacher named Joan. The program's coordinator had spoken highly of her and said the class was one of the best for this age group.

Joan smiled down at Kenny and said, "What a handsome little boy you are." Kenny started tugging on me to leave, but she was able to coax him in and took his hand.

He looked back at me as he walked with her to be sure I was right there with him. I gave him a reassuring smile. While Joan was trying to get Kenny interested in some toys, I was taking in the distorted features and numerous disabilities of the other children in the room. Needless to say, I was in shock. My mouth was agape with horror and I wanted to turn around and run as fast as I could with Kenny. *He doesn't belong here!* I thought. *He is beautiful and smart and functioning much higher than any of these children.*

I took Kenny's hand and held it tightly as I said to Joan, "There has been a terrible mistake! Kenny would not fit in this program."

She could see I was visibly upset and an aide who had been with another child, approached Kenny as if on cue and diverted his attention playfully. Joan took me aside and asked if I would just stay a bit longer, just to see how Kenny might respond to the other children.

He seemed so curious and willingly went off with the aide, so I robotically agreed and followed Joan through the classroom. She explained to me about the different children and what they were doing in their program to help them.

As my initial shock subsided, I looked beyond the abnormalities and saw very positive factors. I saw how dedicated the teacher and the aides were and how they really seemed to care about the kids. Some of the children were coming up to me out of curiosity, but I felt myself shrink away from them. Perhaps I was afraid to acknowledge there could be some truth that Kenny might belong here as well.

I cried as I carried Kenny out of the room and to the car. I hugged and kissed him before I placed him in the car seat. I would be doing a lot of crying from now on it seemed.

I was asked to bring Kenny to class the next day and stay for awhile, until he felt at ease. Then I could wait in the play yard and come back in the room if he got to upset. Joan assured me that he would adjust as the other children had done. *I still haven't made up my mind*, I thought as she spoke. I continued to observe the classroom and was impressed with the supervision and how comfortable the children seemed while trying to do their tasks in spite of their handicaps.

After discussing everything about the school with my husband, we agreed to enroll him in Joan's class. Each day for a few weeks I would leave the room and be gone just a little longer than the time before. In the beginning, I heard him cry for me. Just when I thought I couldn't stand it another minute, I would peek in and see that the teacher had engaged him in something that made him focus, although I could see he was very distracted by the other children. Sometimes, I would watch him when he couldn't see me and it broke my heart to have to leave him, as if there were any pieces left to break.

After a few weeks, I saw he had made a new little friend, Billy, a Down's syndrome boy who was about four years old. He had latched on to Kenny. They

29

seemed to have some kind of comradeship going on and it made me feel better to think of Kenny able to have his own little friend. Although neither of the boys had language skills, they had their own way of communicating. Sometimes it was just a pat on the arm or they playfully tumbled over and over each other. Kenny seemed to enjoy his aides, the teacher and his new little buddy.

About a month later, I was told that Kenny should ride the bus to and from school. The teacher said the transitioning would be less emotional for him and it would further help with his independence.

I thought he was too young. *He is only three years old, how can I let my baby ride a school bus?* How hard this was for me, most parents don't have to let their little ones go until they're five or six years old when they begin kindergarten or pre-school at age four. Those children are able to talk, feed and dress themselves. Kenny was completely dependant on Ken and I and the thought of sending him off with a stranger was more than I could take. But once again, I reluctantly gave in for the welfare of my precious son.

The bus was arranged to pick Kenny up on the following week. The first day I rode with him and he loved it. Big and noisy! The next day, I fought back the tears and waved him off while smiling and acting silly for him as he peered out of the seat at me.

All I could see was the top of his brown curly hair and two little brown eyes peeking back at me through the bus window. There was no squinting of his eyes, so I knew he wasn't smiling, however he wasn't crying either, but I was.

Each year as he grew bigger and a bus came for him, I would little by little see more of his head through the bus window, until eventually it was his head and shoulders.

Now that I had a little more time to myself, I started making phone calls and going to the library, trying to find out about Kenny's condition. I researched seizure disorders by reading books about them and extremely hyperactive behaviors. I wanted to learn what effect seizures had on the body, even though he didn't seem to have them as often now, and he was off the medication. I also looked into special nutritional diets and supplements for him.

The doctor treating Kenny at the time suggested I take him to a specialist in neurology at Kaiser in San Francisco, so I made the appointment. Doctor appointments and tests were becoming a way of life for us, partly, because I was pursuing the professionals relentlessly for answers.

When this doctor was confronted with my son's opposing behaviors, he tried hard to abolish the look of astonishment on his face as he questioned me about Kenny.

By this time Kenny was rebellious about any visits to doctors or behaviorists and was always at his worst. It was so hard to hold him in restraining positions while talking about him to a professional. He kicked at us, screamed, scratched and whatever else he could think of. I told him, "My child has suffered brain damage. I'm sure it was from his last d.p.t. booster shot."

"No" he said, "That's impossible. There had to be something wrong with him before he got the vaccine." My husband immediately responded by telling the doctor, "Just the opposite was true. Kenny was the smartest, healthiest and most curious toddler before his vaccination."

He still admonished us. "You must have overlooked something." I then asked him, "Have you studied Kenny's medical records?" He answered, "Yes." So I said, "The tests they did on him showed no previous abnormalities. What else could it be?"

Remaining persistent to his theory, the doctor stated, "I think you and your husband should have your brain waves tested to find out if there might be any contributing factors to Kenny's condition."

That really got my dander up! "My son went into convulsions 24 hours after his vaccination and never had problems previous to that and now you want us to have brain scans? It sounds to me as if you want his problem to be anything but the obvious!"

His ideology only proved to me that Kaiser was trying to avoid a possible litigation because something terrible did happen to Kenny, and they knew it, and did not want to be held responsible. He further added insult to injury by stating, "You should think about institutionalization for Kenny. He will only be a burden to you both and will never get better. Trying to raise a child like this would be a living hell."

Although there was some truth in his last statement, we replied, "Kenny has a home and that it is with his mother and father. He is our son and we love him! Neither one of us would ever dream of placing him in an institution!" We left the hospital feeling more alone in our dilemma with Kenny and more determined to fight whatever battles that came our way to help our little boy.

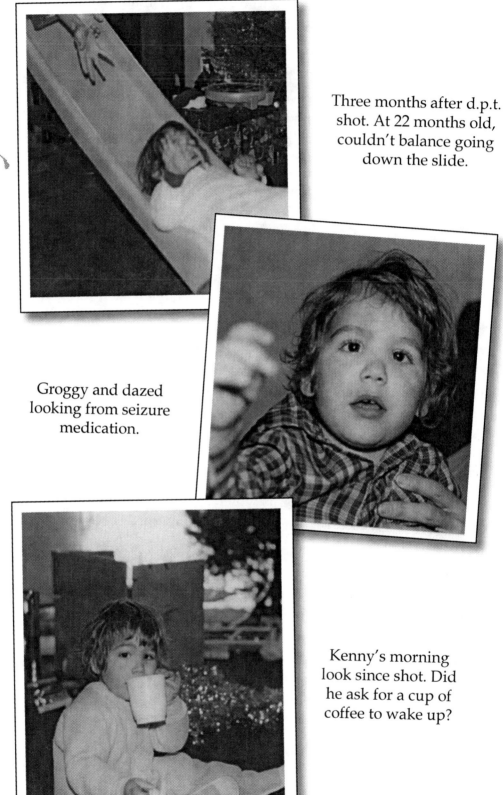

Three months after d.p.t. shot. At 22 months old, couldn't balance going down the slide.

Groggy and dazed looking from seizure medication.

Kenny's morning look since shot. Did he ask for a cup of coffee to wake up?

22 ½ months

Going to first special ed.
Class at three years old.

Kenny (left) and first
friend, Billy, at school.

Kenny in first
Special Olympics.
Kenny and I in
front (middle).

Trying to do Real
Estate calls at
home with Kenny
into everything.

CHAPTER FIVE

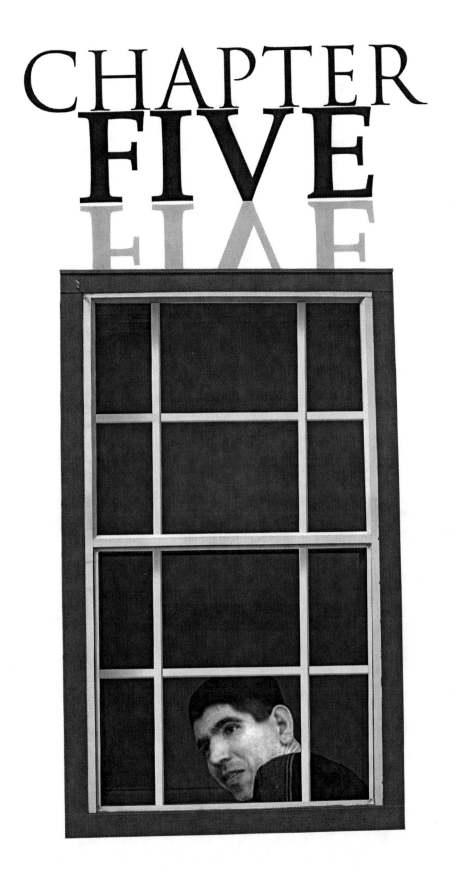

THE BOY IN THE WINDOW

*O*verall, Kenny seemed to be enjoying his environment at school. His energy was being channeled in a purposeful direction and I knew the teacher and aides were diligent with their newest challenge. I felt the socialization was helpful, but there were no major breakthroughs. His language still had not improved and no one, including the school's speech therapist, could tell me if he would ever talk.

For now, Ken and I could understand his baby babble enough to figure some things out that he wanted. The way he had manipulated our world into his regime was certainly a way of communicating. But I couldn't imagine my son having to go through life without normal conversational skills. I thought about times when he might be in pain and I wouldn't know. How would I know what he was thinking or feeling if he couldn't tell me? There were so many things to agonize over and I was always a step ahead of my worries.

I found out through the school district about the North Bay Regional Center and the different services available for behavior problems in children. I made an appointment with the psychologist at the Northern Solano Counseling Center in Fairfield referred by North Bay so they could evaluate Kenny. They would determine if we needed help. Fairfield is about thirty minutes away from Vallejo and a long ride for Kenny, especially when he isn't familiar with the scenery.

Upon entering the waiting room, Kenny was already in a state of high activity after the long ride. He was making it clear he didn't want to be there. He immediately began running around the coffee table in the waiting room and was jumping from one chair to the next. Attempting to restrain him only made him protest angrily. Luckily, we were put in a waiting room without other patients.

The psychologist asked my husband to wait in the outer office with Kenny so he could interview me. During that time, we could hear Kenny through the closed door, kicking and yelling. His voice sounded so distorted and primitive and seemed to explode through the building. I shuttered with despair and could not concentrate on the questions being asked of me.

The psychologist suggested we finish the interview later and for me to try to calm Kenny down and bring him back in the room so he could begin testing him. After a while Kenny settled down and my husband and I brought him to the psychologist where assorted toys and objects of interest were used to entice Kenny. Then he asked us to wait outside the room, which I thought was a brave request on his part. Reluctantly, we did, and I felt grief as I heard Kenny protesting. Through the closed door I could hear different musical sounds and bells and whistles and sometimes whining from Kenny.

Then for awhile I couldn't hear anything at all and I was feeling very apprehensive. My husband reminded me about the sound proof room the doctor mentioned so the noise wouldn't bother other patients. Soon they both appeared and I felt relieved.

The examiner told us he was able to coax Kenny into the sound proof area but was unable to test him. He said Kenny quickly resisted all attempts to get him interested in the toys and ran to the door. He also said Kenny stood at the door yelling for us and that he showed little coherence as to what was being asked of him as well as not seeming to understand any of the directions. He described his display of behavior with the likeness of a young, wild animal held in a cage. I was beginning to wonder if Kenny had been one in a previous life.

He kept talking through Kenny's tantrum and I listened as attentively as I could while still trying to console my little cub. He further stated, "It is quite obvious that both of you have tolerated a considerable amount of disruptive behavior from this youngster, as I was amazed at his tenacity and determination to leave the testing room. No matter what was presented to him, I just could not deter him." *Well*, I thought to myself, *what else is new?*

But this examiner was not giving up yet. He still wanted to try some other tests and Kenny was calming down due to exhaustion from his outbursts. This time I was left in the waiting room while my husband assisted with the Alpern-Boll Developmental Profile that Kenny, at four years old, ended up scoring approximately between 12 to 20 months. This was his physical, self-help, social and academic age. Other attempts at testing were without success. Through that short and quick profile of Kenny, he gave him an IQ equivalency of 33.

This was just the beginning of many more evaluations to come for Kenny and how he would be assessed on his aberrant behavior and non-compliance.

CHAPTER
SIX

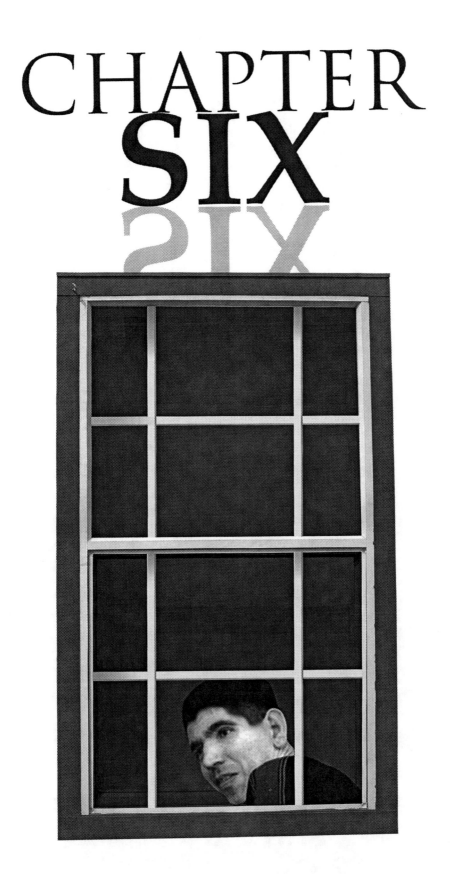

THE BOY IN THE WINDOW *the boy in the window*

I think the day I realized the full extreme of Kenny's disability came in the emotional form of embarrassment. Kenny had been in Joan's class over a year and was four. The other children in the class were between the ages of three and seven. That is how the special ed classes are separated, by age, not disabilities or grades.

Her classroom was going to take part in a Special Olympics event and she thought Kenny would do well at running. That was very apropos for him. Of course getting Kenny to do what you wanted when you wanted it, was another story. But the event was about participation, not winning, so everyone was a winner.

There were activities such as wheelchair races, sack hopping, and disk throwing, etc. I had no idea it was such a popular attraction, not being very sports minded myself, and I could not believe the hundreds of people that came from all over to join in the enthusiasm that was abundant. I assumed since Joan's class was made up of three to seven year olds, it would be another classroom or two of children the same age. But I was wrong.

There were children of all ages with different disabilities from total paralysis and wheelchair bound, and those that were ambulatory that made up the competition, along with their family, friends, and teachers who would assist them and cheer them on. And then there was my little boy, who looked perfect by any standard, who was a part of this strange melee.

I tried to feel jubilant for Kenny and the other children by cheering when each of their events ended, but my heart was torn apart seeing him among the majority of children with visible disabilities, unlike him. I wanted to grab him and take him home, still feeling that he didn't belong there. I wasn't considering the fact that he was still in diapers, couldn't use a fork or spoon to eat, couldn't play with toys appropriately or do anything other children his age were doing.

Suddenly, through the huge and boisterous crowd I spotted someone I recognized from a very long time ago when my daughter was little. Her name was Rose and she had been a big part of our lives.

My first reaction was to run over and greet her, but instinctively I cringed, realizing she would see Kenny. I didn't want her to know I had a child who was

41

participating in the Special Olympics. I went out of my way to avoid her that day and hoped she wouldn't see me. My God! I was ashamed of Kenny's disability and ashamed of myself! How could a mother be ashamed of her own child? What had happened to me?

This was a wake up call for me. I decided then and there I would develop a kind of sense of humor regarding my precious son. I loved him no matter what! There was no question about that! From now on, when Kenny drew attention to himself in public with his grunting or screaming, I will ignore the stares and comments. And instead of trying to rush him off to the car so people wouldn't have to witness his tantrum, I will just look for a spot away from the maddening crowd and let him cool off. If people still stared, and of course they will, I'll just smile back at them. I will remind myself that he is only four years old and can't talk. He is frustrated and has brain damage!

Though I yearned for Kenny to be normal like other children, the reality was that his demeanor could upstage any surrounding attraction. I told myself, *If I didn't know him, I would probably stare in amazement too!*

We got the assistance we needed from the North Bay Regional Center for behavior modification due to the report about Kenny from the Center in Fairfield where he was evaluated. They sent us Julie, who specialized in behavior therapy, and she was a God send.

The first issue we tackled with Kenny was potty training for daytime, using an intense three-day period that consisted of putting him on the toilet every 20 minutes and having him drink liquids all day so he would have the urge to go.

This was no easy undertaking as Kenny was not allowed to leave the upstairs area where the bathroom was located. His bedroom and the master bedroom, a guest room, and the landing completed the upstairs, along with the porch off his bedroom. There was ample room for him, but he was still confined, not understanding why he couldn't go downstairs.

He cried and threw his usual temper tantrums when made to go into the bathroom. The idea was computing the pattern of using the toilet on a regular basis in his brain while being rewarded with a food snack when he would sit on the throne. It's a good thing he liked his little snacks because that was the main reason he eventually gave in. You could call this a kind of "brain washing." But Julie said it would be a major breakthrough for him if we could stick it out and she guaranteed success. I thought how wonderful it would be if he didn't have to wear diapers anymore.

Overall, he fought the situation and it was hard not to feel pity for him, though I understood the necessity. I forced myself to be brave and not give in to his tears. Julie understood how hard this extreme measure was for a mother to comply with but it was best for Kenny in the long run.

Finally, the three days were up and Kenny was going into the bathroom when he needed to go without crying or throwing a tantrum. I would help him with his pants and seat him. When he finished, his hand was out, waiting for his reward. The three of us were exhausted! Of course I would continue working daily with the training, but Kenny got it.

This was a huge milestone for him, not only because of the importance of being potty trained, but he was able to learn a useful skill. To me that meant he could learn more.

Julie came back a few days later, after a much deserved rest, to incorporate the "time out" program. When Kenny exhibited unacceptable behaviors, we were to take him to a corner and make him remain until he calmed down. It was for just a few seconds starting out because of his lack of focus and increased in time with age.

It took a lot of discipline and hard work, but once the pattern of time out for naughtiness was developed, I felt encouraged as I saw progress and had some "tools" to work with. Though bad behaviors were seen less around the Coppo home, Kenny was still Kenny.

Although Julie was the first real help we had in "taming" Kenny, he needed more than just behavioral help. His speech at four years old was only verbal with baby sounds. He said "Maa maa," "ca" for car, "ca ba" for come back. He had a very limited vocabulary that still had not improved.

I found the Center for Communicative Disorders in Napa for speech therapy, realizing that the amount of work on speech at school was not enough. Eventually, I was able to get the Regional Center to fund the cost of taking Kenny there, knowing it would be a lengthy process and it was so expensive.

The initial evaluation was done by Dennis Mordecai, Ph.D. speech/language pathologist and after two one-hour sessions, he came up with this observation:

"Kenny exhibited severely disturbed attentional and behavior deficits. Eye contact was frequently difficult to establish and he often looked away when requested to look at the examiner. Though attention could inconsistently be maintained for up to 60 seconds, it required frequent social-verbal reinforcement and maximal attentional cueing to the target stimuli (e.g., via gesture, vocal inflexion, physical manipulation, etc.) Difficulty to secure attending behaviors was observed for both visual and auditory stimuli.

Motorically, Kenny moved about the room constantly and initially needed to be physically placed in the chair. At both the beginning and end of the session he screamed "ba bai, ba bai" incessantly.

This handsome child exhibited receptive and expressive language skills between the one year and one year, three month level. His attentional and behavioral deficits co-exist and may be contributing factors to the serious language delay."

I drove Kenny to his office twice a week for six months. Dr. Mordecai suggested we increase on-task behavioral management techniques by creating a need for verbalization via structured play and exploration activities. He said those activities may help increase expressive vocabulary. And then we were to eliminate modes of interaction with Kenny that reinforce immature forms of communication. I understood the last part, (quit babying him mother!) *Well,* I thought, *if I can catch the little rascal I certainly will work on these tasks.*

My husband and I have always valued any suggestions through the years that might help Kenny in any way. We have worked hard on everything we were trained to do, and everything we were not trained to do. And many times we failed the expectations we had of ourselves through pure exhaustion.

I knew Kenny understood more than he could express, or communicate. In fact, sometimes he was hauntingly perceptive, but after a year without developing any new language, the speech pathologist agreed we should end the sessions but to continue other avenues, such as sign language.

So Ken and I signed up for a class. It was actually fun, but trying to teach Kenny at home was not successful. All he could do was pat his chest really hard to communicate "please" or "want." His motor skills were too limited and so was his patience.

Before that year was up, however, I took my brother Frank's advice about looking into the possibility of a lawsuit. It appeared that Kenny might have a lifelong problem that could and did get a whole lot worse. We thought about the multitude of expenses that had already cropped up and wondered how we would manage to pay for all of his future needs.

But it was hard to fathom the stress of a lawsuit on top of everything else as our world had been turned upside down. Our family life was anything but the "American Dream," and it seemed as if all of the problems we had swept under a convenient rug before Kenny had his booster shot had now reared their ugly head. Emotions were raw and riding high! No one is ever prepared for the kind of pressure we had been under the last few years.

My focus in life had become a search for "Lorenzo's Oil" for Kenny if there was any. Even the professionals were scratching their heads.

CHAPTER
SEVEN

THE BOY IN THE WINDOW

the boy in the window

*H*aving decided the best option for Kenny's future would be to file a lawsuit, I needed to do some research on attorneys. I picked the most prominent one in San Francisco at the time. He had recently won several large personal injury cases against well known corporations. His reputation was impressive, so I made an appointment to see him. I wanted to know what kind of chances we had, if any, to pursue a lawsuit.

In our initial appointment he was more than positive and wanted to get started right away, which made me feel hopeful. He was a lot older than I had realized and somewhat eccentric in nature, but I kept thinking about his triumphant successes.

I went home and began the staggering task of gathering all of the information he needed; documents from Kaiser, baby records, etc.

My husband and I made many trips to his office. On each trip, there were more forms to fill out. In complete trust we signed our names to all of them. He filed our suit with the state, which turned out to be a huge deterrent by not filing federal. We, of course, had no knowledge of that at the time.

As time moved on and I didn't hear anything, I was worried and would call the office, but he was never available to talk. I had to resort to appointments and drive the stressful congested freeways to S.F. to his office, questioning him about our progress.

With each visit, he seemed to be having a hard time remembering who I was. He needed one of his associates to refresh his memory on our case the last few times I saw him. It was then that I realized his health was deteriorating and I had lost all confidence in his abilities as our attorney.

Soon after our disheartening discovery, the media announced his illness and the fact that his files were being turned over to his junior attorneys. I was tired of traveling to the city only to find chaos at his office. We cancelled them as our representing attorneys after being tied up for almost two years with no progress.

Feeling so discouraged at that point and drained from just keeping up with Kenny, I just continued my own research on seizures, their causes, and brain damaged babies. My mind was constantly in pursuit of what I could do to help Kenny and my antennae spiraled when an article in a news magazine featured a million dollar settlement that had recently been won for a child who suffered brain damage from the d.p.t. vaccine! Bingo! I wasted no time tracking down the attorney in the article.

After sharing all of the information I had regarding what happened to Kenny, and his condition, Andrew Dodd, one of three attorneys that specialized in children that suffered brain damage or who had died from the vaccinations, felt Kenny was indeed another victim. He thought I had good documentation which was needed to warrant his acceptance of our "case."

We made our arrangements to fly to Los Angeles to see him and brought all of the files that he requested on Kenny. By that time we had not only the hospital records, but behavioral evaluations and school and doctor reports as well.

He explained all the ins and outs of a lawsuit of this nature and that he would keep us notified every step of the way. He said we would be able to communicate over the phone, as my concern was the distance of his office. But I shuddered when he, of course, stated we would have to take Kenny to be examined by doctors there in L.A. Finally, I found someone in the professional field who believed in the correlation between vaccines and brain damage that talked to me openly about it. It felt good to have an ally. My husband and I walked away from our first meeting at Dodd's with more information than we had ever encountered regarding what happened to Kenny. Finally, it had a label, "acquired autism from post-pertussis encephalitis with a chronic seizure disorder." Kenny was far from being the only victim of this man-made poison.

When I returned home my emotions were running wild. I felt the satisfaction of an actual diagnosis after all of this time from a professional, who not only had researched the flaws of the vaccine, but had witnessed other tragic results in children like Kenny and were trying to help them.

But I was heartbroken at the news about Kenny. It sounded so bleak and it was very, very bleak! I had never heard about autism or about the association between autism and the vaccine.

I went back to the library and looked up autism. It was a psychiatric disturbance in which the subject is withdrawn into himself. It includes indifference to external realities and fixations on "objects," often accompanied with language disorders and obsessions without meaning.

Kenny displayed most of the symptomatic behaviors listed, but once we weaned him off his medication, he didn't seem as withdrawn into himself, but a better description was he could "draw you into his world." He definitely had obsessive fixations on certain people and objects though.

Unfortunately, autism was not understood that long ago and there wasn't much information on how to treat it. Once again, I found myself hitting a brick wall.

THE BOY IN THE WINDOW

the boy in the window

CHAPTER
EIGHT

THE BOY IN THE WINDOW

By the time Kenny was four years old his existence became a multitude of extreme obsessions. The family who lived across the street from us on Lancaster Dr. in Vallejo, where we lived until Kenny was 12 years old, was one of insurmountable turmoil, much to Kenny's delight.

The upstairs part of our home had a large open porch secured by wrought iron railings that was accessible from two bedrooms, one being Kenny's. This was the front of the house and the porch was the attraction for us when we purchased it. It was a covered patio over the garage.

From the time he was a baby in his little walker he loved being out there. We had comfortable chairs, a little table and there was still ample room for him to scamper about and a perfect area to play with his toys when he became a toddler. It seemed like a hundred years ago when we gathered there as a family, enjoying the progress of our baby who was so darling and so content.

But now, our existence was far from content. From the balcony, Kenny had a bird's eye view for his obscure fascination with Rick, the neighbor directly across the street. It was as if Rick had become his whole world, not that Rick did anything to encourage Kenny.

Though we barely had time to talk to our neighbors, I think they had a quiet understanding that it would be best not to indulge Kenny with attention. That would only escalate his excitement. All of the neighbors had heard about the tragedy and had witnessed the bizarre change in Kenny. If Kenny just laid eyes on Rick, it would send him into an ecstatic frenzy. Kenny's word for Rick was "wek." We could always count on Rick as a source of entertainment for Kenny when everything else would fail. He loved to just watch him work in the yard or on his car. It didn't matter, as long as Kenny could visually see him. But the downside was the incessant chanting of "wek wek, wek" that frayed all of our nerves as it never diminished. Kenny's voice grew louder as he grew taller.

And if that wasn't enough, Kenny would cry and cry when Rick would leave his house and we heard "wek bac" long into the night or until he returned. We became upset at Rick when he left too, and soon we were all saying "wek bak." *Couldn't he just get a home-based job?*

53

When we were outside with Kenny he could dart away from us as suddenly as if he had been jolted with an electric current. My husband and I spent a good deal of time running after him hoping to catch him before he made it across the street and into a neighbor's house. Sometimes we caught up with him and sometimes we didn't. It was a very dangerous scenario.

Most of the neighbors were used to Kenny running up to them or in their house, but it was annoying to them and they had every right to feel that way. Kenny had a second sense of when someone was coming home or leaving. The neighbors feared the thought of possibly backing into him with their car, because of his lightening speed. We were constantly chasing him and short of tying him to a tree or never taking him outside at all, there were no alternatives.

He was the Great Houdini at escaping from our grasp and from our house. We installed high locks on the door, but somehow he would be right there when we opened it to go out. Invariably, he would manage to squeeze out and fly toward whatever attraction was nearest. Usually it was a familiar neighbor. If he caught up to them before we could snag him, he just latched on and wouldn't let go. People tried to be friendly but I understood their irritation. Trying to keep Kenny free from injury or worse has been a lifelong project in itself. There was probably a huge celebration when we eventually moved from 128 Lancaster Way.

Oddities became a part of our lives, because the only thing that seemed to trigger stimulation in Kenny was his own itinerary of self-imposed interests. Through sorrow for my son and wanting desperately to make him happy, I was only too glad to oblige some of his strange obsessions, providing he couldn't get hurt from them, and hoping anything that got his attention might help reach that damaged portion of his little brain.

Once, while on a walk in our neighborhood, Kenny spotted some tractors-many tractors. New homes were going up a few blocks from our own and there was a lot of land to grade. This is the area we eventually moved into, though I didn't know that at the time. I wasn't sure if it was the movement, or the noise, or the shape of the darn things that attracted him, but he became hooked on those monstrous machines just like a little "junkie" would on their favorite "high."

I was glad he found another interest, any interest besides Rick, so we started walking to the area with the tractors every day. He would jump up and down as if he were on a trampoline and bite his hand yelling in delight while I patiently let him have his fill of the monotonous display. The workmen would glance our way with curious expressions and I was beginning to feel like a "tractor groupie" following the men around as they "performed," bringing my dancing "pogo stick" with me.

Watching tractors wasn't the only form of entertainment I found for Kenny. On a trip to the mall, Kenny discovered escalators. The excitement for him riding on them was a positive reinforcement I could use to do quick errands in the stores. I was happy to find an obsession that would allow me to get things done.

One time while at the mall, he jerked free of my hand and started running up an escalator we had just stepped off. The people riding down quickly moved aside to let him pass, hoping I would catch him without breaking my neck or somebody else's. I thought of so many familiar chase scenes on escalators in movies where the good guys are chasing the bad guys, as I frantically tried to catch mine.

Kenny also enjoyed his outings with his dad and me on our bikes. When the weather was nice, this was his favorite thing to do, and it brought the most "calm-ness" to him-I'm using that word lightly. Kenny "rode" in a bright yellow canvas covered trailer attached to the back of his dad's bike. We covered a lot of miles through the years from the time he was a toddler until he grew to the point his knees were in his face barely fitting inside the trailer.

His favorite riding game was throwing out his "blankie." We would stop and turn around to retrieve it. He kept his "blankie" until he was at least six or seven years old and then he graduated to Big Bird. He took him everywhere and went through three of them, chewing the beak off each one. It seemed his need to chew grew with a voracious appetite as he indulged in the deformity of Big Bird. But beak or no beak, Big Bird would still be Big Bird. It was his first comforting toy. Several years after Big Bird, he graduated to the "Corky" boy doll, "Chucky's" nicer look alike!

As Kenny grew older, not only was he without language or self-help skills, but his ability to socialize appropriately was almost non-existent. On weekends, his dad and I took him to a park in Napa. Going to certain parks was something he seemed to get a lot of enjoyment from. This one had plenty of children, and he loved to watch them play. We pushed him on the swing, and kids wondered why he couldn't push himself, because he was certainly big enough.

The Napa Park had a big sand box where children gathered. Kenny liked to zero in on particularly small boys or girls playing there, and when he had enough of the swing, he would run over and plop himself down beside them.

Because he was twice their size, and his verbalization was strange and loud, it frightened the children and they ran away from him. The ones that were mildly intrigued by him and tried to talk to him were quickly bored as there was no re-sponse that they understood. I remember one boy, who was mad at Kenny because he wouldn't answer him, threw his pail of sand at him and ran off. I wanted to run after him and spank him.

It was heart wrenching to watch my little guy extricate himself from the other children knowing he would win the social outcast of the year award, if one were to be given out. But my love for him gave me the courage to take him anywhere, if I thought he might somehow enjoy or benefit from the venture. I sure was learning how to turn a deaf ear to the unsavory remarks and the dumbfounded stares we attracted everywhere we went.

I have to tell this funny little story about Kenny when he was four years old. We took him trick or treating for the first time on Halloween. I dressed him in a little devil costume all in red and it even came with the devil's trademark, a big black plastic "fork." He loved carrying it as if he had a wherewithal of how to use it.

We went to a few houses nearby, and he started getting the idea that he got something good after people came to the door. He quickly got bored with the process of ringing the door bell and waiting for the treat. On about the eighth house we came to, Kenny flew inside when the owner opened the door and was already heading down some stairs before I could catch him. The stranger was still standing at his front door not quite sure about what had just happened as Kenny bolted with his jet propelled take-off.

He played the devil role to the hilt way past Halloween, and wanted to wear his costume everyday. Boy was that scary! But he was the cutest little devil you ever saw. He also liked to use the "fork" on any company that was staying past their "allotted time." He hurried them along by gently prodding their butts as they were leaving. I knew he had something in mind for that fork.

Often, I had the preposterous notion that Kenny knew exactly why he did what he did, and why he acted the way he acted, aside from the obvious reasons. But if there was some truth in that, it meant he had an amazing amount of intelligence that no one had tapped into.

Although Kenny seems to live in a world of his own, his wisdom goes beyond the scope of his ludicrous behaviors. It took some degree of knowledge to become a master manipulator, which he excels in. He may not have been able to talk, reason, or stack blocks, but he's mastered the ability to take advantage of any situation in order to get his way. And I, of course, am his favorite victim. If I could only extract the boy from the animal! Even though he was as cute as a baby Koala, faster than a lizard's tongue, and was a fox at outsmarting me. I just had to find a way to tame this wild, yet adorable, little beast.

CHAPTER
NINE

THE BOY IN THE WINDOW
the boy in the window

*P*rior to Kenny's inoculation, I hired a wonderful woman named Ginny to become Kenny's sitter, knowing I would eventually ease back into work. Kenny readily responded to her and she adored him. She only watched him a few brief times before the tragedy and she was heartbroken when it happened.

Because of her, I was able to have a break now and then from my chaotic life. Though she feared the seizures that he might have in her care, I was able to convince her to remain his caretaker when needed. She had a very soothing effect on Kenny and he was remarkably calmer for her than for me. She was sympathetic to all of the precarious upheavals we were going through and it was a comfort to me having her in our lives. She continued to watch Kenny periodically for many years, she was a blessing.

Kenny loved her husband Jim, who was considerably older than Ginny. She told me of Kenny's gentle manner with him. She would tell me of things she could get Kenny to do and I couldn't believe it was my son she was referring to. Through her Philipino language she would say, "Kenny, get your zapatos," which is the word for shoes, and he would. She taught him other words in her dialect that he fully understood. She would give him something to take to Jim and he would take it to him. She eventually took him with her to visit her friends, and even then, he was very good.

She managed to tame my highly excitable little charge for the time he was with her. I wondered just what the realms of his comprehension consisted of. It would appear that it was a lot more than he was letting on! *How could he go from one extreme behavior to the other? Is he outsmarting the bleak evaluations from professional diagnostics and us? I hope so!*

I tried to dabble here and there in real estate and have some comradeship with Diana and the business world. Though communicating with adults was stimulating, it was difficult to concentrate on my work.

Calls I received at home from clients were hard to maneuver as the ring of the phone brought forth a deviously playful Kenny, who loved trying to retrieve the phone from me. It was another of his obsessive games. During our struggle, 59 he would sometimes get the cord wrapped around my neck as I fought to pry his fingers away. Sometimes we ended up falling together and rolling over each other, yet I managed to maintain a degree of professionalism and made appointments while I was being scratched, poked and strangled. If only the person on the other end of the line could have seen what I went through to make the appointments, sympathy, if nothing else, would have sold the homes.

As any Realtor knows, it is hard to work part time in this field, but I knew it was merely an escape for a while from the pressures of my life. On occasion, and if I had nothing going on in real estate, I would help my brother at his jewelry store in Concord, mostly just to see him and visit, or work a few hours for him. I enjoyed the jewelry business and learned a lot from Frank. Years later, when he wanted to sell out, my husband and I decided to purchase the business from him. The store had become a kind of security blanket for me, and a comfort zone away from home. Ken was more of a silent partner, still working at Mare Island. I had eased out of real estate to try to make a go of this new venture. Although I knew I wouldn't be able be there full time, because I needed to get Kenny off to school in the mornings, I had my sister-in-law, Linda, cover for me until I arrived. I had a good in-store jeweler, who did repairs and designs. But none of us had the expertise of my brother. A few years into owning the store there was a robbery and a good deal of merchandise was stolen. The insurance company harassed me for a long time and my husband said, "Let's call it quits." But I wouldn't listen, and tried to keep the doors open, struggling to make payments while waiting for the insurance company to reimburse us. Eventually I was paid for some merchandise, but not for the full coverage that I had signed up for. We were forced into bankruptcy, and had to close the doors.

One day while I was still working at the store, I picked up the phone book and let my fingers do the walking through the yellow pages, not really sure who or what I was looking for, but that it was always about Kenny, of course. At random, I came across an immunologist and decided to call him, wondering if he had heard anything about the problems with vaccines.

He immediately suspected that I was a spy for the drug companies and it took a lot of convincing that I was not, but just a mother looking for answers. This person not only had some answers for me, but knew much more than he should have. It seemed from the extensive research that he had been doing for a long time, which included traveling to specific areas, he had been documenting not only the damage this particular vaccine had been causing, but the fact that the percentages of cases were not even being acknowledged as such.

In some cases, the occurrences of death from the vaccine were being labeled as "sudden infant death syndrome" or "crib death." He knew about "bad lots" of the serum that were being injected into innocent and helpless babies that died because of it.

This man put me in contact with many families that lived in the surrounding bay area who had babies that either died or were left like Kenny or worse. There were meetings being held as we spoke for the families to discuss their children, lawsuits and care.

This doctor was going to be a "star witness" for the injured children whose cases got as far as a jury trial against a drug company. Dedicated to the cause, he continued the efforts to represent families, in spite of the harassment by the drug companies involved that were trying to destroy his credibility and his practice. It took a huge toll on him.

Our next meeting with Andrew Dodd in Los Angeles involved three more hours of discussing all of the challenges of a lawsuit of this nature. He would like to have filed our case in the Federal Court, which would have been processed faster than the State Superior Court, but as I mentioned earlier, our first attorney had already filed with the State. Also, we could have been in the San Francisco jurisdiction, which would have been more beneficial in our outcome versus a small community such as Solano County.

The most important thing we had to do at that point was schedule an appointment for Kenny to have blood tests, a cat scan, and a total work up to rule out any other causes, including any genetic or hereditary possibilities as the pertussis damage did not show up visibly in tests. Kenny was also to be examined by Dr. Gabriel, a highly recognized neurologist at UCLA where all of these tests were to take place. If the tests all came back negative, Mr. Dodd would officially be our new attorney.

I was worried sick about the consequences of the drugs I knew they would have to use to sedate Kenny in order to perform the tests and if they would do further damage. I was so fearful for Kenny all of the time now.

With all of the items of entertainment and snacks I brought on the flight, he actually did quite well, which made me feel so guilty knowing the reason for our trip. It was unbearable for me knowing he would soon have to undergo more poking and prodding from doctors and not be able to make him understand why it had to be done.

Second to the weekend of Kenny's initial tragedy, those three days in Los Angeles were the most hectic and burdensome of my life. Rushing from one test to the other, trying to make them on time, while trying to appease Kenny, and getting him to hold still for the technicians, was exasperating!

When we returned to the hotel at the end of each day he screamed to go home until the wee hours of the night. The three of us were bedraggled. Finally, the last remaining and the most crucial test, which was the Cat Scan, was scheduled on the day of our flight home. Kenny had to be fully immobile for the test and was to be sedated. Because he was so high strung, the doctor and anesthesiologist were discussing the amount of sedatives to give him. My fear of something terrible happening to my son all over again was overwhelming. They administered the drug while I held him, and we waited what seemed like an eternity, for them to take him into the room for the scan. Kenny was in a deep sleep now. I kept wiping the tears falling from my eyes and down my face and I wanted to scream.

I was a nervous wreck when we found out the doctors were behind schedule and Kenny's sedation was starting to wear off. Then to my upset, they wanted to give him an extra dosage in able to finalize this nightmare. Our only choice was to either allow the additional drugs or reschedule and have to make Kenny go through all of this again. They increased the sedative and assured me it was safe. Is it as safe as the vaccine? I wondered.

The tests were finally over and we barely made it to the airport for the flight home with our now semi-conscious, nauseous, and over-tired guinea pig.

I made up my mind then that I would never put Kenny through the extreme of those types of tests again. I hoped all of the attorneys from both sides would have all of the medical documentation they needed. I just didn't feel I could stand to see Kenny go through this again. Of course, this was only one in the beginning of a multitude of anticipatory results that we would anxiously await before moving on with our suit. There would be hearings, motions, cancellations and a surprising judgment against us.

We understood that a lawsuit of this contention was not only staggering for the attorneys going against one of the largest drug companies in the United States, and against the grain of the American way that was about inoculating children to save them from infectious and deadly diseases, but that the American public was not supposed to hear about the dangers of the vaccines, and the extensive damage they could cause.

Kenny's tests showed no abnormalities, genetic problems or anything else to prove that his condition was from any other source than the vaccine. The doctors wrote their testimonials to that effect in Kenny's medical file and these reports could only hurt the drug companies at a trial, so we were told these doctors would not be called to testify in our behalf. I couldn't believe my ears! But we were told this was standard procedure, unjust as it was.

While the rest of the world was in shock at the news of the Challenger that had just disintegrated, our personal history, which was anything but of monumental proportion, was being scrutinized for two straight days of tedious and insinuating questions from the drug company's attorneys at our depositions held in Oakland.

They were trying their best to conjure up another reason for Kenny's brain damage, which was their job of course, but did they have to put us through hell in the process? We were treated as if we were trying to hide something from our pasts that may have contributed to Kenny's problem.

Questions were asked such as: Was my husband sure he was the father? Did I sleep around? What other children did I have that I might of "hidden away" because of a "brain" problem?

The asininities were revolting, disgusting and never-ending. Through the stress and tension from the interrogations, I would sometimes forget important dates, etc. So then they further humiliated me by asking if I "did drugs," something I have never done in my life, but thought if I had to listen to much more of their unfounded and ridiculous accusations, I would be driven to it!

We were beginning to feel as if we were in a chamber for a penitent and that we would be resolved of our crimes if we just confessed.

The attorneys representing the drug companies in question wanted us to bring Kenny to San Francisco to be visibly assessed. This interview was called a "confirmation of evidence" to determine if indeed there was a case of brain damage, and to what degree.

The meeting was held in a judge's chamber. I was represented by one of Dodd's assisting attorneys and the drug companies had three of their own, one being a woman meticulously dressed in a smart suit and heels, perfect make up and a becoming hairstyle. The men were equally well-groomed and I couldn't help but recognize the expensive suits and the smug faces they were also wearing. It was all very intimidating, especially because my husband and his steadfast demeanor could not take off work for this meeting. I was already frazzled from the long and tedious drive from Vallejo with my backseat counterpart! Fortunately, my attorney was patient and comforting.

Kenny was not happy at all with this conglomerate of strangers. I tried hard to answer questions while trying to keep him entertained on my lap as he fidgeted and resisted my attempts, pulling my hair, scratching at me and squealing with utmost annoyance.

Suddenly, Kenny's reaction to the coldly austere and unfamiliar surroundings that might have reminded him of the possibility of more examinations, brought out his Mr. Hyde behavior and in a matter of seconds he broke loose from my fierce hold and headed straight for the judge's desk, where he immediately demolished every file and threw anything within his reach up in the air. It was as if a tornado had struck without warning as mounds of papers sailed across the room.

While everyone tried to catch flying debris, Kenny had jumped off the desk on to "his honor's" lap and slid down where he made a mad dash and escaped out an unlatched door that opened to a side street alley.

No one could believe the lightening quickness of this little guy and I was the first one to start running after Kenny. I was followed by four attorneys, one in high heels, and a judge. *America's Funniest Home Videos* couldn't top this one!

After we all gathered back inside the room, there was a lot of "throat clearing." A sense of humility filled the stifling air and tears rolled down the now mascara smeared face of the attractive woman who might end up defending the drug that created the monster she just witnessed.

I continued to answer more questions as Kenny continued to act out his agitation as only he can, the sound of their voices had softened, though the attorneys tried hard to be diligent.

I was asked if this was an example of my daily life with Kenny, I nodded and said, "This is just the tip of the iceberg!"

The display of oddities that all had observed during those few hours had left an overwhelming impression. The compassion I was shown by my attorney who walked me to my car in the parking lot with Kenny in tow would never be forgotten. He told me he didn't know how I could deal with this every day and he hoped for the best outcome with our suit. I felt as if he would have laid down a plush red carpet for me to walk on if he could have. He expressed concern over my ability to manage the long hard drive home with Kenny who was totally overwrought and tired. This man had sensed the encompassment of my silent suffering.

It made me think about the movie Mask that Cher had starred in. It was about her son born with debilitating deformities as bizarre as Kenny's behaviors. A stranger had observed the mother of this boy and saw how she looked past the deformities and the staring public and treated him normally. The stranger developed adulation for her.

I recently had been standing in a long line with Kenny at J.C. Penney's to get his picture taken. While I struggled to defy his vociferate attempts to get us out of there, other mothers and their kids glared at us. Exhausted from entertaining him until our turn, I was proud of myself for sticking it out, not giving in to his behavior, even though it was also at the expense of others.

The photographer managed to make him smile a few times for his picture. I looked around to see if there was a stranger somewhere in the crowd adulating me like in the movie Mask.

CHAPTER
TEN

THE BOY IN THE WINDOW

*T*he first motion presented in our case was from the drug companies who wanted to prevent Kenny from being at the trial. Their concern was that the jury would be swayed if they saw what the vaccine had done to Kenny, otherwise referred to as the "sympathy factor." Nevertheless, we had made up our minds. If the judge ruled against him being at the trial we would bring him anyway, even if we were fined for contempt of court.

But before we ever got a chance to wage that battle, a major conflict came about when Kaiser couldn't say positively that Wyeth Laboratory made the vaccine serum that was given to Kenny, although most of the research had pointed in that direction. But there was a small possibility that it could have been Connaught Lab.

So our attorneys had to file against both companies. Three years of the suit were tied up with the attorneys trying to establish which drug company was responsible, and eventually a new motion was granted by the judge to hold a trial for a jury to decide which manufacturer we should proceed against.

Connaught offered a settlement of $10,000 to us if we dropped the suit against them. They justified the offer by stating that if the jury found that it was indeed Connaught who manufactured the vaccination, their final settlement would still be $10,000.

Of course we refused that offer. The two companies were angry that they now had to fight against each other to determine whose vaccine caused Kenny's damage, which actually took a big load off our attorneys for the time being.

This motion had constituted several trips to the Fairfield courthouse which was about thirty minutes from Vallejo. On one occasion we were asked to bring Kenny who was about eight years old at the time. Our attorneys wanted to be sure as many possible jurors and opposing team viewed our son while deliberations were going on inside the courtroom.

The spacious forum overlooking a circular staircase to the lower level and entry of the courthouse was grandiose on a small scale. It proved to be a wonderful playground for Kenny. Unfortunately there was a postponement but not before everyone involved on this particular court calendar day had a chance to meet Kenny.

Our grand entry was made as our attorneys, Ken, Kenny and I emerged from an elevator onto the foyer made of marble floors. Kenny immediately discovered his shoes were making an echo and he jumped and stomped to increase the volume. Herding him along, we sounded like an Arabian stampede entering the composed quiescence of the judicial halls.

The drug company's attorneys were there in large numbers from back East, and they were an impressive sight in Solano County in their once again fancy suits and polished shoes.

Gaping mouths and shushing gestures toward Kenny did nothing to dismay his frolicking about the open and adventuresome arena. The clackity clack noise from his shoes delighted him. But once that novelty wore off, amazingly, he singled out a few of the fastidiously dressed attorneys representing the drug companies and managed to grab and tug at a few of their fancy suit sleeves albeit leaving traces of crumbs from his cheerio snacks. That was one day I didn't try hard to restrain Kenny from his naughtiness.

The next date at the courthouse was the trial itself with a selected jury that would determine who made the serum. I could sense the compassion of the jury as the injury to Kenny was briefly discussed. The emphasis was quickly referred to the manufacturers involved.

Listening to the suppositions of the defending attorneys and the rebuttals of ours was so tense. I was getting a taste of what it might be like if we were to go to trial on Kenny's behalf. It was awful! I had a hard time refraining myself from protesting with my own litany of objections while listening to pathetic excuses from billion dollar companies, whining about their innocence, while my baby was suffering.

There was always the possibility that the jury wouldn't be able to find the proof that it was one or the other. Although there were other manufactures of vaccines out there, these were the major two at the time. There was a chance it could all backfire and poof! There would go our lawsuit!

The injection nurse at Kaiser Clinic was the deciding factor in the case. Her testimony gave the proof needed against Wyeth because her records showed that they had not purchased Connaught drugs recently and all previous purchases had been from Wyeth. When she got new shipments in, she always put the new lot in the back of the refrigerator and the older drugs were in front. She had used up all of the drugs from Connaught before Kenny was inoculated. She had been the only person to give shots at Kaiser for the last 20 years.

After three days of this trial, the jury found Wyeth responsible for manufacturing the serum. It was decided the suit shall indeed be against Wyeth.

At the end we were approached from members of the jury who wished us well in our continuation of the suit. Some had tears in their eyes and didn't know what to say but we felt their sincere compassion.

Connaught was not happy that they had spent the time and effort and money in the trial. They went to the judge and asked for a judgment against us for the amount of $20,000 to cover their expenses to defend themselves. The judge granted their request. To me, this was a good example of judicial tyranny.

Yes, we were finding out about "lawsuits" alright! Now, we were in a pickle because we didn't have $20,000 to fork over. We immediately homesteaded our house so they couldn't touch it. We knew they couldn't attach my husband's wages as he worked for the government. Thank God!

This was a terrible added ordeal! We worried about that debt for a long time until the end of our suit. From the time we signed up with the first attorney, to the very end, it was seven long years.

Whenever it seemed that we were getting closer to a trial date, another motion or hearing would come up and the waiting period for us to go to trial would be prolonged. When a date would be set, there would be a cancellation. Some of the cancellations were at the very last minute. We or our attorneys would already be at the courthouse.

Andrew Dodd and his partner Richard Denver (Bob Denver's brother from Gilligan's Island) made six trips from Los Angeles to Fairfield for trial dates and six of them were cancelled without notifying attorneys.

Through it all we were comforted with "a light at the end of the tunnel," the phrase our attorney often used. I thought about the possibilities of being rewarded enough money to get the best help in the world for Kenny on a daily basis. I also thought of how we could lighten our workload and have a little more freedom to do "normal" things. The thought of a vacation sounded good too, but I couldn't leave Kenny for more than a few hours a day to work, let alone for a vacation. But, still I had my hopes and dreams.

Then the day of reckoning was finally upon us and there were no postponements, no delays and the jury had been picked. At this point, Wyeth Lab requested we try to resolve this conflict without a trial.

After hours and hours of fitful anticipation, there were finally some serious offers coming in. Negotiations were taking place and the atmosphere was intense. Though we were "guided" by our wonderful attorneys, Kenny's future depended on the choice we would make as his parents. This was a day like no other.

The concentration and the mental intensity were unbearable. My husband compared it to running a 26 mile marathon, something he participated in six times.

The last and final offer was being presented to us by our attorney and though it was mediocre in comparison to my dreams, we had to consider this one.

Sitting outside the courtroom hour after hour weary from thinking so hard, weighing every factor of this latest monetary enticement was excruciating beyond belief, we had to think about the fact if we went to trial we could lose and not get anything. Our attorneys had just lost a case in Utah. Although the circumstances were different, and involved religious overtones, it was still a possibility.

Fighting the drug companies was also getting harder as they were spending fortunes on their attorneys to win the cases while our attorney did not have fortunes to garner in fighting against them. *Why couldn't they just give us the money they spent trying to fight us? Then we could all go home,* I thought. But life isn't that easy.

We had to weigh every possible pro and con. This was the hardest and most stressful decision of our lives and we were exhausted. We had debated all day long.

Dodd said we had to think with our brain and not our hearts. He felt though it was not a just offer, it provided security for Kenny when he was older.

After 14 hours at the courthouse and being of sound mind and body, though mentally drained, we accepted this final settlement. I am not at liberty to divulge anything about the amount or terms.

The *Vallejo Times Herald* had obtained our names from the Solano County's court calendar in Fairfield and wanted to do a story on Kenny. We were interviewed in our home by the reporter and we did the best we could explaining all that had happened and how it had affected our lives.

The reporter told us about a mother whose child had contracted the whooping cough and had been very ill. He asked me how I felt about that. I asked him how the child was now. He answered, "Just fine."

When our story came out in the newspaper on the front page, I was shocked to read that he had turned our story into a debate! He had focused on the terrible illness of the other child, disregarding pertinent information I had given him about high risk babies who should by no means have the vaccine, and the risk to any baby like Kenny who either got a bad lot or whose blood brain barrier is not developed enough to fight the toxins.

He stated that the dpt shot was less harmful than contracting whooping cough! But he didn't mention the countless babies that were damaged from the dpt vaccine because of terribly flawed statistics. Many parents or doctors didn't realize or admit that brain insult, seizures and retardation was attributed to the "P" component, or pertussis, (whooping cough), so it wasn't reported.

Pertussis was an epidemic killer when its ravages were first described decades ago. The vaccine came into wide-spread use in the U.S. in the 1950's but was never improved upon until recent years when Japan came out with a much safer version, however, the "old" vaccine is still in general use today.

The reporter went on to state, "Solano County Public Health Director Dr. Edward Lopez says that although there are problems with the vaccine, it is better than no vaccine at all." He said in a press conference last year a mother decided to forego vaccinating her child. The child became very ill with whooping cough but recovered. The key word here is "recovered," unlike Kenny, who had no chance of recovery after his final shot.

The reporter pointed out that several attempts to reach the FDA for comment were unsuccessful. It was disheartening to see that our attempt to draw attention to the problem with the dpt vaccination had turned into an argument for use of the drug without any consideration of the consequences.

During our lawsuit we were exposed to information the public is never meant to know. One interesting topic that we found out was it is a ploy of the drug manufacturers to use scare tactics by announcing whooping cough outbreaks, whenever there is a recent suit against them regarding this issue, and whenever the media discusses brain injured children via the vaccine.

A few months after our settlement we were contacted by producers of a morning show on K.T.U.V. channel 2 for an interview about Kenny but it was cancelled two days before we were to go on. A television network A.B.C. owned by American Home Products also owned Wyeth!

And at the same time, a popular doctor on A.B.C. news was talking "whooping cough epidemic" without certified cultures confirming it, required by the health department. This was more than likely stated because our newspaper article mentioned four other cases in Vallejo and Benicia that were in litigation against drug companies for manufacturing the potentially toxic pertussis vaccine. (I have more documentation on the vaccine issues in chapter 29.)

THE BOY IN THE WINDOW
the boy in the window

CHAPTER
ELEVEN

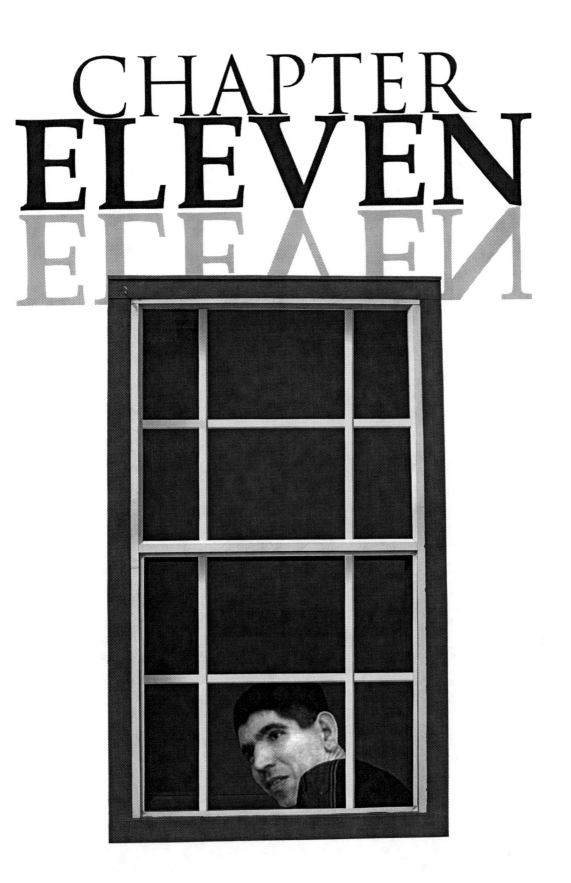

THE BOY IN THE WINDOW

the boy in the window

*K*en and I, as his parents were Kenny's main source of entertainment, other than the few hours he was in school. He was not interested in television, nor could he play with other children, he could only observe. There wasn't much available in recreation for children like Kenny, so I tried to engage him in activities that "normal" children participated in.

I was able to find a gymnastics program that was held in a large gym when he was six or seven. I thought Kenny might "blend" with the children as all the other mothers would be busy helping their kids and not watching the inept behaviors of mine. But he couldn't do the most basic summersault, unless I physically rolled him over, which only made him mad.

He simply wasn't interested in the program because of the degree of difficulty, even though I tried hard to make it fun for him. The other children became distracted by his crying and his obvious differences. Other parents were not open to Kenny, and he was distracting their children.

I went back several times with him, not being one to give up easily, and each time he acted as he had before. The last visit was the worst. The cold stares from the other mothers followed Kenny and I to the door. With Kenny practically dragging me, we left. I felt as if we were from another planet.

Once, not long after the gymnastics fiasco, I took him to a zoo, as he enjoyed going before he became "brain hurt." I wanted to see how he responded to the animals, since he wasn't responding to other things he previously had. But instead of the animals it was a huge fountain surrounded in water ankle deep that attracted his attention. It wasn't long before I found myself chasing after him into the slimy cesspool where we were both christened in animal gook.

I was with a friend and her disabled son, Chris, who Kenny adored. She was laughing while I carried Kenny to dry land. She told me it was the funniest sight she had ever seen. I laughed too, although my pants and shoes and Kenny's were filthy. I sloshed around the rest of the day in my wet shoes. I changed Kenny. I never took him anywhere without a change of clothes.

75

Escorting Kenny through populated places was not without its drawbacks, especially when his need to throw a tantrum sparked the interest of the well-meaning public.

On several occasions, as Ken and I tried dragging him to the car from a mall, because he wouldn't get up and walk, we were stopped by people who thought he was being kidnapped. It appeared to those watching that we were attempting to lure him into the getaway vehicle because he was kicking and screaming. Perhaps we should have let them "rescue" him while we made our escape.

There are many stories through the years about our outings with Kenny that have been funny and tragic to me at the same time. One that I will never forget is when a small girl, who was about eight years old, had been observing Kenny from a distance. His persona had bewildered her so much that she scrutinized him intently as he made his usual spectacle, running, jumping up and down and trying to communicate with grunts; a language not of this earth. Ken was entertaining Kenny while I took my turn in a public pool that was off the beaten track. I saw that she tried hard not to stare at him, but her curiosity got the best of her and she finally went up to my husband and asked if our son was an "Indian."

Ken said, "No, he is not an Indian." And before he could explain why Kenny acted the way he does, she walked off and studied Kenny some more. After a while, she walked back up to him and said, "Excuse me sir, but I think he is going to be one when he grows up!" I laughed until I cried! Then realized I was crying because it made me envision Kenny in the middle of painted tribal warriors chanting their war cries! Yes, I thought he just might grow up to be an Indian too.

CHAPTER
TWELVE

THE BOY IN THE WINDOW

*T*ime was marching on and we marched along with it, and to the tune of a different drummer. While our lives in general were chaotic, to say the least, the contentment of knowing Kenny was in a good school setting eased my mind somewhat. But I would learn throughout his special education years not to rely on that contentment too long in any classroom for him.

Whenever Kenny seemed to be finally adjusting to a positive environment, "stuff," or I could use another word, would happen. In this case, Kenny was turning seven years old, which meant he had to move on to another program, with new teachers and students.

This was the beginning of endless battles we would engage in with the school district, because what they considered an acceptable classroom for him was by no means acceptable to us.

As I reviewed the potential programs in accordance with Kenny's age, I quickly reminisced on the safe environment and structure Kenny had in Joan's classroom. This had to be my first consideration, because Kenny was a fast and furious little guy. One minute he might be intrigued by something, and in a flash he could be off to another venture, or worse, out a door.

It seemed that the older the children became, the more crowded the classrooms were, which left them terribly understaffed. Some of the sites were close to busy streets, and unless the teachers were track stars, I couldn't chance it.

While visiting different sites, I made sure that I was looking into the realm of possibilities for Kenny, and past the emotional issues I felt when viewing them. But I hadn't seen anything remotely resembling a place I would care to leave my son for even a few hours, and I was dreadfully disappointed. How I wished he could have stayed in the class with Joan where he was happy.

Feeling so discouraged with the special education system, we had one more class to visit. Once again, I brought Kenny along so I could get a feel from his standpoint, whatever that was. He sat unhappily on my lap. I knew almost immediately this was not the place for Kenny. Even though I wanted to leave, I was required to remain for a short while to ensure the school district I had given just consideration to each class.

Glancing around the room, I saw several children who were engaged in sorting bean bags by color. Their fleeting successes were met with loud clapping from their peers. Then I took in a very tired looking woman who was trying to round up about six hyperactive children. She was making attempts at getting them to eat their lunch. There was food all over the floor where the lunch table was.

There was also an abundance of miscellaneous disabilities in these children, including hearing, sight and speech deficits. One boy wearing a protective helmet was having a seizure and was being attended to by an aide. Another child, bone thin and drooling, was sitting in a wheel chair alone in a corner. A little girl with matted hair was running circles around others, screaming and holding onto her head as she did. How could anyone of these children attend to their tasks at hand with so much going on at once?

Then suddenly we were engaged in a pandemonium that overwhelmed every nook and cranny in the large room, confirming the initial intake I had upon entering.

In one corner, four students started pounding and banging away on a variety of musical instruments. One sound came from a child who gleefully banged away on his jingling tambourine. It was totally nerve wracking!

The staff and teacher that accommodated this melee were far too few and I didn't see any organization amongst the chaos. I also wondered how a special ed teacher could cope and still keep her sanity. I wondered if I could keep mine if I remained in this room another minute.

As if Kenny was reading my mind, he jumped off my lap and ran toward the door. But before he ran out, he went back and grabbed that most annoying tambourine from the little boy's hand and threw it on the floor, then continued his escape as I made my mad dash after him. My son had some uncanny observations of his own.

I just didn't understand why there weren't classrooms that fit the children's intellectual levels and disabilities, instead of lumping them together by age. And why were there not more classrooms for our unfortunate loved ones. I know school budgets are always a problem, but is that a reason to put 25 or 30 children who are extremely challenged in one room? How could they possibly improve with the amount of turmoil going on?

Without ample adult supervision, what I observed so far was merely a babysitting situation, at best, and not what I considered a safe environment, let alone a "learning one."

Kenny was not born with his problems. Doctors and any professional person I took him to see, other than our attorney, had not even heard of Post-Pertussis

Encephalitis. Somewhere inside my son was intelligence that no one understood how to obtain, but it was there in his eyes. I wanted him to be exposed to more than he might be able to comprehend-not less! And I knew he needed one person working on skills with him at all times and to keep him safe. He needed a one on one aide. He needed everything these programs couldn't deliver.

With much dismay, we met again with his program coordinator and staff at the school district. I told them what I thought about the appalling conditions I had witnessed and that I would keep Kenny at home before I would send him to any of these "classes."

I was told the only alternative was looking at the possibilities of classes out of town, but that was not favored by the school district because of already depleted funds. I didn't cherish him being that far from home either.

Someone mentioned to me a site that was an integrated class in a regular public school here in town. Although, I was advised the students were higher functioning and Kenny may or may not fit in. As a last resort, I wanted to see it, and I was glad I did.

It was more what I had visualized for Kenny. He would have role models there, and I thought he might emulate them. The class seemed well organized and I could see most of the children were more attentive to their surroundings. There was a combination of academics on a very small scale, but at least it was something. Self-help skills were learned, which was an ongoing challenge for Kenny. I liked the pictures on the wall and the bright colored alphabet letters that bordered the chalkboards. Instead of the typical atmosphere of an insane asylum, the room was cheery and reminded me of a Kindergarten class. There was much less mayhem going on.

The district agreed to assign a one on one aide for Kenny, at my insistence, and his itinerary would be incorporated within the boundaries of the teacher's plans for the entire class.

Unfortunately, it only lasted about eight months. Kenny was wearing out the aide, though she was trying her hardest with him. Kenny was too busy keeping an eye on all of the other children and what they were doing instead of focusing on what he should be doing.

My little control freak wanted everyone to do the same thing, at the same time, which caused upset to those that were trying to do their tasks. When his aide kept him from the others he had tantrums. It disturbed the balance in the class that was plentiful before Kenny, and created the chaos that took over after Kenny. Yes, he was a handful, and nobody knew that better than my husband and me.

81

Following is a poem I wrote about Kenny. It sums up in a nutshell what daily life was like during these years.

"Impossible Kenny"

We call our son "Impossible Kenny,"

This brown-eyed boy, so strong, so skinny,

His energy level never drains,

And he plays, oh so many games,

But not the kind most seven-year-olds play,

These are things that turn hair gray,

His favorite is flushing socks down the toilet,

And make-up and teddy bears and daddy's wallet,

His hands are quicker than the eye can see,

As he reaches out to grab my hot tea,

And while I'm mopping up the spill,

He'll run out the door and up the hill,

We can't sit down or use the phone,

Because he knows he runs this home,

This child cannot talk or dress himself,

But he can manipulate most adults,

While I run upstairs, he's turned on the water,

And he ran downstairs to turn the TV up louder,

To go for a ride is even a chore,

We change him three times just to get out the door,

'Cause he wets and takes off his shoes and runs,

And we're tired before we've even begun.

Once on our excursion or "impossible mission,"

He does lots of screaming, we try not to listen,

So we buy him a milkshake in hopes it will please him,

He dumps it on my head, now I need appeasing,

We walk in the house, more laundry to do,

I'm putting away groceries; he's grabbing hot stew,

His hands never stop getting into disaster,

We try to keep up, but he keeps getting faster,

He can snatch food off your plate without any shame,

And at the same time pour his milk down the drain,

We sit down at the table with our little "Rambo,"

Can we eat in two minutes; it's really a gamble,

'Cause he's finished already, eaten two platefuls,

Kenny loves his food, for that I am grateful,

But oh what a mess, what do I clean first?

My dinners still waiting; now he's quenching his thirst,

With wet dirty dishrags I used cleaning the floor,

Oh please God, can I take anymore?

Then we struggle through the shower, washing with care,

He's pulled plug to blower while I'm drying his hair,

In my bathroom, all over, toothpaste he's spread,

Thank goodness it's almost time for his bed!

Look, he's rubbing his eyes, could this kid be sleepy,

Or is it just a disguise?

Now with shear exhaustion we tuck him in bed,

We kiss him and hug him and what's that Dad said?

That he wasn't such a bad little guy,

As we gaze into adorable, innocent eyes.

And now my angel is finally sleeping,

My heart breaks for him and I feel like weeping,

We check him through evening, make sure he's alright,

So that we can enjoy what's left of the night,

But what do we find, the bed he has wet,

More changing and laundry, our works not done yet,

So this is our life 24 hours a day,

Not a lot of time for fun or for play,

But even though frustrations are many,

We wouldn't trade our "Impossible Kenny." – 12/10/85

CHAPTER
THIRTEEN

THE BOY IN THE WINDOW

the boy in the window

I love Kenny so much. But sometimes even love is not enough, if it were, he would be healed to perfection.

All of the books I read on brain damage, seizures, or behaviors hadn't given me the answers I'd hoped for. Nutritional diets that were supposed to be helpful were not. Even researching the stories of similar problems in children, and trying to apply the methods used on them, did not bring major changes in my son.

Kenny still couldn't talk or dress himself, or use utensils to eat. His lack of dexterity left more of his dinner on the table, the floor, and himself than in his mouth. Mostly, he used his fingers, because it was easier and didn't require any effort from him. If he would only just slow down and not be in such a rush all the time. I feel he could do more but won't. It makes me feel like a failure as his mother.

We struggled day after day trying to teach him to use his fork and spoon on his own. Many times we gave up and let him go ahead and use his fingers out of tiredness. I spent more time cleaning up after him than I did eating. The three of us raced through dinner, like everything else in our lives, so Kenny could move on to the next routine. Dinner time has never been a peaceful or relaxing time of day for us as a family, to say the least.

What he really needed was intense structured daily teaching and time was going by, but time was not on Kenny's side. I knew that much! Each day that he wasn't learning something, was a step backward for him.

My antenna that seemed to be guided by a higher source honed in on "yet" another book I found at the library. It was about a brain-damaged child who had been labeled autistic, and though he had some language, his deficiencies were severe. This sounded very much like Kenny.

The couple in the book had taken their son to The Institutes for the Achievement of Human Potential. It turned out to be a successful treatment for this boy. He even eventually went on to college. I could hardly contain my excitement. I quickly pictured Kenny in a graduation cap and gown receiving his diploma. *How handsome he looked. Wow! I would be grateful just to see him get through high school.* I had to find out everything about this place, if it was still available, and if it was, could they help Kenny too?

The book, called *Todd* had explained the intensity of the program that involved certain tasks that had to be taught by the parents in the home, daily and all day long. I felt exhausted just reading about the regimental schedule, but I knew that wouldn't stop me from calling.

The Institute was located in Philadelphia and I instantly flashed upon Kenny running up and down the aisle of the plane terrorizing the passengers while he looked for ways to escape. There was a lot to agonize over about a trip of this length, and the duration of the stay once there, which was about a week.

I got the phone number from the operator. Feeling a little shaky, I blurted out Kenny's story to the person who answered. I was immediately transferred over to a counselor who listened to me vocalize my frustrations. Then she began to explain the hardships of the program. She gave me a brief description of very stringent tasks that must be done daily with Kenny, all day without faltering. They only accepted the most sincere and dedicated parents that were willing to make extreme sacrifices to incorporate this program.

Of course Ken and I had been making sacrifices in our lives for so long, if this program could help Kenny, we were willing to do whatever it took for Kenny's sake.

The first thing I was required to do was order their book called, *What to do about your Brain-Injured Child*. She said they would send me an information packet all about the institute along with the book. Then, if I was still serious about bringing Kenny after reading it, I had to write a letter explaining our situation and convince them of our seriousness.

The title of the book alone gave me hope I had never felt before. Once I read it, I could truly understand why it must have helped so many children.

I was so excited and desperate to have Kenny involved in the program that I frantically scribbled out this letter to the Institute:

Dear Institute,

Kenny was alert and strong from the very beginning of life. The doctor said he rated very high on the apgar scale.

He smiled at me in recognition at one week old. By two weeks he was smiling at me, his dad and his sister. At three weeks he cooed and tried hard to communicate with us.

He could hold his head up from very early on, when put on his stomach. Before one month of age he would dig his feet in while on his tummy, and pull with his arms as if attempting to crawl, gaining movement.

He was observing objects at a month old, whatever room in the house, the wallpaper, paintings, stuffed animals, etc.

The doctor commented on his strength at his three week checkup. He rolled over at six weeks, sat alone by six months and crawled then crept about seven months. He was managing the stairs by pulling up and sliding down. He cruised in a walker at seven months. He walked at 14 months. His first word was at 10 months old. I was eating an ice cream cone and gave him tastes of it and he said "mor," then "ma ma" and shortly thereafter came "mor ma ma." (Kenny always loved his food).

Overall, Kenny was a good and healthy baby, except for a few ear infections, and was happy and well adjusted. He was delightful and beautiful in every sense!

Up to 19 months old his vocabulary consisted of approximately 20 words or more and some two and three word phrases.

Then came his 19 month old booster d.p.t. vaccination and 24 hours later, he started having seizures off and on for three days. I became hysterical and what followed was years of trauma! Kenny's behavior changed and he "lost" what he could do or say. His fine motor abilities diminished and he couldn't feed himself or hold things like he did before his shot. He lost attention span, became hyperactive, and his language was back to baby babble. We are currently involved in an ongoing lawsuit against the drug company responsible.

Kenny was put on Phenobarbital in September of 1979 and was weaned from the drug in February, 1980 and he had another seizure. He was back on the medicine for another year to March, 1981. We tapered off again and the next seizure I observed was in September of 1982.

During this time he averaged a grand mal about once a year with an illness and fever. He was back on the Phenobarbital until September of 1985 and we weaned him off again. His last grand mal as a child was January, 1985 with a fever.

Kenny is eight years old now and there have not been many changes in him. Although he is more than eager about life, so enthusiastic and happy, but extremely frustrated because he can't talk. He is quite loud and tries so hard to say things. "Ga" means truck, "ga ga ga" means potty. He can clearly say "ma ma," "bye bye," and "car." He is constantly verbalizing. His dad and I are the only ones who can distinguish the sounds and know mostly what he wants but he is unintelligible to others.

Kenny's motor abilities are good, he can run, he is always running and so are we to keep up, but he gets faster as we get older.

He is 80% potty trained in the daytime, most accidents are purposeful. He plays these games with us and I could write a book about them. I can see he is extremely bright but I'm afraid others don't see that. His behavior gets in his way and keeps him from advancing. He can think ahead and plan and he can control situations. One woman who watches him on occasion can teach him things that others can't. He can attend to some tasks now for 20 minutes.

I hope this is all making sense as my thoughts are moving faster than my pen. I think to sum up many years of frustrations, struggles, and sacrifices while trying to raise a child like Kenny has been because of our sheer love, devotion and our willingness to give anything a chance that might help him. Even in spite of professionals advising us to think about state hospitals or private institutions for placement because he is getting so strong and we might not be able to control his ability to hurt himself or us or others.

But we have not gone through what we have to give up now and we realize that we as his parents are his only hope. Your book has given me new insight and I pray that Kenny will be considered as a candidate for your program. It would kill me if he had to be taken from us for the reasons stated above and my life would not be worth living.

My husband and I are ready to make whatever other sacrifices necessary to get our son "well." If ever a child could have been cured or made whole again by the love his parents bestowed upon him, then surely Kenny would be the miracle of all times.

Sincerely and Gratefully,

Barbara Coppo

I also had enclosed a list of things Kenny could do and could not do per their request. To summarize, what I wrote was that he could run, get into mischief, make messes, have tantrums, and obsess over people, but he couldn't talk, dress himself, feed himself, groom himself, toilet himself, or do anything appropriately for his age.

What to do about Your Brain Damaged Child goes into great detail about the institute's philosophy behind their methods of treatment and how it works. It is one of the most informative books I have read regarding this subject, and I've read many.

One of the main and crucial exercises to do for brain damaged victims was something called "patterning." The child is positioned on the floor as if he were to start crawling on hands and knees-left hand forward as the right knee moves ahead, right hand coordinating with the left knee. The parents make the movement happen by guiding the child along in this direction. (Crawling in a cross pattern activates cells in the midbrain, that are responsible for normal neurological development.)

Children were treated with non-surgical means through specific programming of the brain with physical and visual stimuli that had to be done with frequency, intensity and duration to increase the flow of information to the brain.

There were breathing techniques that required masks to be used to force the child to breathe deeply, which helped to develop their lungs in order for their systems to absorb more oxygen that is so beneficial to the brain. Many of these methods pioneered by the Institute are in broad general use all over the world.

While I was agonizing on all of the hardships that would be involved if we were to take our little "Indian" boy to Philadelphia, I found out from the information packet that Glen Doman, the chairman of the Board of Directors of the Institute, had a nephew named Robert Doman. Robert had a program called The National Academy for Child Development that was based upon the Institute's own Doman-Delacato methods and was a modification of it.

This modification had been devised through the efforts of Robert Doman Jr. and Robert J. Doman, M.D. Their philosophy was whether you have a normal, gifted or "handicapped" child each is capable of learning more at an accelerated rate. Each, given the opportunity, had the potential to improve his or her function. This is the belief on which the National Association for Child Development (NACD) was founded, and it works when this opportunity is nurtured in the home by parents and family members. The NACD was in Salt Lake City, Utah (much closer) and we were going!

It wasn't just happenstance that gave Ken and me the courage to take on this monumental journey with Kenny, even if it had been to Philadelphia. But it was a combination of the perseverance of our hopes and dreams that he would improve, and the teamwork that enabled us to pursue the impossible for him. It had become a "search and siege" comradeship between my husband and me that we may not have had as man and wife, but we had it for Kenny as his mother and father.

Through Kenny's school years, up to age 22, I was the one who researched the programs that seemed the most suitable for Kenny at the time, not the school district. We knew there would always be a battle, also called "fair hearings."

Ken had developed a great knowledge of the law regarding developmentally deficient children's rights. He used that knowledge to fight the school board so Kenny could attend these sites. This insight he had not only applied to the school district, but also the North Bay Regional Center who assisted with behavioral and respite hours.

Ken had learned to trust what I thought was good for Kenny. So although he knew the trip to Salt Lake City would be excruciating, and he had already rebelled generously at the Philadelphia possibility, he also knew that it was going to happen.

We packed every imaginable item of familiarity for Kenny and minimum items for us into a 1982 Nissan 280z. It was basically a sports car with two bucket seats in front and a small back seat that could fold down to give a little more storage to the trunk. We loved the look of this car, but emphasis was not big on comfort.

We managed to make the back as accommodating and Kenny friendly as possible; a cushy little bed made with a small piece of foam covered with sheets, pillows and blankets and of course he had Big Bird for company.

The most important thing I should have brought was a helmet for me to protect my head from the hair pulling, toy throwing, neck choking, and face gouging I suffered from the back seat passenger along the way. Most of it was actually aimed at his dad hoping to divert his direction back towards home. It was out of using my body as a shield to protect my husband so he could concentrate on his driving, that I suffered the abuse.

During these long hours I would sing along with mother goose tapes, tell stories, count, and say the alphabet so many times I could repeat it backwards just as easily. I spent the whole trip trying to entertain Kenny the best I could.

Upon arrival, we were exhausted! I looked as if I had just been set free from a prisoner-of-war camp! I had less hair than when we started on our journey, scratches with dried blood on my face and bruises on my arms. Luckily, our appointment was on the next day and once we finally were able to get Kenny to sleep, we had a chance to recover somewhat ourselves.

When it came time for Kenny's evaluation, I was immediately impressed with "Bob" Doman's style. He wasn't intimidated in the least with Kenny's behavior and within a brief time he observed how bright Kenny was in spite of the obvious. I thought about the wild boy who tried to sabotage our trip there and wondered if Bob would still feel that way had he been packed in that small car with us.

My flashback ended as I became encompassed in Bob Doman's theory about patterns of behavior in brain hurt children. He said these children have negative feelings and feel inadequate about themselves. They often develop their own ways of coping, especially in children like Kenny who can't talk but can possess intelligence. This results in inappropriate patterns of behavior, which are readily observable and which, when they persist, can lead to further difficulties. They respond to negative attention as well as the positive and often act very immaturely. They may also concentrate on one narrow and meaningless activity to the exclusion of all others.

The amount of information we were receiving was exciting and overwhelming at the same time. I could see a lot of what he was saying could apply to Kenny and in later years almost everything did apply to Kenny.

The day after the evaluation was over the program was outlined for us in great detail. We left with ample supplies needed to do the work with Kenny, including books, flash cards, tapes to watch, and breathing masks, along with a fresh new outlook on our multi-handicapped son.

Once home, I rebelliously had a tee shirt made for Kenny that read: "If you couldn't talk, (over) you'd act this way too!"

This was to address the tiresome stares of the misinformed public about the little genius wearing the garment.

THE BOY IN THE WINDOW

CHAPTER
FOURTEEN

THE BOY IN THE WINDOW

the boy in the window

*O*nce home and rested from our trip to the NACD, I began the daily ritual of the meticulously laid out and rigorous schedule. It consisted of the patterning that I explained earlier in Chapter 14, six times a day; masking, also explained in chapter 14, eight times a day; tactile exercises with assorted textures, squeezing a soft ball, or playing in a sandbox, with clay, or anything else that made him use his fingers at least four times per day.

He had to wear little glasses that had small pinholes in them for five minutes four times a day, to help strengthen his eyes. Kenny seemed to have "peripheral" vision rather than central, a common malady in "autistic like children."

And last but not least, I worked on giving him encyclopedic knowledge by flashing 11 by 11 inch cards at him that have bits of information, such as our presidents, types of birds, trees, body parts, insects, animals, etc. This was to be done with frequency, intensity, and duration, all throughout the day! I would also flash cards with large black printed words, quickly sounding them out to him, in order for him to learn to read.

I turned a downstairs room in our tri-level home that had been our daughter's bedroom when she still lived with us, into his new learning environment. There were alphabet charts with large letters, number charts and pictures of basic objects without added background and only the name of what it represented in large black letters. Everything we worked on was to be simple and clear of added design or color. I arranged the assorted materials I would be using in separate shelves, labeled them and placed them easily within my reach.

He was to be rewarded with food snacks, which I had readily available when he completed a task. These brought great delight as in the old adage "the way to a man's heart was through his stomach."

I hung the necessary room darkening shade to keep out light and discourage his fascination of looking out windows and used a small lamp that focused on the task we were working on to help keep his attention.

Our rigorous routine began each day with my corralling of Kenny into his new "classroom" that was free from the boisterous atmosphere of previous sites.

I would sit him down at his desk while I sat across from him. Speed was important to help keep his attention and focus on the information.

I would say, "Kenny, this is a maple tree." Or "Kenny, this is George Washington, our first president" etc. This procedure had to be fast, with repetition, and without stopping until the allotted time of 15 minutes was up, then we'd quickly move on to the next task.

When the sessions went well it was so inspiring! I finally felt that I was contributing to the possibility of a brighter future for him. I had no idea if anything was sinking in or if he was merely amused by my determination, but he sure looked adorable in those pinhole glasses, which at times he would leave them on the full five minutes. I think he knew he looked cute.

The patterning or "crawling" that was so important was the hardest out of all the assigned tasks we had to do. I had to wait for Ken to get home to accomplish it. Then there was the daily chase to "mask" him, (to get him to breathe deeper forcing fresh oxygen to his brain as I explained in chapter 14.) That had to be done for one minute, eight to ten times a day.

I also had to take time to prepare his new dairy, wheat and sugar free diet that was supposed to have miraculous results with children that had antisocial and uncontrollable behaviors. God I was getting tired and we were just a few months into the program!

There were days that were harder than others trying to get him focused and to maintain his attention, but it kept his attention longer than anything else that had been tried in the past. On bad days, he demolished the room, throwing everything everywhere and we lost precious time while I had to sort and reorganize before we could start where we left off.

After six months, I did the unspeakable and started testing Kenny to see if he had learned and contained any of the information. Bob said testing was a "no-no," as these children do not feel good about themselves and will often choose a wrong answer on purpose, which discourages the parent. But I needed some encouragement myself. I was ecstatic when he picked the right cards to the questions I asked! It gave me new energy.

I had quite an admiration for those parents who diligently pursued and followed all of the rules of this treatment for their child. I am a strong person, and it took every mental and physical substance I had to employ this routine of tasks and still cook dinners, making sure to fix something special for Kenny's new diet, feed and change him, do laundry, clean and go to the store. It was a daily, all day long venture that became so routine in nature. I hardly knew who I was anymore other than a mother who was hell-bent on helping her son get better, although the cost was high!

Even though, for the most part, Kenny seemed to enjoy the program, except for the patterning, (crawling) and masking, (deep breathing exercise), he still had to put up his resistant barrier to everything, making it harder than it already was. This has been a lifelong trait.

With everything I had going on with Kenny, I started to run out of energy trying to maintain the household duties! So I decided to put an ad in the paper for someone that might be interested in free room and board and a small salary in exchange for cooking and cleaning so I could be totally devoted to the program.

An older woman who managed to get around on a bicycle applied for the position. She was the only call I had. She told me what a great cook she was and she even made her own yogurt. She said there were a few things she had to take care of, but could move in right away.

I had to really talk this idea up to my husband, who was not happy at all about having someone move into our home, but he understood my exhaustion. I was also drained by the daily sparks from his short fuse, and that didn't help matters either. It has always been easier for him to yell about everything than to talk things out. I knew we were both overworked and worried about Kenny, and his future. I understood the pressures of Ken coming home from work tired, and instead of relaxing, he had to help me with Kenny. I thought my husband would benefit from an extra pair of hands around the house, and perhaps with a little less to do, we could learn to be civil to one another.

He also was not a happy camper about the many boxes our new star boarder had packed up for him to load onto his truck! Then of course he had to unload them. We had to store them in our garage, which was already overloaded with "stuff!" "Stuff," I was always nagging him to get rid of, being the pack rat that he is.

But the very wonderful thing about my husband is, he will agree to or do anything I ask of him on behalf of our son, and that speaks volumes about the kind of father he is!

So, not only was Ken unhappy with the new stranger, who supposedly was coming to our rescue, but Kenny showed an obvious dislike by crying and running in the opposite direction at the mere sight of her, as if he knew something we didn't. He really liked most people, in general. We would have saved ourselves grief had we respected Kenny's disproval, but we assumed it was the change in routine that upset him.

We moved her things in and didn't see her for three days! Then she precariously came limping home without her bike and said she had been hit by a car, but would be okay in a few days. Now I was caring for my son, doing the program, the cooking, and waiting on a complete invalid, who was a stranger comfortably propped up on my couch.

After two weeks of this ridiculous scenario, I put my foot down and told her she had to get out, now! We packed up the precarious intruder's belongings and dropped her off at the daughter's house per her request.

I put another ad in the paper for volunteers as suggested by the NACD for the patterning. My husband asked, "Don't you ever learn?" But the intense task really required four people so we could get his arms and legs to crawl. He had to be held down on the floor to accomplish this. It was almost impossible with just the two of us to maneuver Kenny's body in the required cross pattern.

My daughter Rhonda was working full time and so was my sister Nancy. Any relatives that might have been able to help lived out of town.

There were no responses from the ad, not one! It wasn't long before the "patterning" that seemed like a "medieval" application anyway was "gone with the wind."

CHAPTER
FIFTEEN

THE BOY IN THE WINDOW

*C*hristmas has been especially hard through the years. I find myself walking down the same aisle of baby toys, at the same toy stores trying to find something Kenny might be able to enjoy. It was frustrating buying gifts for him because he could not utilize or mechanically operate toys that were age appropriate, though I would always take the time to examine them. It was a depressing reminder of his limitations, no matter how old he got, and my unwillingness to accept them.

Kenny really didn't seem to care what was inside the packages he only liked ripping the paper off, his and everyone else's. I have spent many hours rewrapping gifts under the tree until I finally got smart and waited until he went to bed on Christmas Eve.

Holidays in general have been the ultimate in feelings of loneliness. We have missed many special occasions, birthdays, and weddings, etc. with our families because of the difficulties managing Kenny in other surroundings. It made us feel even more isolated from normalcy. Of course we have had celebrations here with our loved ones, but most of our family members have to travel a good distance. Kenny and his self-imposed curfew expected everyone to go home about 5:00pm. It was far too early to break up the fun. He would begin his annoying and continuous chanting of; "Hom, Hom" and "Baa by" until the company's nerves were frazzled, and he got his wish. He behaves as if other's amusements were at his own expense. What a party crasher!! If you have company that overstays their welcome, we will loan you Kenny!

Venturing out on the freeways where traffic could be backed up, especially because of the holidays, was not an option for us because of Kenny's impatience. There have been times I have wanted to call 911 when we were stuck in severe, bumper to bumper cars, because Kenny kicked and hit at the windows, or us, out of frustration. It has been a no-win situation.

Often, the feeling of confinement has been so great I wanted to jump in my car and just go where ever I felt like at the moment, but couldn't, because of my beloved burden.

I have had overwhelming thoughts of envy for those families who could explore whatever they desired; a zoo, a circus, a restaurant, the beach, or even a new city without the worry of a child who was dependant on them forever. People do not realize the true blessing of freedom, unless they are without it.

There were also times I was filled with suffocating guilt and a world of remorse. After all, I was the one who had taken my perfect son for his vaccinations on that fateful day. During one of these emotional evenings I went for a jog, hoping to relieve some of my stress, while Ken cared for Kenny. I needed to shake off my sorrowful thoughts, and have some time to think alone. I found myself praying harder than ever, asking for strength and guidance for myself, healing for Kenny and a sign to give me courage. Praying was something I did a lot of these days and I found running to be a spiritual encompassment.

After a short time, I looked up and saw a young teenage boy walking toward me across the street. My gaze quickly took in a terribly scarred and disfigured sight; what was left of a face that had obviously been burned in a fire! I wanted to fall to my knees as I took this to be my "sign" from God. My heart and soul went out to that young man and as I focused on what his life must be for him. I thanked my lucky stars for ours, and the power of prayer.

CHAPTER
SIXTEEN

THE BOY IN THE WINDOW
the boy in the window

*I*was insistent about continuing the program with Kenny. Each time he was masked, patterned, and fed information, I knew it was helping his brain. Remembering this is what kept me going. But I was tired and needed help. My husband and I debated whether we should ask the school district for an in-home teacher to help me with the program. It wasn't our fault there wasn't a suitable classroom for Kenny and the legality of the matter was they were responsible for his "education."

It was getting harder to keep his attention. I kept upgrading the cards I was showing him with new pictures, words, and numbers. I could get him to look at the items, but I could sense he was becoming bored. I felt I was letting him down somehow. I tried so hard to be enthusiastic everyday, but he instantly picked up on the times I wasn't, and acted out with his behaviors. I thought a new face incorporated into the program would inspire him again.

We presented the facts to the school committee and we got our teacher, but only for an hour and a half, three times a week. I was hoping for more hours and days, but it was better than no help at all. The board found a male instructor with full credentials willing to do this odd schedule.

The moment the instructor appeared at our door, Kenny was fascinated with him. Just as I had thought, Kenny's curiosity of this intriguing stranger turned him into a willing participant. He seemed anxious to show off his interacting abilities in this highly unusual learning environment. This had become a way of life for him now, and the way it went was totally up to Kenny. All of the shenanigans that I had to put up with while doing this work with him, had been put on hold, it seemed, thank God! Although the teacher followed the methodical tasks of the program as I had requested, the school district did not agree that this was an acceptable itinerary for Kenny.

I squeezed in as many household duties as possible while Kenny was being occupied, whether it was cleaning, cooking or laundry, and then it was back to tutoring Kenny when the "other" teacher left.

After six months, we were denied an extension of the hours for the in-home teacher. I did not think I could resign myself to be Kenny's full time task master again. It had been two long excruciating years and I was mentally drained. I knew I had to give myself a break. I was also wondering if he missed seeing other children at schools, or maybe I was so tired I was just looking for excuses to end the tedious repetitiousness that consumed my existence. I didn't have a personal life anymore and it was taking a toll. I felt lonely and I longed to lead a "normal" life. I was feeling sorry for myself and that wasn't fair to Kenny.

Here I was the mother of an eight year old child who couldn't talk, dress, or feed himself, and who was totally dependant on me. I was trying to maintain a household, be a wife and mother, and teach a child that didn't seem to understand his world or how to act in it. I was torn between guilt, knowing his future depended on me, and the pressure of the confinement I was feeling. I didn't know what to do. I was distraught and depressed, because outside the walls of our prison there was life, and we were not apart of it.

I informed Kenny's program coordinator that I would be looking for a classroom setting again. I had no idea where to begin, as I felt I had exhausted all possibilities. And then one night on television, a segment came on the news show *20/20* about a mother's son who also suffered brain damage from the vaccine and had seizures and behaviors similar to Kenny's.

She had recently established a school in Mill Valley (Marin County) where her own son attended. It didn't take me long to meet with her and visit the school with Kenny. I was very impressed with the functional layout of the small one story building. There was a gymnastics area, a music room that included a piano, and a reading room that looked like a small library. There was a large room for arts, crafts, and science projects.

There were just a few children at a time in each room so they could focus more on what they were being taught. It was such a great way to organize a setting for kids with special needs. *This was the way it should be*, I thought.

There was at least one aide for three children, or one to one, depending on the child's difficulties. She liked Kenny and felt really positive the school would be as beneficial for him as it was for her son. She was also familiar with the "Doman" program and utilized some of his methods. Each staff member I met was warm and enthusiastic. They all greeted Kenny as if they knew him already. He loved it and so did I. She hoped I could convince the school district to approve of Kenny's attendance.

Well, there I was again, biting off a lot to chew. I knew I wanted Kenny to go to this school, but the distance was at least an hour or more from our home, depending on traffic. *Would I survive the daily drives there and back without getting too beat up by the terminator?* That was the "big" question.

No doubt it would be very hard getting him and myself ready so early in the morning. But the major problem would be getting our school district to agree to the placement. This meant another tedious debate, which we had with the board and won, and Kenny went to the school. I got to know the surrounding area well, as I hung out until he got out of school. I started by scouting new stores, did some grocery shopping, and eventually I joined a gym close by.

Things seemed really great in the beginning, and there was no doubt it was a good school for Kenny. There was so much fun for the kids, and so much for them to do, they didn't have a lot of time to get bored. Kenny enjoyed attention and got a lot of it there. He had a one on one aide with him throughout all the activities of the day. Kenny was always more interested in his aides than other children in his classes. He was still very hyperactive and the school's most challenging subject, but he was also cute and very likable. By the day's end he was somewhat calmer and very tired.

After several months, the school director felt Kenny might be having partial seizures, which were causing his behaviors. Kenny still had outbursts and resisted through tantrums, but I always felt it was because he was frustrated and couldn't express himself through speech. She thought it would be helpful for Kenny and the staff if he was calmer. That is when she told me about her son's doctor who had helped him so much. He did talk somewhat, even though it was echolalia, a pathological repetition of words said by others. It was shocking for me to think Kenny was having seizures without me visually seeing them. Maybe I didn't want to see them…

I recalled the times Ken and I would be out on a walk with Kenny and he would start running and before he would come to a stop, he would wobble a bit like a duck and we called it "the funny feet." Maybe they were little seizures. We decided to take Kenny to see her son's private neurologist in San Francisco. After the e.e.g. exam (brain wave test for seizures) was done the doctor felt Kenny was having partial complex seizures and wanted to see about trying him on very low dosages of Tranxene and Depakene. Very reluctantly, we tried this, because both the director of the school and the doctor said Kenny would be able to apply himself more if he was calmer and not having seizures.

He did not do well on the medicine, he was constantly agitated and angry and looked terrible and became more hyperactive. We weaned him off that medication after just three months.

Kenny had been attending the Mill Valley School for at least six months when I started hearing rumors floating around about some very unhappy staff members. It seemed they were having issues with the director that jeopardized the core of the program and how it was maintained. I just assumed it was probably a financial matter, those things usually are, and that it would be resolved as these aides were too wonderful to lose.

Kenny had adjusted to his new routine, and once we arrived he seemed eager to start his day, even though for me, the daily rushing around every morning and fighting traffic with the unhappy camper in the back seat was not without major stress. Long drives have always been difficult for Kenny.

The aides that worked with Kenny had exuberance and patience, mandatory requirements for achieving anything of a positive nature with Kenny. Through Kenny's school years I found out it's actually the aides and how they interact with the child that makes all of the difference in their progress.

But little by little, the tension was growing within the school and the confidence I had in the environment was dwindling. New aides were being brought in to replace people Kenny had grown to love and trust.

When special kids are responding in a program, and then suddenly they become more reactive and start regressing, there is always a reason. It is usually that their structure and security has been breached. I was learning to follow my good instincts with Kenny, whether it was a problem at school, with an aide, or respite care at home. I had found out the hard way it didn't pay not to. With a heavy heart I took Kenny out of the school after a year and a half.

CHAPTER
SEVENTEEN

THE BOY IN THE WINDOW

the boy in the window

*I*t was back to the drawing board with the school district in another search for a suitable place for Kenny. The name Coppo was becoming a household word within the perimeters of the special education jurisdiction.

For this debate, we had to resort to arbitration, and the state had to appoint a mediator. We were so fortunate to have been assigned the kindest and most compassionate man who had a challenged son himself.

He understood the predicament we were in and saw us as the loving dedicated parents we were, not the persistent troublemakers the school board presumed us to be. Yes, we were particular about his placements. And yes, I wanted the best possible education for him in spite of his disabilities.

Our mediator realized and understood the fact that we would not place Kenny in any program just to have him out of our hair, and certainly not in a classroom with safety issues. He saw us as parents that would go to the ends of the earth for Kenny and he really went to bat for us.

The district's position was to enroll Kenny in the classes they deemed adequate for him, (keeping within the budget) and our position was to prove they were anything but adequate.

The crisis was not resolved in a day, as we had hoped, because we had to visit these sites referred to by the district, which I had already refused in the past. Our mediator was to accompany us to these classrooms and give a recommendation himself. He readily agreed they were not suitable for Kenny. Several more meetings had incurred without a solution, until our arbitrator came up with a most heartfelt and generous suggestion that triggered an immediate response from me, which was an emphatic "No!"

He told us about the Neurological Diagnostic School, (NDS) in San Francisco. Its forte, as their title implied, was to figure out a child that didn't seem to fit in, and to find out what makes them "tick" so to speak, (not his exact words, I'm sure). He told us the professional staff was a team of doctors, teachers, behaviorists, and highly trained one to one aides that work on behaviors and daily skills, all day long with the child. After establishing what their special needs are, and what therapies help them to improve the most, these methods are written up as an itinerary for the child's next placement upon leaving the NDS. They were to be implemented in that environment.

Kenny would have to "stay" there during the week and come home on weekends.

When I heard the key word "stay" I instantly panicked! I simply could not agree to that. How could I agree to that? I have never been without him for any lengthy period of time. Kenny was totally dependant on us and he couldn't communicate his needs to strangers. We protected him, watched over him, and he was on the special diet suggested by Doman's program. I just couldn't let him go. I couldn't even stand the thought of it. *I can't, I can't, I can't!*

"Mr. and Mrs. Coppo," the arbitrator said, "this would be the most wonderful opportunity for Kenny. Others have prayed they might be able to get their children in this school because the benefits are astounding. Although there is a waiting list, I have connections. The Center will find out what Kenny's most crucial needs are and work on them. It includes all of the daily living skills, toileting, eating, grooming, behavior, and language. And it is ongoing and consistent every day. I don't mean to sound harsh but it would be selfish to deny Kenny this extraordinary opportunity. They will teach him to engage in play with children and he will make new friends. Please, before you say no again, think about this very hard! I know that I could get him in right away."

"How long would he stay?" I asked. His voice softened and he looked at me with compassion in his eyes. "About eight months is the approximate duration, and remember, he will be home every weekend. And Mrs. Coppo, it will give you some time for yourself and the break I'm sure you need. Go and enjoy some wonderful things you haven't been able to do."

Ken put his arm around me in a tender gesture, knowing how I felt. He told the arbitrator that we would go home and discuss this idea rationally and get back to him as soon as we made a decision.

I must have cried a river of tears as I tried to picture letting him go. I felt as if my heart was breaking all over again; that he was being taken away from me all over again. But all of the reasons I didn't want him to go were about me, and how I would feel. Yes, I realized that was so selfish of me. And I cried another river because I knew I loved him so much, I had to let him go for his own sake. *Somehow I would survive this too!*

The arbitrator arranged our first visit to the Center so we could meet everyone and fill out a multitude of forms on Kenny's history.

114   The diagnostic school turned out to be everything and more than I had imagined. The three of us stayed for three days and nights while Kenny was having his

evaluation done by all of the staff members. While Kenny was enjoying all of the attention he was getting, we were given the tour of the premises and saw the room where Kenny would sleep. The rooms where the children slept were side by side, extending from two large corridors and were shared with two or more children. The rooms were all spacious and meticulously clean.

At night there was a constant vigilance while the children slept with a monitor in each room. There was a bathroom adjoining the sleeping quarters where the aides taught toileting and grooming skills. Each child had their own bed, dresser and closet space. There was a wonderful large kitchen and a huge table where everyone, children and aides, gathered for meals. Laughter and learning commingled.

There were several large play rooms equipped with toys, and a soundproof music room with assorted instruments. The gymnastics area was amazing! The floor had protective padding under some equipment. And there were several class-rooms attended by each child with their own aide. Each child was being taught at their own level and mostly to find out what that level was. Their behaviors and reactions to any stimuli was documented, and then worked on by the aides.

The building was perfect for its temporary tenants and the layout was remarkably well-suited for the tutelage that was so obviously abundant there. A sunny patio outside with a beautiful garden, swings, and slides was visible through a thick glass construction that adorned two hallways.

A complete assessment of Kenny's routine at home and special needs were listed, and of course I had prepared a very accurate schedule for them to hang in his room. Every possible question they had about Kenny, and I about them, had been asked and answered in preciseness. One important bit of information I found out was the aides there were long established and highly qualified. They all had their different shifts and all had extensive knowledge of each child.

Not one minute detail of Kenny's needs was overlooked, even to the dietary supplements he was taking that were questioned and evaluated. He was on a gluten free, dairy free, sugar free diet, and it included Vitamin B6 as well as other vita-mins. All of his food likes and dislikes were diligently noted.

I felt by the time the interview was over they knew as much about Kenny as we did! They also had carefully examined his past school history, which really im-pressed me.

The three days went by very quickly with the exchange of information that was now signed, sealed and a soon to be "delivered" Kenny. Although I felt better about this situation after meeting the wonderful staff, and the confidence I had in them, I still cried my eyes out as I packed my little son's clothes a week later, who was more like two, than the eight year old he was.

When the day came that we were to bring him to the Center, I managed to keep myself together. I stayed enthusiastic for his sake and talked about all of the wonderful friends and fun he would be having at his new school.

Upon arrival, Ken and I unpacked Kenny's things and put them away in his new bedroom. We met most of the children previously and there was a little boy close to Kenny's age who shared his room. Neither the little boy or Kenny would be unsupervised and it was all about learning, even when put to bed, how to pull the cover up, which Kenny eventually learned to do on his own if prompted.

We were not hurried or rushed at all by the staff and were told we could take as long as we wanted settling him in.

I set all of his familiar toys, and radio on his night stand and hung pictures of us over the bed, and of course Big Bird. My large printed list of Kenny's day was taped inside his closet for my reassurance that the aides wouldn't forget anything. But I knew Kenny would be in good hands, otherwise I never could have agreed to the arrangement.

I also made a tape with my voice talking to Kenny and telling him how much I loved him and reassuring him I would see him in five days. Then I told him I was hugging and kissing him good night. The staff thought it was a wonderful idea and they promised to play it at night or any time that he might call for me.

On the ride home, I lost it. The image of my darling little boy wanting to drag the last little suitcase to his room with one hand and clutching Big Bird in the other was instilled in my brain. What a trooper he turned out to be!

No mother should ever have to be separated from her child like this, ever! My tears flowed as the sorrow I was feeling for myself and Kenny engulfed me. I knew these were extenuating circumstances, but it didn't hurt any less. I had to keep reminding myself this was for Kenny's good, but I was suffering so much I can't put into words how suddenly alone and lost I felt.

Suddenly, I was being replaced by strangers I had to trust to take over the constant care I had given to my son for eight long years. I wondered how I would get through the next five days without Kenny, who filled each of my days with every possible emotion a mother can feel! Now, I was filled with an emptiness that was hard to bear.

In the beginning, I called each day to see how he was adjusting, but I realized it was an imposition for the busy receptionist to try and track down someone for me to talk to. I knew they were busy with the children, and I was informed the notebooks would be coming home each week when we picked Kenny up. His daily reviews of what took place, how he reacted and what was accomplished was in the notebook, along with any personal suggestions or comments from the aide. I could write back with any concerns or ideas I might have about his care or progress, and they would be addressed.

Kenny was kept so busy with his agenda that it helped to ease the homesickness that most children experienced at first. Kenny seemed to have the hardest time at night, his aide informed us, but the tapes I made really did help soothe him.

Each week when we picked him up and I read his notebook at home, I felt despair when they talked about him being whiny, and calling for me at certain times. I would have driven to the school immediately to get him, had I known at the moment. As it was, the hardship of packing him up each Sunday and driving him back, knowing it would be another five days I would have to endure without him again, was a roller coaster of emotions for me. I didn't even know if he understood how much I loved and missed him. What if he was thinking that I didn't want him any more and that someday I wouldn't come for him at all? Oh God, it was such pain for me! I was heartbroken, again.

I tried hard to busy myself in different projects to keep from going crazy while he was away. My daughter was working as a nurse full time, so we couldn't spend time together. I also did not want to burden her with my pain and struggles with Kenny. My sister and brother both worked also.

Occasionally, I got together with my friend Diana. But I had become so used to multi-tasking that the days just dragged by and I felt myself slipping into oblivion. I felt like a robot sometimes getting the necessary things done and not feeling anything while doing it. I didn't feel like a whole person without Kenny near me. I made myself dabble again in Real Estate and that helped a little, but my heart was not in it. I found myself rushing back home to see if the school might have left messages for me in case of an emergency. There were no cell phones then.

"Have some fun, do things you haven't been able to do, go places, now is the time!" Everyone chided. *How could I possibly enjoy my newfound freedom in this way?* It was a little easier for Ken, because he still worked everyday. Though I knew he missed his son with all of his heart, he was able to deal with it less emotionally. He tried to encourage me to quit worrying so much, but he also knew I wouldn't, couldn't!

Today, at 65 years old, I reminisce over the restricted and difficult life style I've lived while caring for Kenny. I would rather have not gone through that separation from him. I missed him so much! I never want to be without him like that again. But I knew it was the right thing to do at that time. Today, there is still a great need for a program of this propensity for the challenged.

When Kenny was home on the weekends we were to continue working on certain skills they were trying to teach him at school. The first time I saw him place his thumb into his sock to initiate the removal, I was flabbergasted! Then one evening when he was at home he tried to clear dishes from the table, even though it was while we were still eating. It was so cute. He never tried anything on his own without some prompting. It was so exciting for us and we were so proud of him!

He was also learning to take off his shirt, and succeeded with a little assistance. I noticed he was learning how to chew his food more to help discourage swallowing chunks at a time. They told us sometimes he was trying to join in games with other children and would actually place himself in the middle and would lightly touch their hand. They were also trying to teach him to pull the blanket over himself at night while in bed.

There were field trips in groups. Some he enjoyed and some he didn't. My main concern was how exhausted he looked each weekend when we picked him up. This school was like a boot camp for Kenny, but he definitely was improving in many areas.

I had more twinges of guilt not understanding why I couldn't accomplish some of these amazing feats with Kenny at home, as hard as I tried. But my husband kept reminding me that each staff member got to go home at the end of their shift and they had the support of everyone at the establishment. But as bedraggled parents, we had the care and worry 24 hours a day for life.

The months were going by and my fears had eased some. I was delighted, no, ecstatic over the improvements in his behaviors and self-help skills. Kenny didn't cry anymore when he was driven back to the center each weekend. I knew all of my suffering was worth the gains he had made.

When Kenny's stay at the Neurological Diagnostic School in San Francisco was over, we were presented with a summary of 32 pages from their evaluation. It was accomplished through the assessment team consisting of a school psychologist, speech, language and hearing specialist, educational specialist, pediatrician, ophthalmologist consultant and an occupational therapist.

In spite of some improvements in areas that were consistently worked on every day, most of the report was so disheartening:

"Severe deficits in performance were found in the areas of cognitive (12 to 18 months), social-affective behavior (8 to 12 months), pre-academics (1 year 9 months), language/communication (few meaningful verbalizations), and adaptive behavior in all areas of independent functioning skills."

They described Kenny as an "attractive youngster who has difficulty understanding verbal instructions". Even when he appeared to comprehend simple requests, such as imitating a movement with a toy, he typically showed non-compliant behavior by grabbing the toy before demonstration was finished and refusing to return object when requested to do so. This he would do with good eye contact and with a big smile on his face. This type of "teasing" and testing behavior was continuously expressed throughout the assessment week. He was more interested in his teasing and non-compliance than with obtaining examiner's praise with successful performance on the task.

Kenny appeared to be more interested in relating to the examiners than with the large variety of toys. Toys and other objects did not seem to have as much attractive value as people did. (I saw that as a sign of intelligence).

(That's my son, "Mr. Personality.")

They said, "Kenny demonstrates no restraint when his desires are not met immediately, (that is so Kenny)! He enjoys some specific activities, especially taking things apart. He is adept at unscrewing nuts from bolts.

Despite his higher level functioning as seen in his awareness of the concept of objects and his discovery of new means for problem solving, Kenny was unable to demonstrate his use and ability to combine established behaviors to imitate a model, even though only one physical movement was involved.

Kenny was able to search for a hidden object, even though he did not see where it was hidden. This would indicate that he is able to maintain an image of an object while it is out of view.

Kenny is a significantly developmentally delayed nine year old boy with a seizure disorder. He is essentially nonverbal and manifests behaviors which interfere with his ability to benefit optimally from educational instruction and social interaction."

They did not think the Doman-Delacotto program that I had been working on for such a long time, was appropriate for Kenny. They advised the goals for a home and school program that would meet all of his critical needs. And then we would have to find a school for Kenny that would incorporate these goals into his itinerary.

Following was page after page of how these goals should be implemented. The hard part would be to find a site that had the "manpower" to execute these goals. I knew if a school like this existed, I would be the one to find it, but I didn't have great expectations.

A very important issue that I must address at this point, and one that I didn't grasp until Kenny was much older, is the behavior he consistently resorted to when he was being evaluated. Whether the testing was psychological, medical, educational, or in the case of our "lawsuit," legal, Kenny would not share information when I knew he understood what was expected of him. Either out of fear, frustration or pure rebelliousness, he always responded as the imbecile they assumed he was.

There was no doubt in my mind that Kenny was capable of learning. He did learn at the school, but it was the consistencies and intensities of the task at hand that made all of the difference, like the Doman program had stated.

The biggest problems in most special education classes are the downtime and the turnover of aides working with the children. Kenny would come to know and trust the aides. When they were diligent in their teaching, he improved in behaviors and skills. When they moved on, it left a big impact, and he immediately regressed with his "old behaviors" like hand biting, grabbing at others, and tantrums. He couldn't talk, so he couldn't communicate in words how he felt in his loss, therefore he acted out through aggression toward others.

The next step was meeting with Kenny's program coordinator. Then the search would begin for a magical site capable of addressing all of the special needs in Kenny's itinerary.

CHAPTER
EIGHTEEN
EIGHTEEN

THE BOY IN THE WINDOW
the boy in the window

While I was still in search of another school for Kenny, who was then nine years old, I found out about Canine Companions in Santa Rosa. They raised wonderful dogs specifically for the blind and disabled. The dogs offered emotional gratification for children like Kenny. They were trained to protect and assist their handicapped owners. The dogs were outfitted with a special pack that could allow the dog's attendant to be secured with a wrist attachment to the leash, if needed.

It was the companionship for Kenny that appealed to me so much, and I made the appointment for the interview by phone. They said they would have to meet us and Kenny to find out if he qualified for a dog.

At the appointment, they wholeheartedly agreed it would be very beneficial for Kenny to bond with one of their canines. They felt it might have a calming effect on him. Good, I thought. Although I have never cared for animals in the house, it was a small sacrifice I was willing to make if it helped Kenny. It was no problem for my husband, as he loves dogs. We were to start "boot camp," which was the name given for the program, in three weeks.

For 14 straight days, the three of us left at 8 a.m. and drove for an hour to Santa Rosa to "boot camp." We quickly found out why they called it that!

Each morning we were educated and learned everything there was to know about these special dogs. They were preparing us for a test we had to pass at the end of the program. While Ken and I were learning the history of the dogs, the trainers that were not busy with their canines at this time, were assigned to watch our son. They were so compassionate with Kenny, who acted like one of their frisky little puppies anyway.

Afternoons were devoted to working with the dogs. We had to learn how to apply all of the commands with each dog, though the dogs already knew them. The pulling and tugging on the leashes virtually for seven hours each day was grueling, as the dogs were trying hard to figure everyone out. They tested the less aggressive handlers, which was me! Not all of us learned as quickly as others. I am a glutton for punishment!

The whole idea in exchanging dogs during the "camp" was to match up personalities and determine which dog you would eventually pair up with. Not being a dog person, and having a hard time being very assertive with them, I wondered if I would ever be able to make any of them mind me. It was also important for Ken and I both to ascertain which dog responded to Kenny the most, even though Ken would be the main caretaker of the dog.

There were about ten handicapped people in our group with assorted disabilities. As our training progressed with the dogs, certain days were designated for field trips. Going to the mall was big on the list. It was crucial for people to be able to handle their furry friends while out in public. It was quite an impressive sight to see our group with all of the dogs wearing their "packs" that were a colorful blue and gold.

There was so much going on all through the training that Kenny was delighted and loved the dogs. He acted out a lot at times, but there was always help close by. The two weeks of "boot camp" were the longest of my life! By the time we got home each night, we were all exhausted.

We finally paired up with a dog I really felt comfortable with. We had been performing with him the most. It was time to take our "test" dog home for a visit and see how he would fit into the new environment.

His name was Mc-Arthur. He was a dark reddish, gentle golden retriever and he was perfect for Kenny. He followed him around everywhere and was very curious about Kenny. No matter what Kenny was doing, Mc-Arthur would get right in the middle of it. Kenny loved that, and I loved it too, this was the perfect dog for us I felt. I hoped with all of my heart Mc-Arthur would be coming home with us for good. But the final decision was always up to the program coordinator.

It was the last four days of the training and up until that time we thought Mc-Arthur would be ours. But instead he was delegated out to someone that needed to utilize his abilities more than Kenny, as he was an extremely intelligent dog. These dogs could do helpful tasks such as turn on lights, push elevator buttons, and other amazing feats. Mc-Arthur excelled in all of these things and was sent to a wheelchair bound person. Though I was happy for the person, I was so disappointed for the three of us.

Most dogs had been matched up to their new owners, and there were just a few left. My heart was still with Mc-Arthur and I didn't feel any bond at all with the remaining dogs. I left the decision up to my husband who liked the "black sheep" of the clan. His name was Gizmo. He was a cute golden retriever. The trainers were thinking of dropping him from the program because he showed too much aggression at times when he shouldn't have. The room would be filled with dogs lying quietly at the side of their new "potential" owners and the trainers would let in several cats. The dogs were to remain still and oblivious to the cats, which all of them did, except for Gizmo and his quiet bark. Plus he didn't always "obey" the rigid rules of the commands expected from a canine companion. *Great!* I thought. *Another hardheaded addition to our family, just what we need!*

Even though I was not excited about taking Gizmo home, I was not leaving without a dog after all of the hard work and sacrifices we made in the last 14 days. So we literally had to plead for Gizmo and beg them not to "fire" him. He came closest to fitting in with our family out of the few dogs left. And so we got him.

Gizmo turned out to be a great "pet," more than anything else, because it was my husband who cared for him, as of course Kenny wasn't capable.

Gizmo preferred to bond with Ken, no matter how hard we tried to encourage his interaction with Kenny. When Kenny and Gizmo were attached with the special pack, Gizmo didn't have a choice in the matter. Off they went with Kenny dragging the dog along tugging on the leash, and Gizmo not understanding what Kenny was trying to accomplish. The dog didn't know whether to speed up or slow down and would look helplessly back at his "real" master. They looked so cute together even though there was seldom a harmonious stop and go.

Kenny still enjoyed his dog, in his way, and Gizmo was very protective of Kenny. They had a subtle relationship. On the routine weekend drives we took in the mornings, Kenny and Gizmo rode in the back seat of Ken's truck. I think Kenny saw him as a giant "Big Bird" as he could squeeze, love and pull fur out for good measure with nary a complaint from Gizmo.

Being that Kenny really seemed to enjoy his dog, I decided to sign him up for another animal attraction. It was at the Cornerstone Equestrian Center for the handicapped. I heard that it helped to give a child like Kenny a sense of power and connection with their own bodies from the rhythmic movement of the horse. Also, riding was known to help behaviors to improve, kind of like calming the beast within while straddling one. *Imagine the concept.*

We added this venture into our busy agenda that included, looking for a new school for Kenny, working on his behaviors and self-help skills that were taught to him at the Diagnostic Center, and of course there was always cleaning up and chasing after him. Let's not leave out the grocery shopping and cooking for Ken and me and Kenny's special diet. Throw in a little selling of real estate on whatever days of the week I had an opening, and presto! *Wonder Woman is at it again!*

We took Kenny to the stable once a week for his riding lessons. Thank goodness it was in our own town. There was no doubt that the volunteers were the backbone of this wonderful program. They patiently walked on each side of the horse while the children rode. There was a huge indoor arena where ring posts were strategically placed. When the horse stopped there, the child could lean, grasp the ring and try to throw it back on the post.

Kenny had a favorite volunteer, not a horse, as one might imagine. She was a cute blonde and I think he was as excited about seeing her as the horses. Kenny really enjoyed the riding and we got to participate. Sometimes we walked beside the horse or we just watched. The only drawback was he fought the mandatory helmet. He couldn't stand hats of any kind on his head. He constantly fidgeted with it, trying to get it off while still managing to keep a pretty good rhythm on the horse. At times, he managed to shove it over his eyes or halfway off the back of his head, and all of the trailing horses with their riders had to stop so the aide could adjust his helmet.

Kenny enjoyed this program for three years until it closed because of financial difficulties. He was about 13 years old then.

Kenny's first Halloween dressed up. 4 ½ years. Looks like he just used the fork on a visitor who stayed too long.

Still in a crib until six or seven years old to protect him from falling out of a bed with a seizure.

Kenny couldn't use
utensils to eat at six.

Eight years old trying to put
rings on post – listening
to stories on tape –
Doman's program.

Kenny with Dad,
wearing pinhole
glasses from part of
Doman's program.

Kenny didn't want help with the pulling of his belongings into his room at NDC in San Francisco.

Big Bird still has his beak.

Big Bird after Kenny chewed his beak off.

Dropping Kenny off for another week in NDC in San Francisco. Ken and I trying to be brave and all smiles for his sake. I saved my crying for the long ride home.

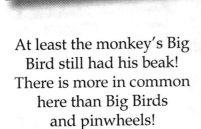

At least the monkey's Big Bird still had his beak! There is more in common here than Big Birds and pinwheels!

129

Train rides at Tilden Park
in Berkeley.

Kenny watching the
boats launch.

Kenny trying to take his
bandage off his hand
he hurt after breaking
a window in his
learning room.

Kenny being pushed on a swing at park by his dad.

Kenny bites his hand when over excited or angry, a lifelong habit.

Kenny's porch overlooking Rick's house across the street. Rick's daughter is visiting.

Trying to take off his shirt at about eight years old.

Our most adventurous outing with Kenny.

Horseback riding for the challenged.

Santa Rosa with Gizmo, our canine companion.

CHAPTER
NINETEEN

THE BOY IN THE WINDOW
the boy in the window

*T*en and I were working so hard on the skills that Kenny had learned at the Diagnostic Center, but we were losing the battle. It didn't take long for him to start back-sliding into old habits and behaviors; hand biting, grabbing and more tantrums. He needed to be in a classroom setting that could help follow up with all of the goals in his itinerary. Our school district still hadn't come up with anything yet, nor had I. The good news was we won the battle for a continuous one to one aide for Kenny that was responsible for his safety, no matter what program we found for him.

I don't remember how I found out about the class in Richmond. It was another out of town location that I knew meant another fair hearing with the Vallejo School District. It was about 40 minutes from home.

How I hated having to see him traveling on the busy freeways and so far from home, but there was no other option.

Kenny's program coordinator went with me to view the class. I liked the teacher and the staff seemed professional, qualified and cared about the children. Several children had one to one aides and it was a very organized learning environment. The teacher welcomed the challenge of the extensive goals for Kenny. The man representing our son agreed that it was an appropriate placement. He also informed me of another boy from Vallejo that could benefit from this school. He said it would help influence our "fight" and necessitate transporting at least two children by school bus out of town instead of just one.

We were able to convince the district in one meeting to enroll Kenny in Richmond. I visited the school often and spent time in the classroom. I could see that Kenny was doing well and eventually thriving, but after a year, parents were asked to write a supportive letter to the Richmond school district as they were planning on selling the building for needed funds. The class would then have to move to Berkeley, which was just too far for Kenny to be able to attend.

This is a letter I wrote regarding that issue. I feel it describes how well Kenny was doing at that time:

Our son Kenny is 11 years old. He suffered brain damage from the Pertussis vaccine at 19 months old. He was born a beautiful, healthy and normal baby. It happens to many babies; it could happen to yours. The affliction left him with severe learning disabilities, seizures, extreme hyper-activeness, a short attention span, abnormal and erratic behaviors that include screaming and tantrums, and no language.

We were told by professional doctors to institutionalize him because caring for him would be impossible for us.

But our love and determination gave us the strength and ability to care for him, even though the past 11 years have been the most emotionally draining, frustrating and at times unbearable for all three of us. But Kenny has improved, and no matter how hard times were or will be, we will never give up fighting for the best for him. Only those of you who are raising a child like this know of the mental and physical exhaustions, the sacrifices, the loneliness, and the continuous struggles and battles you encounter, day in and day out, year after year.

But the most frustrating fight of all for your special child is that child's right to a decent education.

Through the years, classrooms were offered that were not safe or suitable for Kenny's specific needs, and I tutored him myself for two years, on top of his 24 hour a day care. I had no personal life of my own and was exhausted. The lack of competent help, dependable people, and having to do battle for educational support took its toll on me.

The arbitrations and fair hearings with the school district that my husband and I had to prepare in length for and present to the board was precious time wasted in the biological clock of my delayed child, and I resent that.

His last placement was a two hour a day program that wasn't really appropriate because teachers did not have enough help in the classroom and aides came and went, leaving him frustrated and confused. He wasn't learning because of the insecurity in the environment and he regressed.

But our last fair hearing brought us to this wonderful program, a dream come true for us because it was the type of class I visualized Kenny in. The services they provide help the children thrive and grow.

This is what happened to Kenny. He started last June, and they have reached him in a way no previous day school had. He improved rapidly and skills he learned at the Diagnostic Center surfaced again. They work on all areas of his daily living and social behaviors, just like the Center had suggested. We can take him to restaurants with more appropriate eating and actions. He is calmer, and I find I no longer have to run after him every minute. He has more verbalization and listens better. He really seems to be trying to do more for himself and shows pleasure when he succeeds. He also seems happier now. This is the proof when a child is in the right classroom setting and their specific needs are being met they can become the best that they can be and help parents refrain from institutionalization of their child, where they can be demoralized, abused, and drugged. Most of all, they deserve the best.

They can't comprehend the basic fun of life that normal kids take for granted; talking, little league games, ice skating, movies etc.

This class is the best thing for Kenny, it's his fun. Please don't take away something that is helping these children and my son. They have had enough taken from them already.

If these children are uprooted from this environment, they will regress. My beautiful precious son needs this school, I need them, and my life is a little more normal and a little less burdened because of them.

Thank You for Hearing Me,

Barbara Coppo – End of Letter

Well, the letters from the parents bought more time, but eventually the rumors started flying again about the possibility of the building being sold, and evidently it was creating an unsettling tension among the staff. As I visited the class frequently, and through experience, I knew things were falling apart little by little. I saw things I was not happy about and I heard negative comments from the bus drivers, who always had a sense of what was going on in special ed classes.

Then ironically, in October of 1992 I had to write this letter to the Vallejo School Board out of desperation:

We removed our 14 year old, brain-injured son from the Richmond Center because he was in danger. The constant replacement of staff members because of their insecure jobs regarding possible closure of the school created loss of control in Kenny's and other children's behaviors. They were not consistent in their behavior methods, nor did they deal with Kenny's intimidating outbursts, which at one point caused a severe cut on his foot requiring medical attention. Their inconsistencies caused regressions in our son, such as wetting incidents, which had been controlled for a long time, and he is back to hand biting, (on himself) and grabbing strangers, which had diminished when all was well at the school. Kenny was bitten twice on the face by another child, (that broke the skin) which could be a devastating factor for him, because I won't risk more damage from a tetanus shot.

We were constantly being told that his behavior was "good" at school, yet the bus driver would repeatedly tell us of tantrums she had observed before his boarding.

Kenny also was picking up a terrible habit from another child, which was hitting himself in the head very hard.

Many times the children had unsupervised free time outside at recess while staff took breaks, leaving a chaotic and unsafe environment.

Kenny's tantrums at home continued to increase with furor that led to breaking his toe twice, which required a cast to his knee. He was pounding on the windows to the

137

point of neighbors complaining as they could hear him inside their home. He was break-ing glasses and furniture, pushing and hitting me, and biting his hand until it bled.

In September, neighbors (who we had not gotten acquainted with yet), were tired of the racket Kenny made and complained that he always ran after them (because he wanted to give them love). Of course they didn't know that. At one point, Kenny was playing his "grab the cap off a head" game with the neighbor next door, taught to him by a well meaning neighbor across the street. Before I could get Kenny away, his hand missed the cap and latched on to the neighbor's gold chain around his neck, which I had to pry out of his hand. The man called the police thinking Kenny was trying to steal his chain and had attacked him to try to get it.

When the police arrived, Kenny was in his favorite spot looking out the window, de-lighted to see some action on the usually quiet court, as the neighbor animatedly described his ordeal with Kenny. (Note, this family turned out to be the best neighbors anyone could possibly ask for!)

My husband and I were dealing with tantrums that would last up to eight hours. Our life was a nightmare and after 14 years of trying to fight for the best for him, we were ready to throw in the towel. (We wouldn't have.)

It seemed that all of the improvements he had made were lost and I didn't know if I had the strength left in me to bring them back. My husband's anger had escalated from all the tension in our life, and I was ready to call it quits with him. This was not helping Kenny either.

Previous to the deteriorating situation at the school, the director had hired a behav-ioral learning consultant, Pat, and she was good! I met her a few times at the school in Marin County that Kenny had attended. Her methods are uncanny in the sense that she promotes success in these children by treating them as if they already know how to behave, and works with them at that level. She became a part of the success in the program while it was thriving, so she was very familiar with Kenny.

She has been to our house a few times and gave us some very good pointers when dealing with his behaviors.

Late one evening we called her out of desperation. Kenny was going through a terrible temper tantrum that had escalated, and was well into six hours. Kenny had resorted to kicking and hitting anything within reach and my husband had to restrain him by laying his body over Kenny, which took all of his strength to hold him down. Ken was exhausted and all I could do was referee the two struggling contenders. I was so afraid that one or both of them would be severely hurt. We didn't know what to do and there was no one else that could help us with our nightmare.

Pat drove all the way from her home in Marin County to give us relief. She took over with Mr. Hyde, and immediately gathered up pillows and started tossing them at

Kenny. Though he was still to out of control and too angry to respond to her interaction at first, he slowly fell into the brain washing of her "playful" yet assertive demands. He picked up the pillows and tried to throw them back. He reacted forcefully to every spontaneous and ingenious command she threw at him.

Kenny had been in this mode for eight hours. Soon they were both at their wits end, but she never gave up. Finally, he couldn't fight anymore and she sat him on her lap encircling his arms down to his side so he couldn't hit her, and clutched him close to her body. She began to rock him in this position. She called it "baby time."

The following was not in my letter. (I look back now and realize how far advanced her techniques were. In a book published many years later called, Let Me Hear Your Voice, a mother of an autistic child was presented with a "new" method to help cure autism, called "holding therapy." It is about the bond between mother and child that is lost through, in Kenny's case, brain damage. The child doesn't want bodily contact and avoids every effort from the mother when she tries to give it. Holding therapy is when the mother forcibly holds the child against her body and lets the child know her true feelings, which could include her own rage at being rejected. It was to be done an hour or more each day.) End of addition.

She wants to work at home with us and help us get Kenny under some kind of control. She knows if we don't, there could be disastrous results for all of us, with Kenny ending up being drugged and restrained somewhere.

We need an ace in the hole right now, and she is it! So, trained by Pat, we are working hard using her methods and tools, and are encouraged by the almost instant improvements.

She is in the process of getting licensed for her own school in Mill Valley where she is having successes with some very severely "hurt" kids. One, in fact, is another little boy who suffered brain damage from the d.p.t. vaccine. I called his mother and heard a remarkable testimony from her about Pat and her program.

I brought Kenny with me to visit her site and I want him to be a part of it. In fact, his future depends on the person directing it, Pat.

Her program is set up in a fun, yet strict environment that has each child in a continuous activity preventing boredom that leads to behaviors. Her program provides a full schedule implementing total use of the school funds. Her staff is under her direct command, and must follow her regime explicitly because what she does works. There will be no staff conflicts or inconsistencies. That has been a major problem for Kenny in his previous classes.

Her ideas are displayed as a normal kindergarten through third grade setting, including desks for each child, art, music, planting gardens, video room, horseback riding, swimming, and some mainstreaming into regular classes when appropriate. She also will be providing job training skills for older children.

She has set up a parent and caretaker training class so that everyone involved with the child will follow through to achieve optimum results. She documents goals on a weekly basis, not quarterly.

You can see why we have no other choice but to send Kenny to her school in Mill Valley. I will be driving him starting next week, and hopefully we can get his placement approved through the proper channels deemed necessary by your school district within a short time.

Sincerely,

Barbara Coppo – End of Letter

CHAPTER
TWENTY

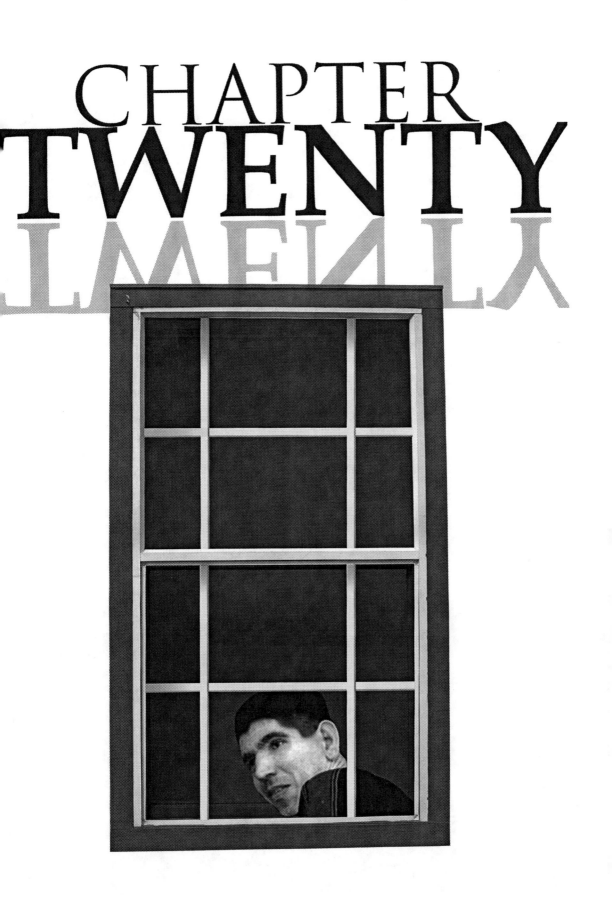

THE BOY IN THE WINDOW
the boy in the window

*I*t was a long drive from Vallejo to Mill Valley in 1992 with Kenny as the back seat driver. There was no Richmond Causeway then, just gobs of traffic, something Kenny couldn't tolerate. At times he managed to put a leg over the front seat grabbing the steering wheel. I don't know if he wanted to drive or just go home. How I got us both ready and out the door by 7:30 every morning was an amazing feat in itself. But enduring the typical neck choking, hair pulling, and arm grabbing from Kenny when traffic backed up, should have won me a spot on the TV series *Survivor*!

Certainly, we were a source of entertainment for those early morning commuters, if they were lucky enough to pull up beside us. We put on quite a show. Kenny's shenanigans included, slithering back and forth like a caged animal and hitting at the windows while I prayed they stayed intact! And me with a happy face and singing, in hopes he would change, his tune!

Kenny was 14, about 5'8", and although he was on the thin side, he was strong. He always looked so much younger than his age, so I doubt the other drivers thought he was an angry boyfriend. I just know I should have won a Nobel Prize for bravery chauffeuring him to   school each day.

But once traffic started picking up, he thankfully settled down. I played his tapes, sang along and did every possible feat imaginable in a car short of tap dancing, to try to please him. *Oh how I longed for Fridays!*

But arriving at the school brought joy to us and I felt instantly uplifted as we were greeted with enthusiasm. Kenny loved his new surroundings and especially "circle time." All the children sat with their aides and all were required to participate in some way. For me, it was amazing to see charts of numbers, letters, maps, the human body, history, plants and other information.

Each child was taught to point to their city on a map and parts of the body on the chart. When the child finished with his or her turn, the whole group would clap. I reveled in the similarities of the Doman program, but this was so much more.

I was encouraged to stay and observe as long and as often as I wanted. I was asked to participate in weekly field trips, which I did. Some days I went to a gym and engaged in strenuous workouts to help relieve some tension. Some tension? Eventually, I was confident enough to drive home and back, if pressing errands warranted that. Of course it was a lot of commuting back and forth, and ultimately Mary, who had become Kenny's most valued respite care person, helped with the driving. We were still waiting for the Vallejo school district's approval of the site. If they did, we hoped they would help us with the cost of transportation.

Several visits from the biased Vallejo School Program Coordinators were scratching their heads over the curriculum that was unlike any program they had viewed before. They were used to special ed kids, "sorting," matching colors, and tossing bean bags, not pointing to body parts and then trying to name them, and identifying plants, numbers, or animals etc.

The visitors from our district felt some of her methods to be "unorthodox." The goal, as usual, was for our school district to finance Kenny's tuition once Pat's licensing was completed. Pat was spending her own money as well as whatever parents could help out with in contributions toward supplies, and lunches. She was to be reimbursed after all the legalities were finalized.

It was at her school that both the good and the bad happened to Kenny. The good was the day I was asked by an aide if I was aware of Kenny's math ability. My jaw dropped. For a moment, I contemplated reporting to Pat that she had an aide who was a little crazy. But since her program was so "out of the norm," I quickly recovered from my thought and burst out laughing. She probably thought I was crazy! When I realized she was more than serious, I straightened my face and looked her square in the eyes and responded, "No. I had no idea Kenny could do math." She said, "Each time I threw the dice, I had a student attempt to pick the answer from several printed choices. Kenny almost always picked the correct amount."

I think I just said, "How wonderful," but I didn't give the credibility to this announcement that I should have. I thought more about the ingenious way they incorporated dice into their math sessions. Parents were always impressed with the originality that was Pat's trademark when working with difficult children. I was just so glad that Kenny was being offered everything that was taught to normal children, to a degree of course. And more importantly, Kenny was really thriving, and seemed to be trying harder in all areas. The kids had fun, were kept busy and were challenged. There was no time for "down time" so prevalent in most special ed classes.

Pat had tried to explain something called facilitation to me one day as I was about to depart with Kenny. It was something about a method of communication on a key board with letters. Kenny's finger would print words. I didn't fully understand what she was talking about as Kenny was pulling at me to leave, and she was rushed. She said we would discuss it when we both had more time. She did tell me she had been training her aides how to do this "facilitation" (FC) with some students.

Shortly thereafter, I caught something on the news about facilitation, and it made more sense to me. A school site in Alameda, near Oakland, which was about a 45 minute drive from Vallejo, was teaching this method to parents to use with their autistic, non-verbal kids. It was just for one day. Because Pat had seemed so excited about it, I wanted to make a special effort to learn all I could. I was so intrigued. I called and found out the day and time and took Kenny, feeling an extraordinary sense of excitement. *How wonderful it would be if I could really communicate with my son!*

There was a long line of parents and their "hurt" kids that couldn't talk. Kenny was not cooperative. *What else is new?* It had been hard occupying him while we waited, and he was tired.

Finally, it was our turn. A kind woman sitting behind a desk held Kenny on her lap to show him a big card with the alphabet in black letters on it. She asked him to point to different letters to see if he had any inclination of the alphabet whatsoever. He just fussed, squirmed and resisted, not showing a bit of interest. But she was not giving up that easily. She tried several more times to get him to point without success. She then quickly picked up two cards to show him. One said "yes," and the other said "no." I had already told her that he couldn't read. Although Pat had said Kenny could read several words. I had felt excited when she told me, but I wondered, *how could Pat know for sure?* I had taken that information lightly also.

The woman said to Kenny, "I know you're tired. Do you want to go home?" Kenny grabbed that "yes" card so quickly off the table and shoved it in her face! "I think he can read!" she said.

It was amazing that he picked the right card! But then again, it could have been a lucky guess. I was definitely going to explore this "FC" further on my own, without Kenny. It was so hard to concentrate on anything when he was with me. Facilitation seemed like such a simple and brilliant method for communication.

The bad news was, when Kenny turned 15 he had a grand mal seizure while on a walk with the class. They called me at the gym and I remember becoming so upset that someone had to help me gather my things from my locker and walk me to my car. I had prayed so hard he wouldn't have the grand mal seizures ever again. I couldn't bear seeing him suffer anymore and I just couldn't deal with the "big" seizures. Tom, who was Kenny's aide at the school and his buddy, came home with us to offer his support.

The waiting game would begin all over again. *Would he have another, and if so when? Should he go on medication immediately, or should we wait and see?* I wanted to scream and scream, why this too? *Isn't life hard enough for all of us as it is?* But when the next seizure came, and the next, I decided to look into alternative medicine before jumping into the nightmare of anticonvulsant drugs and their nasty side effects.

I tried everything from Chinese medicine to acupuncture, and herbal remedies, yet he still had more seizures, and I had less money. Alternative medicine is never covered by your health insurance and is extremely expensive. It was very hard getting Kenny to the appointments, even though I had help. Usually an aide from the school named Moe, who also was assigned to Kenny, would go with me. He worked with Kenny at home sometimes as a side job.

I finally resorted to re-evaluating the traditional drugs that were available. I wasn't happy about any of them. I went with the drug of choice at that time, which was Felbatol. It was fairly new and showed positive results in studies done with the least side affects. I didn't have a choice but to put my complete confidence in his neurologist. The medicine kept him from falling down and going into a full blown seizure. But to this day he still suffers with them. Today, the news is not good about Felbatol. Kenny had been on it for years, when the discovery was made that horrific side effects had occurred, enough to where the drug was not prescribed any longer to new patients. Blood disorders (sometimes fatal) called "aplastic anemia" and liver problems were the most severe. Adding another seizure medication, in conjunction with Felbatol that his neurologist had suggested in order to get better seizure control, increased his risk for aplastic anemia. This disease can also occur after a person stops taking the drug. Imagine living with this fear, alone, for your child. *How can my son escape a future of doom when everything seems to be stacked against him?*

When I heard about an evening catechism class for the developmentally disabled I was so happy. Kenny and I both needed a strong bond with God in our lives. The class was held in the very old St. Vincent's parish in Vallejo, a landmark. Parents and aides could attend with their son or daughter if needed. Kenny seemed fascinated with the Bible stories told in simplicity by the Sisters. They used colorful images made from felt cloth and placed them on a large self-stick background as the stories were being told. The students could visualize the life of Jesus and his disciples for a better understanding. Kenny seemed genuinely happy to be there and enjoyed the circle time where questions were asked of the participants. Kenny of course, took delight examining everyone in the circle and loved the discussions of the evening's lessons.

After the Bible study was over the class was divided into groups and assigned to different tables for crafts. This is when the agitation would begin for him. He wanted the circle time and the stories to continue. He only attempted to color (scribble) pictures if a Sister came over to help him. He couldn't see what everyone else was doing and we would have to leave early because of Kenny's disappointment in the process. My spiritually inclined son was turning out to be a real control freak.

After several months of classes, that were once a week, it was finally time for the whole group to visit the inside of the "big church!" The students had learned that it was the house of God. They were to be familiarized with the procedure of Communion, which was the goal of their studies. Most were quite excited about seeing the inside of God's domain, including Kenny.

A line was formed with the students and parents. And as quietly as possible, we all filed into the empty church via the back entrance.

Upon entering the beautiful sanctuary, Kenny let go of my hand and started roaming the aisles and started calling out loudly for "Ga" (God). It was the best religious experience I've ever had.

When Kenny did get in line for his first communion with the others, the Priest put the piece of bread in his mouth that constitutes the "Body of Christ". Kenny yelled out "mor" (for more bread). This was the second best religious experience!

A very short time later, and we have no explanation as to why, he suddenly did not want to attend the class anymore. My son was a Catechism drop out.

Kenny was and is the mirror to my emotions, and it has reflected on my existence. I am as Kenny feels. When he smiles and seems content, my heart swells with gratitude. When I know he is feeling poorly, I suffer with my silent thoughts. Though I learned to hide my pain well from the world I belong to, I have wallowed in self-pity from time to time, which is contrary to my natural state of optimism. But having to endure the worry and grief over my son so much drained the life out of me. Sometimes I can't separate the boundaries of my fears for Kenny, from the person I know as me.

When in this state of mind, I would try to bring my own identity to a culminating point by challenging myself. Moreover, just to see if I could still meet the challenge. It wasn't enough that I had a real estate license, and later an esthetician's license, (skin care). Maybe I've had to strive for personal achievements to feel worthy of myself because I couldn't "fix" my own son.

Once, during these tense years, I decided to apply for a car sales position just to see if I could pass the required test, never dreaming I would be hired over 15 applicants. I wasn't expecting to become a car saleswoman, and didn't know what the heck I was doing on a car lot, but there I was.

After three days, I realized it had just been something I needed to satisfy my ego, and perhaps a quick escape from my reality. Either way, I found out fast it was important to be able to drive a stick shift when selling cars, which I couldn't, and didn't want to learn. This was the shortest career of my life.

CHAPTER TWENTY-ONE

THE BOY IN THE WINDOW
the boy in the window

We went through a revolving door of respite people, and most didn't want to come back a second time, nor did I want them to. We've had the Nutty Professor, the Mad Hatter, Mo and Curly and even the bad seed appear at our doorstep. Some were of our own findings, and others were from the Regional Center, where our reputation had become much like the school district's when it came to the dreaded "Coppo" name. Yes, I was a fanatic about Kenny's well-being and I was very particular about his caretakers. You can't be too cautious with a child who can't talk.

I had to do a training session with each person that was sent here. It became so repetitious that I began dreading a new face. So many of the workers were unskilled in their custodianship, and lacked any positive enthusiasm. Not that I wasn't grateful for even the least amount of help, but most times I ended up caring for the caretakers too, trying to make them feel welcomed and comfortable. I would know by Kenny's reaction whether someone would work out on a more permanent basis.

Sometimes I would peek in the room where the person was supposed to be engaging him in activities. Many times I found them just sitting and staring at him, while he stared out the window. *Were they waiting for him to entertain them?* In these cases, I knew he would be running from the room calling for me.

I found it easier if we all got in the car and did errands together. Then I treated them to snacks or lunch, and by the time we got home, I never felt like I'd had a break.

Once, a young woman came out, and she seemed fairly capable and Kenny liked her. After getting used to him, she suggested a walk. Though I was a little uneasy, I knew he would enjoy it. He was only about ten-years-old at the time. I gave her all of the firm instructions about holding his hand and not letting him go for an instant and if she had any problems to turn around and head for home quickly. He was still small and not strong enough to resist firm grasps, if needed. I told her the first block is the key to a good walk. Meaning, if he goes that far, he usually does great the whole way. I watched them go down the street and felt proud that I had given Kenny some slack.

I figured I had about 20 minutes, so I rushed around doing little jobs around the house and must have been relishing how good it felt to not be interrupted between tasks. Suddenly, I was aware it had been 40 minutes since they left. I got a shiver when the door bell rang.

I dashed downstairs in a flash, my heart in my mouth, when a man said, "There is a little problem and I think you should come." I grabbed my car keys and drove several blocks to the house he directed me to. There was the respite person standing in front of a house crying. I could hear a tractor from the backyard, but no Kenny in sight.

Oh my God, I thought, *a tractor!* While she was explaining that he got away from her when he heard the tractor, I was already heading for the backyard where Kenny was. He, of course, was jumping gleefully and biting his hand from the excitement, while less than three feet away stood his favorite noisy machine! The distracted driver continued to dig very cautiously, but was not going to let a public nuisance keep him from his work!

After gathering him up and giving the driver a dirty look, I lectured the young woman about leaving Kenny. She begged me not to tell the agency, which I didn't, and I didn't care to have her back again either.

I felt more compelled than ever to keep Kenny by my side. Keeping him safe is not always easy, but at the time all that ran through my mind was, *I know I am the best person for that job! I guess I have to do it all by myself. I can't delegate that responsibility to a stranger.* I wept from frustration, exhaustion and for my son.

I don't remember exactly how long it was before I called for respite help again. I only knew it was inevitable and necessary if I was to retain my sanity.

At first, she was just another stranger coming to my house. I was feeling resentful that I even needed a stranger in my house at all! I was not looking forward to going over the "do's and don'ts" of Kenny's criteria.

As soon as she met Kenny, she exclaimed how adorable she thought he was. She stated that he seemed so normal, until later, when she served him the piece of chocolate cake I had promised him for good behavior. (Not often on his menu). I had totally forgotten to tell her that Kenny needed a lot of guidance when eating because he likes to disregard the spoon and fork. So he quickly picked up the cake with his hand, shoving most of it in his mouth at once. The rest ended up everywhere else. Although it surprised her, we both laughed as I walked into the room and saw the chocolate comedy, sitting so innocently in his chair smiling. What a sight he was with gobs of black goo on his face, teeth and hair.

I ran downstairs to find dishrags and cleaner, and when I got back to the room, she had already found something to clean him up with. She then attacked the rest of the mess. *Finally,* I thought, *someone that can function without being told what to do.*

Then later, noticing that he hadn't come running out of the room yet to look for me, I peeked in and saw him holding the radio I had bought him. He never had showed an interest in it. "He likes the radio." she said, "Do you play it often for him?" "No," I replied, "he pulls the plug before it has a chance to play. In fact," I told her, "Kenny cannot stand plugs in the wall. He goes around the house and unplugs what he can get to!"

There were other things she got him to do and I was so pleased. He liked her. I liked her too and wanted her to come back.

But later when Ken got home from work, she immediately picked up on the household tension. It made her feel uncomfortable. His Italian disposition, or "short temper" had become so commonplace with him, that it was more out of habit, than actual anger. I didn't want to deal with it anymore. That day she didn't think she would be returning, although she really liked Kenny. She told me this many months later, after she had become the most welcomed person in our home.

It had been an extremely stressful time for me. I knew I wasn't good company the first day of Mary's arrival. She was such an easy person to be around, and I relished in the comfort of her. I ended up telling my whole story, what happened to Kenny, and how the only other person that really could handle Kenny was Ginny, who was now busy taking care of her ailing husband.

I told her about the pandemonium that engulfed our lives on a daily basis, while trying to meet Kenny's needs. On top of that, I explained that I was making plans to leave my husband so I could work with Kenny without the added turmoil that described our relationship.

I felt joyless and lonely. I unloaded to Mary. It felt good, because I always tried to retain a cheerful manner with everyone as much as possible. After all, I was an optimist at heart and hated being a "downer." I never wanted to sound like I was complaining about Kenny. I have always loved him so much, in spite of what a well intended psychologist told me a long time ago, "You will grow to resent your son someday, so you might as well institutionalize him now!" I have never resented Kenny, and I never will.

A lot of my frustrations, other than my marriage, were caused from self-expectations. There was always so much do. I ran myself ragged trying to accomplish it all!

Mary changed her mind and came back to care for Kenny on designated days. I changed my mind about a separation. Through the years, she became Kenny's main respite person. She opened doors for Kenny that led to new responses from him. She not only became family to us, but Kenny became a part of her family too. Ken and I had a little more freedom. She helped me with Kenny when he got sick, knowing how much I worried. She would come over, no matter how late it was, and comfort me while I agonized over his seizures. She remains in our life today and hopefully forever. She is our "angel."

CHAPTER
TWENTY-TWO

THE BOY IN THE WINDOW
the boy in the window

W hile Kenny attended Pat's school he enjoyed one of the aides there who was a bright young man I will call Tom. We were fortunate that he was already familiar with Kenny, and knew how to work with him. He had been trained by Pat, so he was very special himself.

Unfortunately, Pat was never able to get the licensing she deserved in time to save her financially drained school. Her aides had to look for other jobs. She wanted them to continue with her and keep the program going in her home. But she already owed them back pay, and couldn't promise how long it would take for her get reimbursed from school districts who owed her. We could not afford to continue taking Kenny. She wanted us to hang in there. But in spite of her pleas, we had to say no. I began my scouring search for another program for Kenny.

The Vallejo School district told me about Spectrum in Concord. It was a behavioral school with some very unmanageable students, but a well-trained staff. The program had a good reputation and seemed to have a decent curriculum. I was able to get Tom, who was out of work, hired as Kenny's one-to-one aide at the school. I enthusiastically expressed how well he worked with special ed students and that he would be an asset to the school. Having Tom with Kenny was the only way I agreed to enroll him at the new site.

Kenny was 16, and though I wished he didn't have to be in a school with some older boys with tendencies toward violent outbursts, I knew he was in good hands with Tom. Kenny behaved quite well for him. I think he saw him as a friend, as well as his mentor. That was so beneficial for the adjustment he would need to make, again, in his new surrounding.

I was happy to find out that Spectrum had computers and some of the students were being shown the new technique of facilitation. There was a class in Marin County where I had learned the history and process of facilitated communication or FC. It was newly brought to the United States from Australia, and was devised to accommodate nonverbal people diagnosed with autism, developmental disabilities, and other related syndromes to give these people a voice, if the ability was there.

157

The method was quite basic. It required a support person that was trusted by the impaired, and was done by pointing to the letters on a computer or keyboard. The hand of the supporter rested gently under the hand or arm of the speller (the impaired), holding up the first finger so it could point precisely. The supporter was to pull back gently on the arm of the speller while the speller aimed toward the letters he wanted. This slight holding back of movement in the arm was to confirm that it was indeed the "speller" expressing himself. The supporter wrote down each letter pointed to by the impaired. Eventually, the support could fade into a bare touch on the shoulder or the speller could go at it alone. The support was merely to engage the impaired into "conversation" and keep them focused.

But with everything good that comes along for the majority, there are always the spoilers in the minority. Controversies had arisen regarding abuse claimed by a few spellers. Some had mentioned sexual abuse, mistreatment, etc. No one wanted to take it seriously, and some were afraid it could open up a can of worms, so it cast a shadow of negative analysis on FC.

Because so many developmentally challenged people have poor motor control or paralysis, they were therefore thought incapable of typing their own work, let alone, making accusations of abuse. (Kenny has complete function of his extremities.)

Other rumors going around at the time were that the work accomplished was that of the facilitator, and not the person responding. Some talked about the possibility the speller could be as capable of lying, as he was of telling the truth. And last but not least, is the ever abundant stigma that society has taught us, that if you don't speak the same as everyone else, you must not be all there. Speech is the communication people are willing to accept as a sign of intellect.

I never thought of Kenny as being retarded, because there is intelligence in his eyes and other reasons that I know. His ability to manipulate a situation to get his way is a huge factor. But I do think of him as a soul locked up in a damaged brain waiting for a key to open it, and if this new method could possibly do this for him, I wanted to make sure Tom incorporated this technique into Kenny's curriculum.

Tom was a quiet, smart and caring young man. He seemed to genuinely like Kenny. He was tall, and a little intimidating to Kenny, which was a good thing. He realized too that Kenny was easily distracted by others, and wanted to work with him in rooms that were not as crowded, when introducing Kenny to the computer.

In the meantime at home I had tried asking Kenny yes or no questions as I was shown at the class in Marin, but he was never one for doing anything his mom wanted. Mary introduced me to her friend Kim, who Kenny already knew and liked. I hired her to see if Kenny might be willing to do FC after school. I showed her how to do the procedure and he seemed even anxious about it. I would soon find out that Kenny was particular about who he wanted to share his thoughts with. Unfortunately, I was not one of them very often. Kenny probably had his fill of working with me during the Doman program. After all, I am just his mother who prayed for the chance to communicate with her son his whole life!! Why should I be privileged? (What a brat!)

The school made me a laminated key board with the numbers and letters like the computer. The letters were large and there was four words added in squares, they read, "yes," "no," "maybe," and "stop."

I had her start out with very basic "yes" or "no" questions. It was so exciting to see him point to his answer. We were not sure in the beginning if he knew what he was being asked, but it didn't take long to see it appeared to be so. Mary also did some FC with Kenny, but he was intrigued with Kim, and she became a new friend to him.

I started thinking of questions that would prove consistency in his answers to eliminate the possibility of lucky guesses. I wanted to be sure he understood what he was answering. *Was it a hot day? Yes or no? Did you have a good day at school? Yes or no?* That could be confirmed from the notebook he brought home from school. We asked any question that could be verified, whether it was about the weather, how he felt, what color he was wearing, or *was his mother's name, Pat? No. Was his mother's name Barbara? Yes!* And we would slip in repetitive questions to see if he answered them the same. This was an extraordinary breakthrough and I was beside myself with enthusiasm for Kenny. Thank you God!!!

We were so excited about all of the questions that he rapidly answered! I quickly decided I wanted to log everything down in a notebook. I wanted whoever was doing FC with Kenny to put their name and date on the pages. After two notebooks of "yes" and "no" questions, it was very obvious Kenny knew things and could express what he knew in this way. I was beyond exhilaration, and I was fascinated and proud of my son.

I wanted to find out what else this kid could do, and what all he understood. I went shopping for workbooks with large print that were for K- 2. (We quickly advanced to higher levels.) I got flash cards and books on different subjects for everyone to read to him. I also bought encyclopedia knowledge books. I wanted to expand on everything they were working on at school with Kenny, which I found out Tom was already doing!

I had Kim work on learning to point without assistance, which he could do on the "yes" and "no" questions, when he felt like it. Everything was when he felt like it, partly because of his seizures and medication, and partly because he has always been resistant to improvement.

Nevertheless, before long, he was proving that his comprehension surpassed any expectation I had. Kenny was using the facilitation method with Tom at school, pointing to answers from very basic questions that were either choices of A, B, C, or D after a short story was read to him.

On occasion, other aides worked a little with Kenny on worksheets along with the computer. He enjoyed working with his favorite teacher, Doreen. When he would comply, he could point to the answers of questions such as, "What is the largest of the two?" or "What number is smaller, two or four?"

I was happy to be able to squelch anyone's thought of Kenny being of vegetable IQ. Early on, he earned that label from professionals because he resisted being tested, and from his extreme behaviors, which he still has unfortunately.

I visited the school often to check on the progress with Tom and Kenny. Kenny was doing some great work. He was doing division problems and math similar to fifth grade. The programs on the computer were designed so one could point to answers on the keyboard with the letters or numbers. Tom used the method of facilitation by folding back all of Kenny's fingers but one, using minimum support to Kenny's hand. Kenny's finger went to the keyboard with such strength that people doing FC with Kenny often complained of a sore arm. Kenny could point on his own if he so desired. Later, when he became a pro at this, he would use the facilitator's finger as a pointer at times.

When Kenny came home from school, worksheets were sent home that he had done with either aides, or teachers. Kenny had answered through pointing, and in most cases he was right. I knew this was all Kenny's good work because he was doing similar work at home with Kim and Mary.

No one could imagine how I felt, it is impossible to put into words. We had gotten through to Kenny and it was only the beginning.

It was about seven months into facilitation with Tom when he called me, and asked me to come to the school and meet with him. I instinctively panicked, thinking he was going to tell me he was quitting. I thought, *just when everything was going great at school for Kenny!* I immediately felt sadness, picturing Kenny without Tom.

I confronted him right then and there, on the phone, and asked if he was leaving. He said "no," but he couldn't talk about it over the phone. He had me so anxious. I didn't have a clue what he was going to tell me and I couldn't sleep at all that night. I went to see him the next day.

"Before I tell you this Barbara," he said, "I have worked on this for three months straight to make absolutely sure there was no other explanation for what I am going to tell you." "Tom," I said, "You are scaring me, what in the world are you trying to tell me?" He shushed me as if what he was about to tell me was the world's biggest secret! In a way, and to me, it was!

He then proceeded to tell me that Kenny was telepathic. I just looked at him. He asked me if I knew what that meant. "Yes," I knew what telepathy was, but I laughed at him, and asked him why he was playing this joke on me? Then he shushed me again, and I could see he was not only dead serious, but very uncomfortable in having this conversation. I could tell this was a very difficult decision he had obviously come to make in divulging this information to me. He said, "I have not told anyone and I don't want you to say anything right now because so many are down on FC anyway!"

Sitting there in a state of confusion, I listened as he told me how he discovered this amazing ability in Kenny. Tom had made some notes and dated his first findings. The following is how he described it to me with as much accuracy as I can remember.

6/14/93 - He thought something was strange one day as I sat next to him and Kenny at the computer. Tom was showing me a comprehension workbook they had been reviewing. Tom said Kenny answered it correctly each time. Tom pointed to a short story which was a paragraph in length and followed with questions about the story. He asked me if I knew which answer was correct. It was a multiple choice. I didn't have my glasses on and I struggled to read the question. I thought of an answer in my head and before I had a chance to express it, Kenny pointed to my choice at that moment. Tom said, "Kenny, that's not right." "That's the answer I was going to choose" I told Tom, not realizing what just happened. Tom did the question with Kenny again and he pointed to the correct answer.

6/15/93 - Tom and Kenny did division software, which up until today, Kenny had been correctly answering. Tom purposely thought of a wrong answer and Kenny printed in what Tom was thinking.

Then Tom decided to think of a person's name to throw Kenny off guard, instead of the math they were doing. Kenny quickly printed the name.

6/18/93 - Tom and Kenny played the Uno card game on the computer. Kenny was told to pick cards he wanted for his hand. They were all cards Tom thought in his mind.

6/21/93 - Tom and Kenny were doing assorted number games on the computer and another male aide happened by. Tom, not knowing this information himself, asked Kenny if he knew how old the aide was. Kenny quickly pointed to the numbers reflecting the man's age. Tom confirmed with the aide and wanted to know who told him. Kenny was right!

While reading a comprehension workbook on the computer showing a picture of two men working, Tom reflected light heartedly in his mind how "odd" one man looked. Kenny quickly printed "odd" before Tom asked him a question about the story.

This type of testing went on for three months, including examples of Tom thinking wrong answers, when Kenny had been putting the right answers. If Tom blanked his mind, Kenny wasn't interested in printing anything.

My feelings were of excitement beyond belief, yet at the same time I felt dubious. *How could this be?* It just didn't make any sense to me that he could possess the rarest of gifts known to man, and be the Kenny I know at the same time. And who would believe it anyway, if it were true?

Tom led me to the computer room to see if Kenny would use his magic with me. With rubbery legs, we went to get Kenny, who was with another aide and students finishing their lunches. We went to the computer room that was empty and sat down. It was always so wonderful to see how good Kenny was for Tom.

I thought of Kenny's name in my mind, and he pulled my arm to the letters of his name before I had a chance to position my hand under his. It was the most amazing experience I had ever felt in my life. I thought of my name, and he spelled that. Tom thought of the sentence "I can read minds" Kenny spelled that out! *Oh my God, this was so incredible!* I wanted to scream it out! But I had to keep the excitement to myself. I promised Tom I would not talk about it at school. *For now,* I thought! I could hardly contain all of the thoughts running through my mind about this phenomena.

At home all of us jumped on the bandwagon. On 7/23/93, logged in a notebook titled "Telepathy with Kenny," my husband thought of our dog's name-Gizmo. Kenny printed that!

7/29/93 - My husband told Kenny to read his mind, and Kenny printed "bath," which was the correct word.

8/2/93 - My husband and Kenny were in the shower, and Ken was wondering about our daughter, who was supposed to call us that evening. Kenny smiled and said, "Ra Ra," (his word for Rhonda).

We also asked Kenny some "yes" or "no" questions like, "does it frustrate him to read minds?" "No."

My brother Frank thought of the words "Harley Davidson," (he had one), Kenny printed H.D. (too lazy to print the whole thing, I guessed).

I thought of the word "milkshake," he printed that. A person has no idea what this feels like, to have someone read your thoughts. It was also a bit scary at the same time. It felt like mind invasion!

It was the family members that I shared this information with first. Although he was not always in the mood, or willing to participate upon request to do his telepathy, he definitely had those fortunate enough to experience this amazing feat with him, convinced!

He now had proven himself with Tom, me, his Dad, my brothers, Frank and John, and John's son, Tommy, who was an army officer at the time.

Of course, none of these family members knew anything at all about FC or its procedures. I showed them how to apply the method by using their hand under his arm with the slightest contact. The contact is what kept Kenny focused, almost in a hypnotic sense. Kenny became very adept at pointing, as if he had used this form of communication his whole life. I think he was saying, "Finally!"

I looked at Kenny's telepathy as a miracle, along with all of the amazing work that he had been accomplishing. I was overwhelmed with what was going on with him and I wanted to share it with the world. There can't be too many people that have this gift, and why was Kenny one of them? I had too many questions bombarding me, and I began calling those in the professional field.

I talked to Dr. Glen Elliot from U.C.S.F. who was a child psychiatrist. He was very negative and told me he did not believe in telepathy. I reminded him about the Aborigine Tribes from the Outback, whose main communication was through telepathy. I spoke to Judy Henderson, assistant of Dr. Cohn from Stanford, who I never heard back from. I also spoke to neurologists from major Hospitals like UC medical center, Stanford, and John Hopkins from back east without a positive response. I talked to a Dr. Vernon Neppe from Seattle, Washington whose assistant said to write to him, but I never heard back. I talked to Parapsychology investigations in California, but could never reach the people that I was referred to. I left messages with the Edgar Casey Foundation, with no return of phone calls. I called Paranormal Investigations, nothing there! I would have called the Ghost Busters but didn't have their number.

No one was interested! And worse than that, in most cases I wasn't believed and made to feel like a "quack!" *Why would I waste my precious energy making these calls if I was a "quack?"* All I wanted was someone to help me turn this gift Kenny had into a way to improve his life. Part of me also wanted some recognition for my amazing son!

My last resort was calling the famous Dr. Bernard Rimland, of the Autism Research Institute in San Diego. He told me he had heard from other parents that knew a vaccination had caused their children's autism, despite the fervent assertions of the medical establishment that the vaccines could do no harm.

When I told him of Kenny's telepathy, he retorted, "That can't be possible, because if he was truly autistic, he didn't have his "own" mind and you have to possess a mind of your own to be telepathic!" (I would bet through the years he changed his tune about autistic people not having their own minds.)

Perhaps the government was plotting to create an army of telepathic soldiers with the vaccine. But the side effects were possible brain damage. (Just kidding!)

He sent me a form to fill out so he could ascertain whether Kenny was autistic or with autistic tendencies. I did the best I could, answering the questions as accurately as possible, and mailed them back to him. The results, according to my answers and his checklist, showed autism!

CHAPTER
TWENTY-THREE

I got past the point of feeling the need to prove Kenny's telepathy to anyone. I was through trying to convince anyone about it, although I asked his neurologist at Kaiser to give it a try. Kenny wasn't in the mood, but he quickly picked a few letters from the word the doctor thought of.

I could tell the doctor was surprised with the correct letters and he said, "Unfortunately, with Kenny's behavioral patterns, it would be impossible to test him in the conventional way." I agreed!

I continued to have him converse through FC with those that came to the house to help out with him. He enjoyed the girls that worked with him at home, Kim, Malia, and Heather. They were friends of mine and Mary's. There were also a few girls from the respite agency that came over from time to time. They were more than willing to try this phenomenal feat with Kenny.

Kenny is not only telepathic, but has extrasensory perception as well. He knows the phone will ring before it does, and makes his phone sound, which is "huh, huh."

I started taking some notes of my own when he reacted to someone sending him thought waves: On February 4, 1995, my husband waiting outside the bathroom for Kenny and was wondering if he should venture off to the store for some ice cream. He pondered this a few minutes and heard Kenny blurt out, "Baa by!" Ken asked him who was going, "bye bye," and Kenny said his word for store.

On January 1, 1995, my birthday, we had company and my niece's husband, Jim, wanted to test Kenny to see if he could respond to a telepathic message sent to him. While everyone was engaged in watching the football game on TV, Jim sent his thought wave to Kenny. A few seconds later, Kenny suddenly bent down and untied the shoe of the man sitting next to him. That was the silent request Jim sent!

I told Malia about this the next time she was over, and she wanted to try this herself. In her mind she asked Kenny to untie his shoe. He did!

On January 27, 1995, I was reaching for an after school snack for Kenny from the freezer. He was not in view of what I was doing and yelled out "pie!" Sure enough, I had grabbed the vegetable pie I had just bought that afternoon while he was in school. It was something I had never given him before that day.

I have a notebook on many more of these ESP and telepathic episodes, too lengthy to write it all here, but eventually, I stopped logging things down from lack of time. Now that we were really paying attention to all the signs, sounds, and gestures he made, it was practically a daily occurrence. It's just who Kenny is, an authentic mystery.

But now, I would like to share with you, the wonderful, tragic, astounding, delightful, funny, and childlike innocence of my son's thoughts as only he can tell them. I wholeheartedly hope you will take the time to read his work. You will be amazed! Everything comes straight from his heart, whether he is being naughty or nice. As his mother, I was shocked, happy, and sad discovering my son all over again.

Especially when I read at the age of ten, he was making up names for stars in his mind to entertain himself while I was still talking to him in baby talk. I would say things like, "Kenny, see the lambs? They say 'baa, baa.' Can you say 'baa?'" Sometimes he would repeat, "ba!"

You will feel his frustrations at times when he tried to make a point, and the support person didn't catch on. Many times, he quit because his brain was thinking faster than his finger could point. He developed his own technique of shorthand by spelling out part of a word, thinking everyone would know what it meant.

For example, when asked what religion he was, pointed to C.D. I took that as Catholic denomination, which he is. Or, when he did telepathy with my brother, Frank, Kenny spelled out H. D. for Harley Davidson, which was the correct word.

When Kenny acted out or didn't want to spell, he either pointed to "stop" or shoved the board away. He still had to be in the right mood. Going through his notebooks, and finding what I thought would be of the most interest to my readers, was hard for me. I wanted to share every page, but that would have been a book in itself. So, I chose material from each notebook, starting with the earliest date. I scanned several pages of his work directly as it appeared in the notebook, so you could see how it looked. Then I decided to print the remaining pages to assure rapid and easier reading. It is all his work and nothing was changed, except the format. In the beginning some of the questions are repetitive because we were still testing his comprehension.

There are remarks made sometimes on the pages by the supporter, such as "great work," or "Kenny was grouchy," etc. But what I hope is that you recognize his own personality surfacing, with his very own style of answering questions no matter who did the FC with him.

Without further ado, I give you Kenny....

CHAPTER
TWENTY-FOUR

THE BOY IN THE WINDOW
the boy in the window

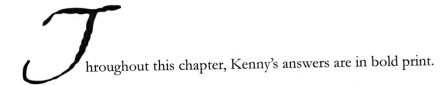

*T*hroughout this chapter, Kenny's answers are in bold print.

⊠   ⊠   ⊠   ⊠   ⊠

APRIL 1994/KIM

Telepathy Continued

WORDS THOUGHT OF	LETTERS POINTED TO BY KENNY
Tall	**T-A-L-L**
Short	**S-H-O-R-T**
He pointed! Oh my God! Yes!	
Mary	**M-A-R-Y**

	YES	NO
Do you think you can point to the letters on the FC Board by yourself?	**X**	
Did you like dinner?	**X**	
Were you happy to see Rhonda today?	**X**	
Are you in a good mood?	**X**	
Were you a bad boy for Mary?		**X**

⊠   ⊠   ⊠   ⊠   ⊠

APRIL 1994/KIM OLIVER

Used facilitation for these questions. I asked them and Kenny answered them on the FC Board.

How are you today Kenny?
Answer: **Fine**

Did you have a good day today?
Answer: **Yes**

Who watched you today?
Answer: **Jenny, Mary**

What is your favorite food?
Answer: **Chocolate**

Question: What is your favorite color?
Answer: **Blue**

Question: Who is your best friend?
Answer: **Mary**

Question: What is the name of your school?
Answer: **Spectrum**

Question: Who taught you how to spell?
Answer: **Me**
I guess it means he taught himself.

Question: If you could go anywhere in the world, where would it be?
Answer: **Zoo**

Question: Who's mind do you like to read the most?
Answer: **Ken**

Saturday April 23, 1994   Approx. 6:16 pm

Telepathy - I thought of the name "Kenny" continuously & repetatively and Kenny kept pointing to the letter "K" over & over again.

I thought of the name "Mary" and Kenny went straight the the exact letters! M-A-R-Y! I resisted but he persisted.

I thought of the word "DOG" and again Kenny went straight to the letters. D-O-G. And again I used some resistance.

I thought of the word Mom & Kenny went straight to M-O-M. I can't believe it! We need to video tape this!!!

I thought of the word "DAD" and Kenny went to D-E-D.

I thought of the word "Toy" and Kenny went to various letters.

I thought of the word "CAT" and Kenny went to C-A-R.

I thought of the word "Book" & Kenny went to various letters.

▨   ▨   ▨   ▨   ▨

SATURDAY, APRIL 23, 1994/KIM OLIVER

Telepathy – I thought of the name "Kenny" continuously and repeatedly and Kenny kept pointing to the letter **"K"** over and over again!

I thought of the name "Mary" and Kenny went straight to the exact letters! **M-A-R-Y!** I resisted, but he persisted.

I thought of the word "DOG" and again, Kenny went straight to the letters **D-O-G**, and again, I used some resistance.

I thought of the word "Mom" and Kenny went straight to **M-O-M**. I can't believe it. We need to videotape this!!!

I thought of the word "Dad" and Kenny went to **D-A-D**.

I thought of the word "Toy" and Kenny went to the various letters.

I thought of the word "Car" and Kenny went to **C-A-R**.

I thought of the word "Book" and Kenny went to the various letters.

◻   ◻   ◻   ◻   ◻

MONDAY, APRIL 25, 1994/TAMMIE

Ken and I worked on Symbols Telepathy words. Ken was asked to spell <u>comp</u>uter and **<u>Ken</u>**neth. *He pointed to underlined letters.

I forgot to tell you about this. Do you remember the forms with blank spaces where Ken had to choose an operative word to fill in space? I don't know if this is F.C. or what, but Ken filled in this sentence: a load of _____.

His choices: Clothes, Soap, Numbers.

Of course, Ken chose **clothes**. This is good!

◻   ◻   ◻   ◻   ◻

Saturday April 23, 1994   Approx. 6:16 pm

Telepathy - I thought of the name "Kenny" continuously & repetatively and Kenny kept pointing to the letter "K" over & over again.

I thought of the name "Mary" and Kenny went straight the the exact letters! M-A-R-Y! I resisted but he persisted.

I thought of the word "DOG" and again Kenny went straight to the letters. D-O-G. And again I used some resistance.

I thought of the word Mom & Kenny went straight to M-O-M. I can't believe it! We need to video tape this!!

I thought of the word "DAD" and Kenny went to D-E-D.

I thought of the word "Toy" and Kenny went to various letters.

I thought of the word "CAT" and Kenny went to C-A-R.

I thought of the word "Book" & Kenny went to various letters.

▫️   ▫️   ▫️   ▫️   ▫️

TUESDAY, APRIL 26, 1994/TAMMIE

Telepathy

Lets start with easy, basic words today. I thought of the word "Boy." Kenny went to **B-O-Y** then stopped for 30 seconds. I then shook his hand and got his attention and he went straight to **B-O-Y**.

I thought of the word "Mom" and Kenny went to "L." I told Kenny to concentrate and he then went to **"M-O-M."**

Let's try something a little more difficult. I thought of the name "Kimiko." It took Kenny a while to get through this one. He almost made it though.

He went to **K-I-M-I-P-O**.

I thought of the name "Kenny" and Kenny went to **K-E-N-N** and then stopped.

I went back to a familiar, basic name to Kenny: "Mary." Kenny, very quickly, went to **M-A-R-Y**.

I thought of the word "Rock" and Kenny went to **"R-O-K."**

Telepathy Continued

WORDS THOUGHT OF	**LETTERS POINTED TO BY KENNY**
Bed	**Keeps pointing to the stop button**
Mary	**Again, keeps pointing to the stop button**

*Kenny and I weren't sitting in our usual chairs. I just made him switch places with me. Now let's see if it works. I'll try using the same two words as before.

Bed	Kenny went straight to the letters **B-E-D**
Mary	**M-A-R-Y**
Gizmo	**G-I-Z-M-O**
Stairs	**S-T-A-I**

Then Ken came in the room and said "Let's go get something to eat." Talk about ruining the moment.

TUESDAY, APRIL 26, 1994/KIM OLIVER

Telepathy Words: **Purp**le and **Car**ve

⬚　⬚　⬚　⬚　⬚

WEDNESDAY, APRIL 27, 1994/TAMMIE

Ken rode on an extremely long flat tri-cycle and totally enjoyed this.

We worked on _____ motor skills and putting together flashlights.

Sorting clothes pins

Telepathy words: **Cl**o**c**k and **Pi**pe

⬚　⬚　⬚　⬚　⬚

THURSDAY, APRIL 28, 1994/TAMMIE

Ken did not do to well with symbols or with F.C. We attempted Oregon Trail in which we have been doing daily this week.

Telepathy: Ken would not participate at all.

⬚　⬚　⬚　⬚　⬚

FRIDAY, APRIL 29, 1994/TAMMIE

Oh Barb, you are going to be so excited!! One of our peer buddies (student aides from the high school), anyway, I was telling her about Ken's telepathy and trying to see if he would do some F.C. with her. Well, with the telepathy thing, I told her to think of a word (clearly) while I held his hand. She thought of "Greg," her boyfriend. Ken spelled GFERG!! Do you think this is exciting or what?

Kim Oliver

May 2   Kim & Kenny

Kenny seems to be in a pretty good mood today. Let's see if he'll cooperate in a little telepathy.

Words Thought of	Letters pointed to by Kenny
Mary	M - A - R - Y Bravo Kenny
Kim (me)	K - I - M Yeah! I'm so hap The first time! ☺
Book	B - O - O - K

* This is really weird Kenny seems totally cooperative & his parents are home.

Dr. McDonald	D- space bar - M - k · D - O - L - D
Car	C - A - R
Door	D-O-O-R
Sky	S- k - y
Smile	S - M - W - back space spacebare - I - L - E

MAY 2, 1994/KIM & KENNY

Kenny seems to be in a pretty good mood today. Let's see if he'll cooperate in a little telepathy.

WORDS THOUGHT OF	LETTERS POINTED TO BY KENNY
Mary	M-A-R-Y
Kim	K-I-M
	Yeah!
Book	B-O-O-K

*This is really weird. Kenny seems totally cooperative and his parents are home.

Dr. McDonald	D- space bar – M-K-D-O-L-D
Car	C-A-R
Door	D-O-O-R
Sky	S-K-Y
Smile	S-M-W- back space, spacebar – I-L-E
Puzzle	P-U-Z-Z-L-E
Food	F-O-O-D

	YES	NO
Did you see Dr. McDonald today?	X	
Do you like Dr. McDonald?		
Do you want to play puzzles?	X	
Can you read people's minds?		
Do you want me to read your mind?	X	
Do you understand when people talk to you?		
Do you want to talk back to people?	X	
Do you think you're a baby?	X	
Do you like being treated like a baby?		X
Does Mommy treat you like a baby?	X	
Does Daddy treat you like a baby?	X	
Does Mary treat you like a baby?	X	
Does Kim treat you like a baby?	X	
Do you want us to treat you like a big boy?	X	
Do you have a sister?	Verbally tried to say "Sister"	
Is her name Rhonda?	X	
Do you want to see Rhonda?	X	
Does Rhonda treat Kenny like a baby?		X

MAY 16, 1996/KIM OLIVER

Telepathy:

Today Kenny had two tantrums at school, but was very calm this late afternoon. He's smiling and hyper, and in a good mood.

WORDS THOUGHT OF	LETTERS POINTED TO BY KENNY
Good	G-O-O-D
Bad	B-A-G
Ugly	U-G-L-O
Andrina	A-N- then he knocked his knuckle on the question mark.
Jenny	J-E-N-N-Y

	YES	NO
Do you like school?		
Is school boring?		X
Do you like Tammie?		X
Did Tammie make you mad today?	X	

⬚　　⬚　　⬚　　⬚　　⬚

MAY 19, 1994/KIM OLIVER

Telepathy

WORDS THOUGHT OF	LETTERS POINTED TO BY KENNY
Car	C-A-R
Key	K-E-Y
Run	R-U-N

	YES	NO
Did you have a good day today?	X	
Are you in a good mood?	X	
Are you hungry?	X	
Did you wet the bed last night?		X
Are your pants black? (His pants are black.)	X	
Are my pants black? (Mine are white.)		X

MAY 20, 1994/KIM OLIVER

WORDS THOUGHT OF	LETTERS POINTED TO BY KENNY
Mary	M-A-R-Y
Kim	K-I-M
Cesar	C-E-S-A-R

	YES	NO
Did you have a good day today?	X	
Was Tammie upset today?	X	
Was Mary upset today?	X	
Is Kenny upset today?		X
Are you hungry?	X	
Is Phil going to call me?		X
Note: Phil hasn't called		
Does Phil like me?		X
Does Lawrence like me?	X	
Note: Lawrence is taking me out tonight.		
Are my pants red?		X
Are my pants black?		X
Are my pants blue?	X	
Note: My pants are blue.		
Is my shirt black?	X	
Note: My shirt is black.		
Is my shirt blue?		X
Did you wet the bed last night?		X
Is today rainy?		X
Is today sunny?	X	
Note: Today is sunny.		

I asked Kenny where he went today after he went to Tammie's house and he pointed to the letters **D-Q-N** three times and then he went to the **"NO"** box! Maybe he doesn't know the name of the place she took him.

I asked Kenny again where he went after he went to Tammie's house and he pointed to **D-O-D-L-D**. Maybe McDonald's? Hmm, this is strange!

Telepathy

WORDS THOUGHT OF	LETTERS POINTED TO BY KENNY
Sunny	Kenny won't cooperate.
	Maybe it's too hot here.
	Maybe he's not in the mood.
	I don't know.

	YES	NO
Is it rainy today?		X
Is it hot today?		
Note: It is hot.	X	
Are you happy today?	X	
Are you sad today?		X
Is my dress green?		X
Is my dress black?		
Note: My dress is black.	X	

WORDS THOUGHT OF	LETTERS POINTED TO BY KENNY
Book	B-O-O-K
Pen	P-E-N
Paper	P-A-P-E-R
Ruler	R-U-L-E-R

	YES	NO
Are my pants red?		X
Are my pants black?		
Note: My pants are black.	X	
Are you happy today?	X	
Is Phil going to call me?		X
Note: Phil hasn't called.		
Does Phil like me?		X
Does Lawrence like me?		
Note: Lawrence does like me alot!	X	

THE BOY IN THE WINDOW *the boy in the window*

Okay Barb, I'm going to try to do some sentences with the Telepathy. Wish me luck.

SENTENCE THOUGHT OF:	KENNY POINTED TO: (NO SPACE BAR)
The Dog is Asleep	**The Dog is Asleep.**

Okay, for this I just kept repeating the sentence over and over in my head. I didn't use any visual pictures of the sentence/words. Yes Barb, you were right. He can do sentences. I had my doubts, but now I'm definitely convinced.

SENTENCE THOUGHT OF:	KENNY POINTED TO: (NO SPACE BAR)
I like puzzles.	**I like puzzles.**

MAY 31, 1994/KIM OLIVER

Telepathy

WORDS THOUGHT OF	LETTERS POINTED TO BY KENNY
Black	B-L-A-K
Red	R-E-D
Green	G-R-E-E-N
White	W-H-I-T-E
Blue	B-L-U-E

	YES	NO
Did you have a good day?	X	
Was Tammie in a good mood?		X
Was today sunny?		X
Note: Today wasn't sunny/nor rainy.		
Was today rainy?	X	

Question		
Did you have fun at Mary's?	X	
Did you wet the bed last night?		X
Do you pray to Jesus?	X	
Note: Verbally says "Jesus"		
Do you know who he is?	X	
Note: Verbally says "Jesus"		
Do you know anything about him?	X	
Do you pray to God?	X	
Note: Verbally says "God."		
Do you know who God is?	X	
Note: Verbally says "God."		
Do you know about God and Jesus?	X	
Note: Verbally says "Jesus."		
Does God ever talk to you?	X	
Note: Verbally says "Yeah."		
Does Jesus ever talk to you?	X	
Note: Verbally says "Jesus."		
Are Kenny and Jesus friends?	X	
Note: Smiling!		
Does Kenny talk to Jesus?	X	
Note: Getting a little impatient.		
Does Jesus live in Vallejo?		X
Does Jesus live in America?		X
Does Jesus live with God?	"Yeh"	
Do you know where God & Jesus live?	X	
Do you ever see him with your eyes?	X	
Do you go to church?		X
Have you ever gone to church?	X	
Do you want to go to church?	**Verbally says "Yeh"**	
Does Jesus talk to you every night?		X
Does Jesus talk to you more than once a week?	X	
Can Kim see Jesus with her eyes like you?	X	
Where is Jesus right now?	On FC spelled **H-E-A-V-E-N.**	

*Based on today's following questions, he is more than capable of answering with his mouth. Definite progress. He knows what the heck I'm talking about.

JUNE 7, 1994/KIM OLIVER

	YES	NO
Did you have a good day?	X Verbally says "Yes."	
Was today hot? Note: Today was hot.	X Verbally says "Yes."	
Was today cold?		X
Did Ken & Barbara come up to your school? Note: Ken & Barbara went to IEP Meeting.	X Verbally says "Yes."	
Was Tami at school today?		X
Did you like dinner? Note: Ate 3 servings of ravioli.	X Verbally says "Yes."	
Do you like your haircut?	X Verbally says "Yes."	
Did you make a big mess in this room earlier? Note: Room was a big mess.	X Verbally says "Yes."	
Is Mary having a girl? Note: Verbally says "Boy."		X
Is Mary having a boy? (Mary did give birth to a boy)	X Verbally says "Boy."	
Did Kenny pee on himself today at school?	X Verbally says "Pee."	
Did you do it on purpose?		X
Did you do it on accident?	X	
Do you know how to go to the bathroom?	X Verbally says "Yes."	
Did you tell someone you needed to use the bathroom?		X

◻   ◻   ◻   ◻   ◻

JUNE 11, 1994/KIMIKO OLIVER

Do you know that every time I ask you a question and you answer back, we are communicating?

Answer: **Yes**

Would you like to communicate with Ken & Barbara the same way you communicate with me through facilitation?

Answer: **Yes**

How come you don't let Ken or Barbara do facilitation/communication with you?

Answer: **Long**

What does "long" mean?
Answer: **Long**

What's "long?"
Answer: **Time**

Would you like for Ken & Barbara to be able to know what you want or need?
Answer: **Yes**

Do you understand that you need to do facilitation with either of them so that you can communicate?
Answer: **Yes**

Well then, why won't you let them do facilitation with you?
Answer: **Long**

If Barbara wants to do facilitation with you so that you can talk to her, will you let her?
Answer: **No**

If Ken wants to do facilitation with you, will you let him?
Answer: **Yes**

Why don't you want Barbara to do facilitation with you?
Answer: **Points to the question mark.**

Don't you think that if you could use facilitation to tell Barbara what it is you want, you would be much more happier?
Answer: **Yes**

Then why won't you do facilitation with Barbara?
Answer: **Buck**

What about Buck?
Answer: **Points to the question mark.**
(Buck was a respite person that Kenny liked)
You act as if you are mad at Barbara. Are you?
Answer: **No**

If you're not mad at your Mom, why do you get so angry whenever she is around or tries to talk to you?

Answer: **Not**

Not what?
Answer: **Mad**

If you aren't mad at Barbara, why won't you let her do work with you?
Answer: **Points to the question mark.**

How come you don't let Ken or Barbara do facilitation work with you?
Answer: **Long**

"Long" what?
Answer: **Time**

"Long time" for what?
Answer: **Help**

What did you want help with?
Answer: **Me**

What about you?
Answer: **Teach**

Spelling:

Directions: Spell Dog:
Pointed to DOG (Very rapid and accurate response.)

Spell Cat:
Pointed to CAT and **verbally repeated cat** while in the process.

Spell Ball:
Again **rapidly pointed to the letters correctly** and **verbally repeated the word ball**, clearly. Oh and yes Barb, I'm blanking out my mind. If he's reading my mind, he would be spelling out Lawrence. Let's see how advanced his spelling is.

Spell Corporation:
He spelled it! He rapidly **spelled corporation correctly!**

Barb, I was joking when I asked him to spell that. I didn't think he actually would do it. Let me sign my name. This is true! Kimiko Oliver

Spell Dictionary:
Kenny went straight to the letters.

Spell Telescope:
Again, went straight to the letters.

Spell Skyscraper:
Right again!

Barb,

Kenny is doing some great spelling on his own, not telepathy. Too bad you guys don't have a blank videotape this evening. Kenny's in a great mood. He had a good day today and the neighbors are out this evening. Tonight would have been ideal. I'm sure he'll keep up the good work throughout the week.

Spelling

Okay, let me see if I can confuse Kenny in the spelling. Let's see how good he really is.

Spell Comfort:
Kenny goes to the letters **C-O-M-F-O-R-T.**

Spell Comforting:
Again, he spells it correctly.

Spell Comforter:
Again, he spells it correctly.

Spell Comfortable:
Again, he spells it correctly. Not telepathy. Very good job Kenny!

Asked to spell the following words and all were spelled correctly:
Addition, Subtraction, Division, Multiplication, Equation

JUNE 12, 1994/KIM OLIVER

Yesterday you told me that you would like to do work with Ken. Do you still want to do work with him?
Answer: **Yes**

How come last night when Ken tried to work with you, you said "no?"
Answer: **Joke**

Do you like to joke around a lot?
Answer: **Yes**

How come Kenny likes to joke?
Answer: **Good**

JULY 5, 1994/KIMIKO OLIVER

When was the last time you talked to Jesus?
Answer: **June 5th**

What does Jesus look like?
Answer: **Me**

When you pray to Jesus, what do you ask for?
Answer: **Life**

How come Ken or Barbara can't see Jesus?
Answer: **Went to the question mark.**

Who is Jesus's father??
Answer: **God**

Who is Jesus's mother?
Answer: **Beth** (asked him twice – same answer).

Does Jesus have brothers and sisters?
Answer: **Yes**

189

Who are his brothers and sisters?
Answer: **Us**

Where do people go when they die?
Answer: **Heaven and Earth** (Very strong and persistent with these letters.)

Do you mean that some people stay on earth after they die?
Answer: **Yes**

◻   ◻   ◻   ◻   ◻

JULY 6, 1994/KIMIKO OLIVER

Did you pray to Jesus last night?
Answer: **Yes**

What did you ask him for/pray for?
Answer: **Life**

What about "Life?"
Answer: **Good Life**

You want a better life?
Answer: **Yes**

What do you want to be better in your life?
Answer: **Family**

What is wrong with your family?
Answer: **Happy**

Is Kenny happy?
Answer: **Even**
Note: I don't know what he's trying to tell me.

What does Jesus say to you when you pray for life?
Answer: **Believe**

Believe in what?
Answer: **Him**

And do you believe in him?
Answer: **Yes**

How often do you pray to Jesus?
Answer: **Every day**

Who is Jesus' mom? What is her name?
Answer: **Beth**

What is her last name?
Answer: **Points to the question mark.**

Isn't Jesus' Mom's name Mary?
Answer: **No**

What color eyes does Jesus have?
Answer: **Gold**

What color hair does Jesus have?
Answer: **Black**

What color is his skin?
Answer: **Brown**

Is he tall or short?
Answer: **Tall**

Is he fat or skinny?
Answer: **Skinny**

Okay Kenny, your eyes are brown and you are light skinned with brown hair, so how in the world does Jesus look like you?
Answer: **He is in me.**

Where is he in you? Where is he at?
Answer: **Heart**

JULY 7, 1994/KIMIKO OLIVER

What do you want to be when you grow up?
Answer: **Jello**. I asked again and he answers: **Ken Coppo**

Where would you like to live in the future?
Answer: **Ken's**

What would you most like to do in the future?
Answer: **Play**

Did you eat your lunch today?
Answer: **No**

Did you eat at all at school?
Answer: **Yes**

What did you eat?
Answer: **Finish?**

Do you want to talk to me with your mouth?
Answer: **My can't.**

Why can't you?
Answer: **Brain**

Do you try to talk through your mouth?
Answer: **Yes**

What happens when you try to talk through your mouth?
Answer: **Are joke.**

What's a joke?
Answer: **I am.**
Note: Oh my gosh Barbara, maybe Kenny thinks he sounds funny when he talks and that's why he doesn't try. Why does he think he's a joke? Did you notice that a couple of times he tried to make a sentence?

JULY 8, 1994/KIMIKO OLIVER

What did you do at school today?
Answer: **Jog** (Does he jog at school?)

Do you have any friends at school?
Answer: **No**

Why don't you have any friends?
Answer: **Points to the question mark.**

Did you wet the bed last night?
Answer: **No**

Do you know what communication is?
Answer:

Do you think you would be happier if everyone were able to understand what you try to tell us?
Answer: **Yes**

What can I do to understand you? What would you like me to do to understand what you try to say?
Answer: **Read**

Read what?
Answer: **I**

Is that how you understand what we try to say to you?
Answer: **No**

What do you do to understand us?
Answer: **Hear**

Do you hear our minds or our mouths?
Answer: **Mouth**

So if you hear our mouths to talk/understand, why do we have to read your mind to understand you?
Answer: **Can't talk.**

Yesterday we spoke and you wanted to know if I liked Barbara. Why did you ask?
Answer: **Fight**

Who got into a fight?
Answer: **Barbara Kim**

Do you know what we were fighting over?
Answer: **Job**

It wasn't a fight Kenny. It was a disagreement. Do you understand that it had nothing to do with you? You didn't do anything wrong.
Answer: **Yes – I work**

Yes, you are my work, but I also have other things to do for my work that don't directly involve you. It wasn't your fault in any way. Okay? Do you understand?
Answer: **Yes**

Was it upsetting to you when Barbara and I were upset?
Answer: **Yes**

Why was it upsetting?
Answer: **Barbara, Kim end**

I know I ask you lots of questions. Is there anything you would like to ask me?
Answer: **Yes**

What would you like to ask me?
Answer: **Kim Friend**

What about Kim Friend?
Answer: **Good**

Do you want to know if I'm your good friend?
Answer: **No**

Do you want to know stuff about my friends?
Answer: **Yes**

What would you like to know about my friends?
Answer: **Happy People**

Then I explained: My friends and I are happy people. We have lots of fun to-gether, laughing and joking around.

Is there anything else you'd like to ask me?
Answer: **Yes**

What is it?
Answer: **Do you like Barbara?** His exact words: **Do like Barbara** My answer: Yes, I like Barbara.

CHAPTER TWENTY-FOUR
chapter twenty-four
chapter twenty-four

    ⊡   ⊡   ⊡   ⊡   ⊡

JULY 16, 1994/KIM AND KENNY

Do you remember your parents interviewing Lincoln today?
Answer: **Yes**

Was Lincoln nice?
Answer:

Do you like Lincoln?
Answer: **No**

Would you like Lincoln to work with you?
Answer: **No**

Was Lincoln tall or short?
Answer: **Tall**

Did you show him your puzzles?
Answer: **Yes**

Do you know what reading is?
Answer: **Yes**

Do you know how to read?
Answer: **Yes**

Picked up an action card and asked him what it said. It happened to be the # four.
Answer: **He said it and spelled it.**

⊡   ⊡   ⊡   ⊡   ⊡

JULY 16, 1994/KIM AND KENNY

Would you like Tami to ask your questions like I do so she can get to know you better?
Answer: **Yes**

Do you want to get to know Tami better.
Answer: **Yes**

Does Tami want to get to know you better?
Answer: **No**

What would you like Tami and Cory to teach you at school? Something that you would like to improve on?
Answer: **Math**

The other day you told me "long time for help." Did that mean you wanted help from Ken & Barbara?
Answer: **Yes**

What kind of help?
Answer: **Learn**

Do you know that Barbara is always trying to get help for you?
Answer: **Yes**

⊡   ⊡   ⊡   ⊡   ⊡

JULY 19, 2004 – KIMIKO OLIVER

How was your day?
Answer: **Fine**

Did you learn anything new at school?
Answer: **No**

Was Kenny in a good mood at school?
Answer: **Yes**

Was Tami in a good mood?
Answer: **No**

Did you like dinner tonight?
Answer: **Yes**

Would you like to do some work with Heather today?
Answer: **Yes**

Do you like Heather so far?
Answer: **Yes**

So when are you going to start doing FC with Ken & Barbara?
Answer: **No**

In fact, when are you going to start doing FC with everybody that cares about you like Tami, Mary, Rhonda, etc?
Answer: **No**

▦　　▦　　▦　　▦　　▦

JULY 19, 1994/KIMIKO OLIVER & KENNY

Do you feel as if Spectrum school is teaching you enough?
Answer:

Would you like Spectrum to teach you more?
Answer: **Yes**

What is your favorite thing to learn in school?
Answer: **Workbook**

Do you feel as if Spectrum is helping you get smarter?
Answer: **Yes**

Do you like going to Spectrum?
Answer: **No**

What do you most like about Spectrum?
Answer: **Like Tami**

Do you like math, reading or history?
Answer: **Math fun**

What about reading or history?
Answer:

Does Kenny know how to read?
Answer:

Are you happy now that you are communicating with me?
Answer: **Yes**

Do you know that Ken & Barbara are happy that you are communicating?
Answer: **Yes**

Would you like to tell them anything or ask them anything?
Answer: **Yes**

Tell them or ask them?
Answer: **Tell**

Okay, what would you like to tell them?
Answer: **Good Barbara Ken Work**

CHAPTER TWENTY-FOUR
chapter twenty-four
chapter twenty-four

JULY 25, 1994/KIMIKO OLIVER

How have you been?
Answer: **Fine**

Did you miss Kim?
Answer: **Yes** (I can't believe he said yes!)

Do you like your new workers?
Answer: **No**

Have you been doing good work?
Answer: **No**

Do you know why Kim hasn't been coming?
Answer: **No**

How has school been?
Answer: **No**

Have you been working on communication at school?
Answer: **No**

Does Heather think that you are a lot of work?
Answer: **Yes**

Why does Heather think you are a lot of work?
Answer: **Points to the question mark.**

Is that what you meant when you said "Friend—believe me work?"
Answer: **No**

Well, what did you mean by that?
Answer: **Points to the question mark.**

When you got kicked at school last week, where on your body did you get kicked?
Answer: **Butt**

What was the boy's name that kicked you?
Answer: **Won't answer**

199

Were you alone in the room or was someone else there?
Answer: **Yes**

Who was in the room with you?
Answer: **Big Man**

Was "big man" upset or mad?
Answer: **Yes**

Why was he mad?
Answer: Kenny wouldn't answer.

Did that scare you?
Answer: **Yes**

What was Big Man doing?
Answer: No

Did Big Man hurt Kenny?
Answer: **No**

Was Big Man the boy that kicked you?
Answer: **Yes**

Was Tami gone for a long time?
Answer: **Points to the question mark.**

Does Tami leave Kenny alone a lot?
Answer: **Yes**

How come you've been in such a great mood lately?
Answer: **Fun**

What's fun?
Answer: **Life**

Do you enjoy having a lot of different workers come over?
Answer: **Yes**

200   So now you ask me something. I'm tired of asking all the questions around here!

Saturday No

Answer: No, I won't work this Saturday, but maybe next Saturday.

No Friend Boy

Answer: Yes, I have a boyfriend and that's why I can't work next Saturday. And yes, you are a boy and you are my friend.

Mary Friend

Answer: Yes, Mary is your friend and my friend, and she has lots of friends.

⊠   ⊠   ⊠   ⊠   ⊠

JULY 30, 1994/KIM OLIVER AND KENNY COPPO

How have you been?
Answer: **Fine**

What's been up? What's new?
Answer: **Points to question mark.**

How has school been?
Answer: **Fine**

Are you doing good work at school?
Answer: **Yes**

Have you been happy?
Answer: **No**

Have you been unhappy?
Answer: **Yes**

Have you been sick?
Answer: **No**

Did someone/something make you angry?
Answer: **Yes**

Who?

Answer: **Mary**

Why did she make you mad?

Answer: **No, No, No**

You did pretty good work with Mary. Are you willing to work with other people now?

Answer: No answer

What would you like to work on at school?

Answer: **Math**

Would you like Tami to help you with math?

Answer: **No**

Who would you like to work with?

Answer: **You**

You work with me at home and work with Tami at school. Okay?

Answer: **Points to the question mark.**

Does Tami know how to work with you? Can she help you learn math?

Answer: **No**

Why can't she help you?

Answer: **Stay Alone**

Who stays alone?

Answer: **Me**

You want to be left alone?

Answer: **No**

Does Tami leave you alone?

Answer: **Yes**

When does she leave you alone?

Answer: **Am scared.**

Scared of what, who?
Answer: **Man**

What man?
Answer: **Big**

What's his name?
Answer: **Points to the question mark.**

Is the Big Man mean to you?
Answer: **Yes**

What is so scary about him?
Answer: **Loud**

What's his name?
Answer: **No**

Ask Tami about a big man. I don't know what he is referring to. He doesn't want to talk too much about it. Maybe he sees something they don't or someone they don't. Is Cory big?

▨   ▨   ▨   ▨   ▨

AUGUST 1, 1994/MARY AND KENNY

Kenny, did you have a good day?
Answer: **No**

Did you do a lot of work at school?
Answer: **Yes**

Is the Big Man in your class in school?
Answer: **Yes**

Was the Big Man good today?
Answer: **No**

Do you like all the kids in your class?
Answer: **No**

Do you like Big Man?
Answer: **No**

Do you like Tami?
Answer: **Yes**

Do you like me?
Answer: **I'm not sure.**

Did I get mad at you today?
Answer: **Yes**

◻   ◻   ◻   ◻   ◻

AUGUST 10, 1994

How was school today?
Answer: **Fine**

Was Big Man there?
Answer: **Yes**

Did you like Ed today?
Answer: **Yes**

Do you like the computer today?
Answer: **Yes**

Do you want to do more work on the computer?
Answer: **Yes, More!!!**

What were you trying to tell me and Ed at the table?
Answer: **QU...Question?**

You had a question?
Answer: **Help!!!**

Do you want Ed & Me to help you with math?

Answer: **Yes**

WORDS THOUGHT OF	LETTERS POINTED TO BY KENNY
Car	C-A-R
Bus	B-U- (Stopped)
Truck	T-R-U-C-K

Barbara,

We need to continue this computer work with Kenny. His enthusiasm is over-whelming! He literally asked for help through the F/C board. When we were in the room with Ed, Kenny was trying to spell something out to us, which he was pointing. He was trying to say H-E-L-P. Help with math I assume! He worked with me so well today… I am so flattered. He did F/C with me. Questions = GREAT!!! Telepathy = Good. Stopped on BUS, but that's the only one. I am so proud! Also, on next page, Kenny traced his name. I helped him by holding his hand, but he was very intent! Awesome Day!

❖   ❖   ❖   ❖   ❖

AUGUST 16, 1994/MALIA AND KENNY

Did you have a good day at school?

Answer: **No**

Do you like your one to one aid?

Answer: **No**

Do you want your parents to try to get you a different aide at school?

Answer: **Stop**

Do you want Kim to be your one on one aide?

Answer: **Yes**

Are you glad that your parents are trying to get you another one on one aide at school?

Answer: **Help**

Do you want your parents to help by getting you a different aide?
Answer: **Yes**

Kenny, do you think that you may work with Ken & Barbara someday?
Answer: **No**

Will you try to for them?
Answer: **No**

Kenny, would you like to learn to play the piano?
Answer: **No**

Do you remember my mom?
Answer: **Yes**

What's my mom's name?
Answer: **J-O-A-W**
Very good! "W" could be upside down "M?" Not sure!

Telepathy

WORDS THOUGHT OF	**LETTERS POINTED TO BY KENNY**
Eric	**E-R-J?**
Jaime	**J-A-I-Q**
Ken	**K-said word**

Funny though. Look at notes.
P.S. Instead of finishing word, he simply said it!!! Great job!

Barb,
It's funny, Kenny started spelling Eric and I started thinking of who next to think and Kenny started spelling that (Jaime) instead!
He even started spelling my sister's name right. Most people spell it Jamie. When Kenny eventually writes, he'll be the best speller. With the word Ken, he just said it instead! Amazing!
We worked on the letter "D" and "d" in spelling and writing tonight. In math: Brain busters. We did pages 81 & 85.

206   In "Explode the Code," we worked on pgs. 54 & 57 and part of 62. He did so good today!

Barbara, please listen to music tape! It's so beautiful. Melodious! If you listen carefully, you will hear songs in what he plays.

❑   ❑   ❑   ❑   ❑

AUGUST 23, 1994/KIMI AND KENNY

What would you like to do today?
Answer: **Work Q**

What Kind?
Answer: **Questions**

Is there any special place that you would like to go?
Answer: **Go?**

So, I hear you know how to write. Is it true?
Answer: **Yes**

Who taught you to write?
Answer: **Me**

Do you like writing?
Answer: **Yes**

Do you know that writing is a form of communication?
Answer: **Yes**

Do you remember what communication is? How important it is?
Answer: **Yes**

Okay, then you tell me why it is important?
Answer: **To me what I want.**

So how is Malia working out? Is she cool or what?
Answer: **Yes**

Do you like working with her?
Answer: **Yes**

207

Why haven't you been eating like you know you should? What's the problem?
Answer: **Points to the question mark.**

Have you been sick?
Answer: **No**

What's been going on?
Answer: **Mad**

At who?
Answer: **Verbally says Barbara**

What's Barbara done to make you mad?
Answer: **Were pot fell?**

That doesn't make any sense. Explain better.
Answer: **Were pot?**

Did anything exciting happen on the last day of school?
Answer: **Yes**

Well, what happened?
Answer: **Fun Sick**

Too much fun made you sick?
Answer: **Yes**

Did you have a seizure?
Answer: **Yes**

Did it hurt?
Answer: **Yes**

Where did it hurt at?
Answer: **Head**

Did you cry?
Answer: **No**

At the time, did you know what was happening?
Answer: **Yes**

How did you know?
Answer: **Felt**

Felt what?
Answer: **Come**

What did it feel like?
Answer: **Light**

Explain what "light" means.
Answer: **Light mind**

Do you know why you had the seizure?
Answer: **Points to the question mark.**

So do you know you're going to have a seizure before you have a seizure?
Answer: **Yes**

◻   ◻   ◻   ◻   ◻

AUGUST 25, 1994/KIM AND KENNY

Barbara, brace yourself. These questions and answers are real tear-jerkers. It took a lot to get him to open up.

Do you like the weather today or do you prefer sunshine?
Answer: **Sun**

Are you excited about starting a new school year next week?
Answer: **Yes**

What do you like most about school?
Answer: **Leave Home**

What are you most looking forward to when you return to school?
Answer: **Tami**

What are you least looking forward to when you return to school?
Answer: **Work**

Are you enjoying the summer of 1994 so far?
Answer: **Yes**

What most have you enjoyed about this summer?
Answer: **Water**

What least have you enjoyed about this summer?
Answer: **Bored**

If you could change one thing about this summer, what would it be?
Answer: **Kim Work**

If you could change one thing about your school/education, what would it be?
Answer: **Nicer people.**

If you could change one thing about your life, what would it be?
Answer: **More friends.**

Someone told me that you may be able to turn yourself into anything you want. A molecular change or something. That you can leave your body and become something else. What do you think about that?
Answer: **No**

Can you make yourself become part of a chair, or an animal or maybe a tree?
Answer: **No**

If you could change into or become part of something else, what would it be?
Answer: **Bird**

Why would you choose that?
Answer: **Free**

⬚   ⬚   ⬚   ⬚   ⬚

AUGUST 25, 1994/MALIA AND KENNY

Kenny, you grabbed the board. Do you wanna talk?
Answer: **Yes**

I heard that if you could choose to be an animal, you would be a bird. Why?
Answer: **F-L-Y**

Who do you wanna fly?
Answer: **F-R-E-E**

What do you want to be free from?
Answer: **L-O-V-E**
Note: What could this be about?

Why do you wanna be free from love?
Answer: **H-E-L-P**

If you could fly like a bird, would you not need help with anything?
Answer: **Yes**

Do you need help with something Kenny?
Answer: **Yes**

What do you need help with?
Answer: **Pointed to question mark.**

Do you want me to help you? Yes, how?
Answer: **Already**

I'm already helping you. Is that what you mean?
Answer: **Yes**

Would you want your parents and friends to be birds too?
Answer: **Yes**

Do you like school?
Answer: **No**

Do you like working with Kim?
Answer: **Yes, Help**

Is Kim helping you already?
Answer: **Yes**

Outline of Work Completed

1.   Worked with puzzles
2.   Questions
3.   "Big Get Ready Book" pg. 217 (Didn't want to finish.)
4.   Letters (Writing) See attached page (Aa-Gg)

Barb, on workbook, Kenny stopped. Did not want to continue. Great questions!

Kenny, what music do you like the most?
Answer: **West-E**

Do you like piano music?
Answer: **Yes**

Do you like to play the piano?
Answer: **Yes**

Do you ever get frustrated because we don't always ask the right questions?
Answer: **Pointed to yes twice!**

Will you help us by trying to spell out what you want to say on the F/C board?
Answer: **Yes**

Do you like to write?
Yes

What is some of your favorite things to do?
Answer: **Puzzles**

Besides puzzles?
Math? Pointed to Yes.

What subject of books do you like us to read?
Answer: **E-D Stopped**
Note: Could be educational maybe?

Why won't you do F/C in front of your Mom & Dad?
Answer: **Pointed to question mark.**

Telepathy

WORDS THOUGHT OF	LETTERS POINTED TO BY KENNY
Dog	d-o-g
Cat	c-a-t
Rabbit	r-a-b-b-I-t
Mouse	m-o-u (stopped)

Barb & Ken,
Pg. 226 in "Big Get Ready" book.

We worked on the letter L & M. Kenny did great job with questions. He was a little hesitant with the writing part of the lesson. We will work on that tomorrow.

Good F/C and telepathy. Loves puzzles. Did lots of puzzles. Make sure you look at the questions. Very interesting!
Malia

❖   ❖   ❖   ❖   ❖

AUGUST 27, 1994/KIM AND KENNY

When you were mad at Barbara because "pot fell," what did that mean?
Answer: **Points to the question mark.**

What does "pot fell" mean?
Answer: **No**

No What?
Answer: **Stop**

Why do you want freedom from Barbara?
Answer: **Bad**

Who?
Answer: **Barbara**

Why is Barbara bad?
Answer: **Alone**

Who's alone?
Answer: **Me**

Are you lonely?
Answer: **No**

You want to be left alone?
Answer: **Yes**

Barbara doesn't leave you alone?
Answer: **No**

She wants to help you. Do you want her help?
Answer: **Yes**

Then will you quit tantruming and crying when you are upset?
Answer: **Yes**

▢   ▢   ▢   ▢   ▢

AUGUST 28, 1994/KIM AND KENNY

Are you excited about going to Marine World today?
Answer: **Yes**

Have you ever been there before?
Answer: **Yes**

Who did you go with?
Answer: **Mary**

What did you like best about Marine World?
Answer: **Fun**

What are you most looking forward to when we go today?
Answer: **Fish**

Is it okay with you if Monica (my cousin) goes with us?
Answer: **Yes**

Are you having a better summer since we've been having fun lately?
Answer: **Yes**

Are you still bored?
Answer: **No**

Did you have fun at Playland on Saturday?
Answer: **Yes**

What did you like best about Playland?
Answer: **Childs**

Would you like to go again?
Answer: **Yes**

Have you been behaving for Ken & Barbara?
Answer: **Yes**

Why is it important to behave for your parents?
Answer: **Good life**

And is Kenny having a good life since he's been behaving?
Answer: **Yes**

What is good about your life?
Answer: **Free**

Free from what?
Answer: **Bad**

What needs improvement in your life?
Answer: **Brain**

Do you like me yet?
Answer: **No**
Note: I'm gonna hurt him

AUGUST 29, 1994/KIMI AND KENNY

Okay, tell me about Marine World. Did you have fun or what?
Answer: **Yes**

What did you like best about Marine World?
Answer: **Elephant**

What did you like least about Marine World?
Answer: **Hot**

Which show was your favorite? The bird show, the wildlife show, the elephant encounter or the whale and dolphin show?
Answer: **Whale**

Why was that your favorite show?
Answer: **Good**

I know you liked the elephant ride, but why? What was so fun about riding an elephant?
Answer: **Fun**

Describe the elephant to me. What did it feel like when you touched it?
Answer: **Hard**

What did it smell like?
Answer: **Points to the question mark.**

Did it make any noise or was it quiet?
Answer: **Quiet**

Did the elephant travel fast or slow?
Answer: **Slow**

So is Marine World a place you would like to visit again someday?
Answer: **Yes**

Was there anything you didn't get a chance to do yesterday that you would like to do the next time you go?

Answer: **Water**

Were you disappointed that Monica didn't stay with us?

Answer: **No**

▨   ▨   ▨   ▨   ▨

AUGUST 31, 1994/KIMI AND KENNY

Do you like playing your keyboard?

Answer: **Yes**

What do you like about your keyboard?

Answer: **Music**

Do you know any songs to play on your keyboard?

Answer: **Yes**

Do you want to learn how to play your keyboard better?

Answer: **Yes**

So why were you so tired yesterday?

Answer: **Points to the question mark.**

Have you been getting enough sleep?

Answer: **Yes**

Why have you been so tired?

Answer: **Points to the question mark.**

Why didn't you want to swim yesterday?

Answer: **Points to the question mark.**

Was it because you were so tired?

Answer: **Yes**

Well, would you like to go back another day when you aren't so tired?

Answer: **Yes**

Do you still feel tired today or are you better?

Answer: **Better**

217

Molly is coming over to give you a music lesson. Would you like that?
Answer: **Yes**

What do you like about Molly's music?
Answer: **Sing**

⬚ ⬚ ⬚ ⬚ ⬚

SEPTEMBER 2, 1994/MALIA AND KENNY

Are you excited about going to Playland?
Answer: **Yes**

Do you want to go with me to Playland?
Answer: **Yes**

Do you wish Kim were going like yesterday?
Answer: **Yes**

Do you want to go by my house afterwards?
Answer: **Yes**

Would you like to see my new apartment?
Answer: **Yes**

What do you want to do at Playland?
Answer: **F-U-N**

⬚ ⬚ ⬚ ⬚ ⬚

SEPTEMBER 5, 1994/KIMI AND KENNY

Why were you so grouchy yesterday?
Answer: **Hot**

What was wrong with you?
Answer: **No/Stop**

218

Did someone make you mad?
Answer: **Yes**

Who?
Answer: **Ken**

Why did you fight with Barbara?
Answer: **Mad**

Is Barbara your mother?
Answer: **Yes**

Are you supposed to hit Barbara?
Answer: **No**

Are you supposed to hit anyone?
Answer: **No**

Then don't. Understand?
Answer: **Yes**

If you were mad at Ken then why did you hit Barbara?
Answer: **Points to the question mark.**

What did Ken do to make you mad?
Answer: **Ride**

Ken took you for a ride and that made you mad?
Answer: **No**

Did Ken take you for a ride?
Answer: **No**

Did you want him to take you for a ride?
Answer: **Yes**

You mean to tell me you hit Barbara because Ken didn't take you for a ride?
Answer: **Yes**

Well, didn't Ken & Barbara take you to the water front to watch the boats?
Answer: **Yes**

That wasn't good enough for you?
Answer: **No**

Are you a spoiled brat?
Answer: **No**
Yes you are!!!

◻   ◻   ◻   ◻   ◻

SEPTEMBER 6, 1994/KIMI AND KENNY

Did you do work at school today?
Answer: **No**

Did Tami or Doreen do math work with you?
Answer: **No**

Was Tami in a good mood today?
Answer: **Yes**

What did you like about school today?
Answer: **Bus**

What about the bus?
Answer: **Ride**

Was Tami nice to you today?
Answer: **Yes**

Did you run on the treadmill?
Answer: **No**

Well, what did you do all day?
Answer: **Points to the question mark.**

Are you tired?
Answer: **Yes**

◻   ◻   ◻   ◻   ◻

SEPTEMBER 8, 1994/MALIA AND KENNY

Did you have a good day today?
Answer: **Yes**

Do you know what I did today?
Answer: **Yes**

What?
Answer: **D-E-N-T-I-S-T**
That is so funny. I thought he was going to say work, but I did go to the dentist.

Did you have fun sleeping at Mary's house?
Answer: **Yes**

So I understand you were hot at Playland? Is that true?
Answer: **Yes**
Note: It was hot!

So if I take you there again sometime when its not so hot, you'll play?
Answer: **Yes**

Did you like my apartment?
Answer: **Yes**

How come you didn't want to swim?
Answer: **Cold**

What do you mean cold?
Answer: **W-A-T-E-R**
Note: The water was cold! You gotta tell me these things! Good job!

Do you want to work on writing?
Answer: **Yes**

Worked on letters (writing) – see attached
Puzzles of course.
The Big Ready Book pg. 219

SEPTEMBER 8, 1994/MALIA AND KENNY

Kenny, are you upset about something today?
Answer: **No**, but then he slammed it (f/c board) down and away and wouldn't do any more questions. He's hiding something Barbara. He is upset about that boy.

Worked on puzzles.

         ⊡   ⊡   ⊡   ⊡   ⊡

SEPTEMBER 8, 1994/KIMI AND KENNY

Do you like Mitchell?   (Mitchell is a down syndrome boy Kenny met)
Answer: **No**

Did Mitchell say something to you earlier?
Answer: **Yes**

Did Mitchell make you cry?
Answer: **Yes**

What did Mitchell say to you?
Answer: **Bad**

Bad what?
Answer: **Ass**

What was the word?
Answer: **Ass**

Can you read Mitchell's mind?
Answer: **Bad**

Can Mitchell read your mind?
Answer: **Yes**

Can you and Mitchell communicate?
Answer: **Yes**

How do you communicate with Mitchell?
Answer: **Brain**

How old is Mitchell?
Answer: **B-O- then stopped**

◻   ◻   ◻   ◻   ◻

SEPTEMBER 12, 1994/KIM AND KENNY

Did you do anything new or exciting yesterday?
Answer: **No**

What did you do yesterday?
Answer: **No**

Barbara said you and Ken went to the park. Did you have fun?
Answer: **Yes**

What did you like about the park?
Answer: **Kids**

Did you swing?
Answer: **No**

Were you grouchy yesterday?
Answer: **No**

Did you behave for your parents?
Answer: **Yes**

Did you do work at school today?
Answer: **No**

What did you do at school today?
Answer: **Nothing**

You just sat around all day and did nothing?
Answer: **Yes**

Are you telling the truth?
Answer: **No**

Well then, what did you do today?
Answer: **Nothing**

Why won't you tell me what you did at school?
Answer: **Yes**

Did you have fun at school?
Answer: **Yes**

What was fun at school?
Answer: **Tami**

What did Tami do that was fun?
Answer: **Points to the question mark.**

⬚   ⬚   ⬚   ⬚   ⬚

SEPTEMBER 14, 1994/KIMI AND KENNY

What's up?
Answer: **Nothing**

Anything new or exciting you feel like talking about?
Answer: **No**

Did you do work at school today?
Answer: **Yes**

What did you work on?
Answer: **Nothing**

Did you work on some math?
Answer: **Yes**

Did you do good work with Tami?
Answer: **Yes**

Do you want Kim to come work with you at school?
Answer: **No**

Why not?
Answer: **Tami**

What about Tami?
Answer: **No**

Kim and Tami will both work with you. Okay?
Answer: **Yes**

Did you work with Malia yesterday?
Answer: **No**

Why not?
Answer: **Tired**

You were tired?
Answer: **No**

Malia was tired?
Answer: **Yes**

Are you telling the truth?
Answer: **Points to the questions mark and starts laughing.**

Are you being funny today?
Answer: **Yes**

◻   ◻   ◻   ◻   ◻

SEPTEMBER 15, 1994/MALIA AND KENNY

Kenny, did you have a little seizure or just chills today at Mary's house?
Answer: **Seizure? No** (by himself)

Did you just have chills?
Answer: **Pointed to question mark.**

Maybe he doesn't know what the chills are.

Were you cold?

Answer: **No**

Remember the boy named Mitchell that could read your mind?

Answer: **Yes**

Did he try to tell you something about his life?

Answer: **No**

Or did he just call you a bad name?

Answer: **Yes**

Kenny, do you know what I am excited about tonight?

Answer: **Pointed to question mark.**

Did you stay cool at school today?

Answer: **Yes**

What would you like to do on Friday after school?

Answer: **Pointed to question mark.**

Would you like us to go to the park?

Answer: **Yes**

Telepathy

WORDS THOUGHT OF	LETTERS POINTED TO BY KENNY
Walk	**W-A-K**
Work	**W-O-R-K**
Write	**W-R-I-T-E**
Math	**M-A-T**

Barb & Ken,

We worked on puzzles, as well. Good questions, he did! Good telepathy!

SEPTEMBER 24, 1994/KAREN COMPTON, RESPITE WORKER

Kenny wasn't very into this exercise today. He did recognize the following words thought of.

Telepathy

1. Pet
2. Cat
3. Dog
4. Sun
5. Ronnie
6. Kenny (not identified)

Crossed my name Karen between it (spelled KK). The word Ronnie was not an intentional mind word, but it was my personal thought at that time and Kenny picked up on that, which was ironic because I had just received a page from Ronnie, a male friend. At this point, Kenny lost interest due to the fact my own mind was not at his <u>full</u> attention.

*Considering the fact that I am not a trained expert and was able to do this exercise with Kenny and received excellent feedback, I'm more than sure that this matter should be looked into further (Telepathy).

SEPTEMBER 30, 1994/KIM AND KENNY

Did you enjoy the project on elephants today?
Answer: **Yes**

What was one thing you learned about elephants?
Answer: **Skills**

Do you remember where elephants live?
Answer: **Yes**

Where do elephants live?
Answer: **Zoo**

How do elephants drink water?
Answer: **Trunks**

Did you do some good work with Malia last night?
Answer: **No**

What was nice about your visit with Malia yesterday?
Answer: **Points to the question mark.**

Did you eat a good dinner last night?
Answer: **None**

Can you tell me what you had for dinner last night?
Answer: **Restaurant**

What was the name of the restaurant?
Answer: **Points to the question mark.**

Are you feeling better or do you still have a cold?
Answer: **Yes**

Yes, what?
Answer: **Better**

What kind of schoolwork would you like to start with today?
Answer: **Read**

Would you like to go anywhere special tonight?
Answer: **Restaurant**

How about if Mary cooks you dinner?
Answer: **None**

What would you like for dinner tonight?
Answer: **Pop**

OCTOBER 4, 1994/KIM AND KENNY

What did you make in Speech class today?
Answer: **Pizza**

What were the names of the ladies in speech class?
Answer: **Kim**

Who else?
Answer: **Kathleen**

What were some things that you put on your pizza?
Answer: **Sauce**

What else?
Answer: **Cheese**

And?
Answer: **Meat**

What were some colors on your pizza?
Answer: **Red and White**

What did you smell?
Answer: **Sauce**

What did you do when everyone was asked to help make the pizza?
Answer: **Points to the question mark.**

There was a special task that you were asked to do. What is it?
Answer: **Cheese**

What did you do with the cheese?
Answer: **Cut**

Do you know what kind of cheese was used?
Answer: **White**

What did the cheese feel like? Hard or soft or wet or dry?
Answer: **Soft**

How did you cook the cheese? In the oven, in the stove or in a microwave?
Answer: **Microwave**

How much time did it take to melt the cheese?
Answer: **Seconds**

How many seconds?
Answer: **Points to the question mark.**

What did the pizza taste like after the cheese was melted?
Answer: **Good**

Was the pizza hot or cold after it came out of the microwave?
Answer: **Hot**

Do you like going to speech class?
Answer: **Yes**

What's great about the class?
Answer: **Fun**

Why does Kenny need speech class?
Answer: **Talk**

Why is communication important?
Answer: **Life**

◻   ◻   ◻   ◻   ◻

OCTOBER 5, 1994/KEN & MALIA

You do such good work at school and with me. How did you teach yourself to tell time?
Answer: **C-L-O-C-K**

What is it about your classroom that bothers you most?
Answer: **S-P-A-C-E**

Is there not enough space?
Answer: **Yes**

What type of work did you do?
Answer: **Pointed to question mark.**

What caused red marks on your chest and arm today?
Answer: **Pointed to question mark.**

Were you hot?
Answer: **Yes**

Why didn't you want to go to park with me earlier?
Answer: **Stop**

What makes you get so cranky and upset at times?
Answer: **A-L-O-N-E**

Do you feel alone?
Answer: **No**

Do you want to be left alone?
Answer: **Yes**

Is it because something inside your body is bothering you?
Answer: **No**

Do you mean that you learned to tell time by looking at the clock?
Answer: **Yes**

When did you learn to tell time?
Answer: **L-T/Stop** (Means long time ago)

Who taught you how to tell time?
Answer: **No answer**

OCTOBER 6, 1994/KIM AND KENNY

Was I at school yesterday?
Answer: **No**

Do you know why I was absent yesterday?
Answer: **Sick**

I'm curious about how your day went yesterday?
Answer: **Fine**

Did you do some good work yesterday?
Answer: **Yes**

What type of work did you do?
Answer: **Read**

Did you answer any questions?
Answer:

Were you cooperative during academics?
Answer: **Yes**

Who did you do work with?
Answer: **Tami**

Was that the only person you worked with?
Answer: **No**

What's the name of the other person you worked with?
Answer: **Points to the question mark.**

Was it Lisa?
Answer: **Yes**

What was something you learned yesterday?
Answer: **P-U**

What does P-U mean? Is that an abbreviation?
Answer: **Pig-U**

Was there a part of work that you would have liked to do more of?
Answer: **Sport**

More PE?
Answer: **Yes**

Was there a part of work that you would have liked to do less of?
Answer: **Write**

Did you miss me yesterday?
Answer: **No** (Stinker!!)

What does the U stand for?
Answer: **U-U-U**

Does the U stand for a word?
Answer: **Yes – U points to the question mark.**

The U stands for "you?" Are you asking me something?
Answer: **Yes**

Oh! What did I learn new yesterday?
Answer: **Yes**
*Note: Kenny is smiling and clapping. I guess happy that I figured it out.

Do you know why your Dad left tonight?
Answer: **Yes**

Why?
Answer: **S-T-O-R**

Do you know what he's buying?
Answer: **C-O-M-P-U-T-E-R**

Do you know what it's for?
Answer: **M-O-R-E**

More? More what?
Answer: **W-O-R-K**

Are you excited about work?
Answer: **No**

What does a computer do for you?
Answer: **S-P-E-A-K**

How does a computer help you speak?
Answer: **R-T**

What is "R-T?"
Answer: **R-E-A-D**

O.K. What is "T?"
Answer: **T-H-O-U-G-H-T-S**

What are your favorite stories about?
Answer: **P-E-O-P-L-E**

What kind of people?
Answer: **M-E**

People like you?
Answer: **Yes**

Would you like Barbara to get any special type of books?
Answer: **Yes**

What special kind?
Answer: **H-E-R-O-E**

You want books about heroes?
Answer: **Yes**

If there are no books about heroes, what is your second choice?
Answer: **F-U-N-N-Y**

Kenny, when you say "heroes," what exactly do you mean?
Answer: **T-E-A-C-H**

234   You want books about heroes who teach?
Answer: **Yes**

What do they teach?
Answer: **M-I-N-D**

☒   ☒   ☒   ☒   ☒

OCTOBER 7, 1994/KIM AND KENNY

Did you enjoy the walk we just took?
Answer: **Yes**

What did you like about it?
Answer: **Fun**

What made it so fun?
Answer: **Free**

Free what?
Answer: **Points to the question mark.**

Did you dislike anything about it?
Answer: **Yes**

What?
Answer: **Short**

It was too short?
Answer: **Yes**

How's the weather today?
Answer: **Cool**

What kind of weather do you think we'll have over the weekend?
Answer: **Hot**

What were some things you saw on the walk?
Answer: **Trees**

What were some things you heard on the walk?
Answer: **Mouths**

235

OCTOBER 8, 1994/KENNY AND HEATHER

Do you like the computer that Ken got for you to work on?
Answer: **Yes**

Do you want to learn the computer?
Answer: **No Work**

Do you think the computer can help you to communicate?
Answer: **Yes**

Are you mad at Ken for taking too long to go to the park?
Answer: **No**

Do you still want to go to the park?
Answer: **No**

Working on the computer can help you to communicate. Do you understand that it can help you?
Answer: **No work! (W.R.K. NO!)**

How can we make work more fun for Kenny?
Answer: **He said: Kim? (K.M.?)**
I think it's easier for him to do. Questions with Kim maybe? Good effort!

OCTOBER 11, 1994/KIM AND KENNY

How was your weekend?
Answer: **Fine**

Did you do anything special or fun?
Answer: **Yes**

What?
Answer: **Ride**

With who?

Answer: **Ken**

Are you glad to be back in school after three days?

Answer: **Y-Then points to question mark.**

How'd you like speech class?

Answer: **Yes**

Do you remember what you made today in speech?

Answer: **Tuna**

Tuna what?

Answer: **Tuna Sandwich**

Was tuna something you enjoyed making and eating?

Answer: **Yes**

What's one great thing about tuna?

Answer: **Taste**

What about it?

Answer: **Good**

Do you know what kind of animal tuna is before it goes in a can?

Answer: **Sea**

What else can we call it?

Answer: **Fish**

Do you know where the tuna fish lives before it becomes your meal?

Answer: **Sea**

Besides a sandwich, can you tell me what other kinds of dishes tuna can be used for?

Answer: **Soup**

What are some condiments that you enjoy with tuna?

Answer: **Pickles**

What did you mix with your tuna today?
Answer: **Mayo**

What else?
Answer: **Celery**

Is there anything in particular you would like to talk about or mention to me?
Answer: **Yes**

Ask away! Or tell me about it.
Answer: **Weekend**

Which weekend?
Answer: **This**

This past or this upcoming?
Answer: **Coming**

What about it?
Answer: **Work**

What about work?
Answer: **Kim Work**

You want me to work with you this weekend?
Answer: **Yes**

Which day would you like me to come; Saturday or Sunday?
Answer: **Sunday**

Saturday would be better for me. Is that okay?
Answer: **No**

Why not?
Answer: **Malia**

What about Malia?
Answer: **Coming**

Malia's coming on Saturday?
Answer: **No**

Do you want Malia to come on Saturday?
Answer: **Yes**

What were some things you smelled on the walk?
Answer: **Points to the question mark.**

Did you touch anything during the walk?
Answer: **Yes**

What?
Answer: **Bush**

What did it feel like?
Answer: **Rough**

What kind of neighborhood was that?
Answer: **Quiet**

Was it similar or different than your neighborhood?
Answer: **Same**

In what way was it the same?
Answer: **Houses**

Can you think of any ways that it was different?
Answer: **Name**

Name of what?
Answer: **Street**

Why is it important to take walks?
Answer: **Points to the question mark.**

Why are walks good for you?
Answer: **Exercise**

OCTOBER 12, 1994/KIM AND KENNY

I heard you got a new computer. Is that true?
Answer: **Yes**

Well, are you happy about it?
Answer: **Yes**

Have you been able to use it yet?
Answer: **No**

Why do you think your parents bought you something like that?
Answer: **Points to the question mark.**

Can you tell me what a computer is used for?
Answer: **Fun**

What else?
Answer: **Work**

Why is a computer an important thing for you to have?
Answer: **Words**

Words meaning?
Answer: **My words.**

What can a computer help you do?
Answer: **Teach**

Teach? Explain.
Answer: **U-U-U-U**

Teach you? Teach Kenny or teach Kim?
Answer: **Kenny**

What does your computer look like?
Answer: **TV**

Is it similar to the computer here in your class?

Answer: **Yes**

In what way(s) is it similar to the computer here at school?

Answer: **Color**

What color is it?

Answer: **White**

Is it different than the one here at school?

Answer: **Yes**

In what way(s) is it different than the computer here at school?

Answer: **More**

More what?

Answer: **More better.**

In what way?

Answer: **Points to the question mark.**

Have you seen or felt the keyboard of your new computer?

Answer: **Yes**

Does the keyboard remind you of something else that you use everyday?

*Hint, they both have the alphabet.

Answer: **Yes**

What?

Answer: **Board**

Can you tell me one difference between your FC Board and the keyboard on the computer?

Answer: **Point**

You have to point to both of them, so that's a similarity. What's something different?

Answer: **Size**

OCTOBER 13, 1994/KENNY AND MALIA

Can we talk about the type of books you like to read?
Answer: **Yes**

Do you like mystery?
Answer: **No**

Do you like westerns?
Answer: **No**

What's your favorite type of books you like us to read to you?
Answer: **Westerns**

I thought you said you didn't like westerns. Do you?
Answer: **Yes**

Do you enjoy us reading to you?
Answer: **Yes**

Do you enjoy the workbooks we do?
Answer: **Yes**

What's your favorite workbook?
Answer: **M-A-T-H**

What do we need to do to help you have a better time?
Answer: **L-E-A-V (Stopped)**

You want us to leave?
Answer: **Yes then pointed to "No" and "Help"**

Do you want help during bad moods?
Answer: **Yes**

Do you know that we sometimes worry about you?
Answer: **Yes**

Do you know that I want you to have fun during work and play with me?

Answer: **Yes**

When you're in a bad mood, what should we do to help you?
Answer: **No**

So no help when you're in a bad mood?
Answer: **Pointed to "Yes" and "Stop"**

Stop helping you? You want us not to help you when you're in a bad mood?
Answer: **Yes**

▫   ▫   ▫   ▫   ▫

OCTOBER 18, 1994/KIM AND KENNY

What would you like to talk about today?
Answer: **Fun**

What about fun?
Answer: **My fun.**

Your fun in the past, present or future?
Answer: **Future**

You want to do something fun in the future?
Answer: **Yes**

The future as in later today or another day?
Answer: **Another day**

What is it that you want to do?
Answer: **Play**

Play where?
Answer: **Park**

Who would you like to take you to the park?
Answer: **Ken**

What do you want to play on or with at the park? Swings, slide, monkey bars?
Answer: **Kids**

Oh! You want to play with children?
Answer: **Yes**

Why do you want to play with children?
Answer: **Fun**

How would you play with them? Games or on the jungle gym?
Answer: **Sand**

You want to play in the sand with the children?
Answer: **Yes**

❑   ❑   ❑   ❑   ❑

OCTOBER 20, 1994/KIM AND KENNY

Telepathy

What's up? What do you want to talk about?
Answer: **You**

What about me?
Answer: **Life**

My life?
Answer: **Yes**

About my entire life or on one specific thing or person?
Answer: **One**

A person or thing?
Answer: **Person**

Who?
Answer: **Will**

How do you know that I know someone named Will?
Answer: **Phone**

I don't understand?
Answer: **He Phone**

So anyways, what do you want to know about?
Answer: **Love**

What about love?
Answer: **You**

Are you asking if I love you?
Answer: **No**

You love me?
Answer: **No**

Well, what does love – you mean?
Answer: **Will**

You want to know if I love Will?
Answer: **No**

You want to know if Will loves me?
Answer: **No**

Well, what? Explain.
Answer: **Know**

What or who knows?
Answer: **Kenny**

Kenny knows something?
Answer: **Yes**

Do I know?
Answer: **No**

What do you know?
Answer: **Love**

What about love?
Answer: **Will**

CHAPTER TWENTY-FOUR
chapter twenty-four
chapter twenty-four

245

You know about Will's love?
Answer: **Yes**

How can you know about Will's love if you don't even know him?
Answer: **You**

You know from me?
Answer: **No**

Well, how?
Answer: **You – Love**

What about my love?
Answer: **No**

You think I love Will?
Answer: **No**

You think Will loves me?
Answer: **Know**

You know I love Will?
Answer: **No**

You know Will loves me?
Answer: **Yes, Yes, Yes**

How do you know?
Answer: **Mind**

How does your mind know?
Answer: **Everything**

Your mind knows everything?
Answer: **Yes**

Your mind knows everything about the entire world?
Answer: **No**

Well, everything about what?
Answer: **Friends**

You know everything about your friends or my friends?

Answer: **Kenny**

So I'm your friend?

Answer: **No**

But you know everything about me so I must be. Right?

Answer: **Points to the question mark.**

OCTOBER 20, 1994/KENNY AND MALIA

Telepathy

WORDS THOUGHT OF	LETTERS POINTED TO BY KENNY
Mom	M-O-M
Doctor	D-O-C-T-O-R
Teacher	T-E-A-C-H-E-R
Dentist	D-E-N-T-I-S-T
Dad	D-A-D-D-Y
Kenny	K-E-N-N-Y
Kin	K-I-M

OCTOBER 21, 1994/KIM AND KENNY

What would you like to talk about?

Answer: **Love**

What about love?

Answer: **Who**

Explain better.

Answer: **Who Love?**

Who loves what? I don't understand what you mean.
Answer: **Kenny**

You want to tell me who you love?
Answer: **No**

You want to tell me who loves you?
Answer: **How**

How what? How to love? How love works? How love feels? How love is?
Answer: **Love**

Okay, I understand "love." What about love do you want to talk about?
Answer: **My**

You want to talk about "your love?"
Answer: **Kenny**

So tell me about your love Kenny?
Answer: **Come back**

Who or what "come back?"
Answer: **Love**

Your love "come back?" Or your love is coming back? Or it already came back?
You want it to come back?
Answer: **Friend**

What about friend? What friend are you talking about? Give me a name.
Answer: **Kenny**

You want Kenny to come back?
Answer: **No**

I don't understand what you want to tell me. Help me out a little more. Is your
friend "Kenny" someone else or you?
Answer: **Me**

You want your love for Kenny to come back?

Answer: **No**

You want your love for something else to come back?
Answer: **Yes**

What do you want to love?
Answer: **Friends**

You love your friends and your friends love you?
Answer: **No**

You don't love your friends?
Answer: **No**

Why not?
Answer: **Mad**

Why are you mad?
Answer: **Life**

You're mad at life or about your life?
Answer: **Yes**

Why are you mad at life?
Answer: **Bad**

You think life is bad?
Answer: **Yes**

Why is life bad?
Answer: **No**

No what? What do you mean?
Answer: **Friends**

❖   ❖   ❖   ❖   ❖

OCTOBER 24, 1994/KENNY AND MALIA

What kind of friends do you wish for?
Answer: **G-O-O-D**

What are good friends?
Answer: **T-A-L-K**

Was there any friends you had who had to leave?
Answer: **?**

Good friends talk to you?
Answer: **Yes**

What do good friends talk to you about?
Answer: **L-I-F-E**

Good friends talk to you about life in general?
Answer: **No**

What life do they talk about? Yours?
Answer: **No**

About their lives?
Answer: **Yes**

What do you like to know about their lives?
Answer: **F-R**

What is "F-R?"
Answer: **Friends**

You want to know about my friends?
Answer: **N-O**

What would you like to know?
Answer: **Y-O-U**

You want to know about me?
Answer: **Yes**

I don't understand. What about me would you like to know?
Answer: **e-v-e-r-y**

You want to know everything?
Answer: **Yes**

Can you find out a lot telepathically?
Answer: **Yes**

Do you remember a boy named Patrick?
Answer: **No**

What could we do to make you happier?
Answer: **t-a-l-k**

Talk about myself?
Answer: **y-e-s**

What things can you find out telepathy?
Answer: **Wouldn't answer**. Asked again and he threw board. He stopped for some reason and would not go on.

We worked on reading and puzzles and brain quest cards and music though, too!

Major reading. Kenny loves it. Really enjoys it and I am so happy with the books because he's happy!

Kenny, your bus driver asked me out on a date. Did you know that?
Answer: **Yes**

Is he nice?
Answer: **No**

Do you like him?
Answer: **b-o-r-i-n-g**

OCTOBER 25, 1994/KIM AND KENNY

What kind of friends do you wish for?
Answer: **Points to the question mark.**

Are there some friends you had and they had to leave you?
Answer: **Yes**

Who were they?
Answer: **Points to the question mark.**

Do you remember Patrick?
Answer: **No**

What would you want a friend to do for or with you?
Answer: **Fun**

Like what specifically?
Answer: **Points to the question mark.**

What can any of us do to make you a happier person and enjoy life more?
Answer: **Points to the question mark.**

What would you like Ken and Barbara to do to make you happier?
Answer: **Puzzles**

What about puzzles?
Answer: **More**

Is there something you feel like talking about or telling me about?
Answer: **Ride**

What about ride?
Answer: **Street**

Ride, street . . .?
Answer: **Ken**

You want Ken to take you for a ride on the street?
Answer: **No**

Explain more. I don't understand.
Answer: **Ride**

What do you want to ride?
Answer: **No**

Do you want to go for a ride?
Answer: **No**

Someone else is going for a ride?

Answer: **Points to the question mark.**

Okay, from the beginning, what would you like to talk about or tell me?

Answer: **Boys**

What boys? Boys in your class? Boys that are your friends?

Answer: **No**

What about boys would you like to discuss?

Answer: **Street**

Boys on the street, boys you saw on the street?

Answer: **Yes**

On what street did you see them?

Answer: **My**

On your street?

Answer: **Yes**

Well, did you go over and talk to them or play with them?

Answer: **No**

Why not?

Answer: **Points to the question mark.**

Did you want to play with them or make friends with them?

Answer: **No**

Why not?

Answer: **Can't**

Why couldn't/can't you?

Answer: **Busy**

Are you too busy to make friends with the boys?

Answer: **No**

Were the boys too busy to make friends with you?

Answer: **Yes**

Well, why were they too busy? Were they working or something?
Answer: **No**

What made them too busy?
Answer: **Bike**

They were busy with their bikes?
Answer: **Yes**

What were they doing to their bikes? Fixing or working on them?
Answer: **Ride**

They were busy riding their bikes?
Answer: **Yes**

Do you want to ride a bike?
Answer: **Yes**

Do you know how to ride a bike?
Answer: **No**

Do you want to learn how to ride a bike?
Answer: **Yes**

Who would you like to show you how to ride a bike?
Answer: **Points to the question mark.**

Do you even have a bike?
Answer: **Yes**

I don't think so, are you sure?
Answer: **Yes**

Well, where's it at?
Answer: **Home**

I never saw it before. What color is it?
Answer: **Red**

Is it big or little?
Answer: **Big**

How many wheels does it have? 2-3-4?
Answer: **Two**

Who bought it for you?
Answer: **Ken**

Contratulations!

His Dad bought a new motorcycle for himself, not Kenny of course!

⊡　　⊡　　⊡　　⊡　　⊡

OCTOBER 26, 1994/KIM AND KENNY

What would you like to talk about today?
Answer: **Points to the question mark.**

Did you enjoy the art project we just did?
Answer: **No**

What didn't you like about it?
Answer: **Bored**

Explain further?
Answer: **Draw**

Draw what?
Answer: **Draw More**

Is there anything you liked about it at all?
Answer: **No**

What about the bright, orange paint? Did you like painting?
Answer: **Yes**

Did you know that I won't be at school Thursday and Friday?
Answer: **Yes**

Do you know why I won't be here?
Answer: **No**

Do you think I'll miss out on anything while I'm gone?
Answer: **Yes**

Like What?
Answer: **Party**

Who's having a party?
Answer: **Us**

What's the party for?
Answer: **Points to the question mark.**

What will you be celebrating?
Answer: **Fun**

Do you like parties?
Answer: **Yes**

What do you like about parties?
Answer: **People**

Is there anything you dislike about parties?
Answer: **No**

⬚   ⬚   ⬚   ⬚   ⬚

OCTOBER 26, 1994/HEATHER AND KENNY

Did you have a good day at school?
Answer: **Yes**

What did you do at school?
Answer: **w-o-r-d**

256   Are you hungry?
Answer: **No**

Do you know what I made for dinner?
Answer: **Brad** (Bread maybe)

Do you like what I cook?
Answer: **No**

Do you want to read a book?
Answer: **Yes**

Do you like the book I'm going to read?
Answer: **No**

What kind of book would you like to read?
Answer: **p-e-o-l-e** (people maybe)

Do you want to read or go on the freeway?
Answer: **No**

Then he said **no w-o-r-k** and got up and went and sat on the chair! Then he fell asleep. What a cute kid!
Good Work Kenny!
We also read a few chapters from the bible stories.

So let's talk more about you okay?
Answer: **No**

What would you like to tell me?
Answer: **M-A-D**

Why are you mad?
Answer: **M-E**

Are you mad at yourself?
Answer: **Yes**

Why?
Answer: **B-A-D** Pointed to the more sign.

Well, were you bad?
Answer: **No**

What's wrong? You can tell me!
Answer: **M-O-R-E H-E-L-P**

You want more help?
Answer: **Yes**

Do you want more help so you won't be bad?
Answer: **S-C-H-O-O-L**

Do you want to go back to school?
Answer: **Yes**

Are you just bored on your vacation and that makes you bad?
Answer: **No M-A-R-Y**

Then he said **stop!**

What is it that you are mad at Kenny?
Answer: **H-A-N-D**

Why are you mad at your hand?
Answer: **B-A-D**

Are you mad at your hand because you have been pulling on people lately?
Answer: **No**

Do you know that I am your friend?
Answer: **Yes**

Are you my friend?
Answer: **Yes**

By doing these questions I can help you and I know sometimes it's hard, but you are doing a great job.
Answer: **Pointed to more and got frustrated!**

Is their anything else you want to tell me?
Answer: **H-A-R-D**

258 What is it that is hard?
Answer: **H-A-N-D**

Is it hard for you to do questions with me because sometimes I don't understand?

Answer: **Yes**

Is it hard on your hand?

Answer: **Yes**

Did pgs. 77, 74, 73 in workbooks.

❑　❑　❑　❑　❑

NOVEMBER 4, 1994/KIM AND KENNY

Barb,

Laurie and I presented this question to Kenny, while working on the computer: "Is something at school bothering you or is something at home bothering you?

He typed in: **School**

We asked: What about school?"

He typed in: **"Brad"**

We asked: "How or what is bad?"

He typed in: **"Doreen."**

And he wouldn't respond to any more questions regarding that subject so we gave him a choice of Laurie leaving or staying on a blank piece of paper and **he pointed to "leave"** independently.

So the following is a continuation of questions after Laurie left.

What is bad about school and Doreen?

Answer: **Hurt**

Who's hurt?

Answer: **Doreen**

How is she hurt? Did she hurt somebody or did somebody hurt her?

Answer: **Her**

Someone hurt Doreen?
Answer: **Yes**

Who hurt Doreen?
Answer: **James**

Is that why you tantrumed yesterday?
Answer: **Yes**

Is there a way they could have handled James that wouldn't have upset you so much?
Answer: **Move**

Move who, what or where?
Answer: **Away**

Move away from James? (James is another violent student at school)
Answer: **Yes**

⬚   ⬚   ⬚   ⬚   ⬚

NOVEMBER 9, 1994/KIM AND KENNY

Is there anything you would like to talk about today?
Answer: **Yes**

What would you like to talk about?
Answer: **Jesus**

What about Jesus?
Answer: **Help**

Jesus help what or who?
Answer: **People**

Are you telling me or asking?
Answer: **Telling**

How does Jesus help people?
Answer: **Pray**

Jesus prays for people?
Answer: **No**

People pray for help?
Answer: **Yes**

Do you pray for help?
Answer: **Yes**

What do you pray for?
Answer: **Life**

What about life?
Answer: **Good**

You pray for a good life?
Answer: **Yes**

Do you think you have a good life?
Answer: **No**

Why don't you have a good life?
Answer: **Fun**

You want to have more fun?
Answer: **Yes**

You don't have fun now?
Answer: **No**

How can everyone help you to have more fun?
Answer: **Can't**

Why can't we?
Answer: **Friends**

What about your friends?
Answer: **None**

You don't have any friends?
Answer: **No**

What about your classmates and your neighbors and teacher and respite workers?
Answer: **Different**

How are they different from friends?
Answer: **Play**

Those people don't play or they do play?
Answer: **Don't**

What about the baseball game in PE. We played. Why didn't you join us?
Answer: **Can't**

Why can't you?
Answer: **Hard**

Would you like us to teach you how to play baseball?
Answer: **No**

What would you like to play?
Answer: **Toys**

You want to play with toys?
Answer: **Yes**

Would you like to play with any of the new toys in the PE room?
Answer: **No**

Why not?
Answer: **Little**

You think they're too little for you?
Answer: **Yes**

Would you like some big kid's toys? Maybe toys for teenagers.
Answer: **Yes**

Could you give me some examples of what you want so we can start helping you have fun?
Answer: **Points to the question mark.**

262

Can you name a toy for me that you would like to have?
Answer: **No**

Will you think about it and maybe tell me later?
Answer: **Yes**

⬚   ⬚   ⬚   ⬚   ⬚

NOVEMBER 21, 1994/KIM AND KENNY

What would you like to talk about today?
Answer: **Fun**

What about fun?
Answer: **Walk**

Would you like to go for a walk after academics?
Answer: **Yes**

You can earn a walk after academics. Okay?
Answer: **OK**

So what's new? Has anything made you happy or sad lately?
Answer: **Happy**

What made you happy?
Answer: **Fun**

What was fun that made you happy? What happened?
Answer: **Rolling**

Rolling what? Explain further please.
Answer: **Print**

I'm still not understanding you. Rolling – Print – What does that mean?
Answer: **Play**

Rolling – Print – Play. I still don't understand. Were you playing a game?
Answer: **Yes**

What was the name of the game?
Answer: **st – Then points to the question mark.**

Who were you playing the game with?
Answer: **Me**

Who else was playing?
Answer: **Points to the question mark.**

What was the object of the game?
Answer: **Stars name**

To name stars in the sky or movie stars on tv?
Answer: **Sky**

What did you name them?
Answer: **Imagine**

Imagine what? Did you use your imagination and create names for stars?
Answer: **Yes**

What kinds of names did you come up with?
Answer: **Quowz, Ziry**

Where did you come up with those names? I never heard them before.
Answer: **Me**

NOVEMBER 22, 1994/KIM AND KENNY

How are you feeling today?
Answer: **Fine**

Do you feel sore at all?
Answer: **Yes**

What would you like to talk about today?
Answer: **Yesterday**

What about yesterday?
Answer: **You – No**

I – No – What does that mean?
Answer: **Bad**

What was bad about yesterday?
Answer: **Me**

Why were you so upset?
Answer: **Everything**

You were upset about everything?
Answer: **Yes**

Like What?
Answer: **Walk**

Do you remember why you didn't get to go on the walk?
Answer: **Yes**

Why not?
Answer: **Doreen**

What happened with Doreen?
Answer: **Hair**

Why did you pull her hair?
Answer: **Points to the question mark.**

Was that an "okay" thing to do?
Answer: **No**

What else was upsetting yesterday?
Answer: **Mary**

Why were you upset with Mary? What happened?
Answer: **Kids**

You're upset about her kids?
Answer: **Mine**

The kids are yours?
Answer: **Mary – Mine**

Mary's yours?
Answer: **Yes**

You have to share Mary with everyone that loves her. Okay?
Answer: **OK**

⸙   ⸙   ⸙   ⸙   ⸙

NOVEMBER 23, 1994/MALIA AND KENNY

What should we talk about today?
Answer: **F-R-I-E-N-D-S**

What about friends would you like to talk about?
Answer: **M-Y**

Your friends? Which one of your friends do you wanna talk about?
Answer: **K-I-M**

What about Kim?
Answer: **S-C-H-O-O-L**

Kim and School? What about Kim and your school?
Answer: **I-D-E-A**

Who's idea do you want to talk about? Yours?
Answer: **Kim**

What idea does Kim have? Does it involve you?
Answer: **Yes**

Kim has an idea for you?
Answer: **Yes**

What idea is it?
Answer: **S-C-H-O-O-L**

Okay, Kim's idea is about you at school?
Answer: **Yes**

What's her idea?
Answer: **Question Mark**

Is it about herself or only you?
Answer: **No**

It involves both of you?
Answer: **No**

What is it Kenny?
Answer: **Question Mark**

Is it about work for you and her?
Answer: **Yes**

What kind of work?
Answer: **?**

Did she tell you about her idea?
Answer: **No**

How do you know?
Answer: **R-T**

What's "R-T?"
Answer: **R-E-A-D T-H-O-U-G-H-T-S**

You read Kim's thoughts?
Answer: **A-L-T-I-M-E**

Do you read Kim's thoughts all the time?
Answer: **M-O-R-E**

Are you excited about Kim's idea?
Answer: **Question mark**

What is it?
Answer: **Question mark**

More than others?

Answer: **Y-E-S**

◻　　◻　　◻　　◻　　◻

NOVEMBER 25, 1994/KIM AND KENNY

Did it hurt when the doctor took the stitches out?

Answer: **No**

Are you happy to have the cast off?

Answer: **Yes**

How does it feel?

Answer: **Good**

Did you have a good Thanksgiving or what?

Answer: **Yes**

What did you like best about your Thanksgiving Day?

Answer: **Food**

Which dish was your favorite?

Answer: **Jello**

Did you enjoy all the company that came over?

Answer: **Yes**

What were you thankful for yesterday?

Answer: **Life**

You're thankful for your life?

Answer: **Yes**

Can you think of anything else you're thankful for?

Answer: **People**

People, like who?

Answer: **Mary – Ken – Barbara**

What about me? Aren't you thankful for me?

Answer: **No**

*He should be!

Have you named anymore stars lately?

Answer: **Yes**

Did you name one for Barbara?

Answer: **No – can't**

Why can't you?

Answer: **Rules**

You have rules that you play by?

Answer: **Yes**

Can you tell me one of the rules?

Answer: **No – People – Names**

No people names for the stars?

Answer: **No**

What kind of names do you give the stars? Where do the names come from?

Answer: **Space**

⊡   ⊡   ⊡   ⊡   ⊡

NOVEMBER 26, 1994/HEATHER AND KENNY

So how was your Thanksgiving?

Answer: **No**

Did you like all the food you ate?

Answer: **No**

I'm going to cook next week so is there anything you would like?

Answer: **Spaghetti S-P-A-G-H-T-I**

What else would you like?
Answer: **G-A-R-L-I-C B-R-E-A-D**

What about dessert?
Answer: **No**

So I heard about your games with the stars.
Answer: **Yes**

What do you do in your game?
Answer: **Count**

You count the stars?
Answer: **Talk**

Do you talk to the stars?
Answer: **Talk**

What else do you do?
Answer: **Zaeus**
I have no idea what this means.
*Kenny was telling her a "star" name he made up!

So tell me about that bad thing that's going to happen.
Answer: **No**

What's going to happen bad?
Answer: **K – M**

Something bad is going to happen to Ken?
Answer: **No I, You, Me**

Is it going to be from God maybe?
Answer: **Yes--Then he said Stop.**

Will you tell me a little more please.
Answer: **V**

What about V?
Answer: **Stop**

So I told him what I did for Thanksgiving and he laughed and I asked him what he was laughing at?
Answer: **Y-O-U**

What about me?
Answer: **L-I-K-E**

Do you like me?
Answer: **No**

What do you like?
Answer: **V-I-T-O- Y-O-U**

Do I like Vito?
Answer: **Yes**

So how was your vacation?
Answer: **G-O-O-D, S-C-H-O-O-L, K-I-M, G-O-O-D, P-E-O-P-L-E**

Tell me about school?
Answer: **G-O-O-D W-O-R-K, K-I-M**

You're doing good work at school with Kim?
Answer: **Yes**

Then Kenny pointed to no and spelled: **H-E-A-T-H-E-R N-O**

No what?
Answer: **N-O W-O-R-K- H-E-A-T-H-E-R**

That was great work Kenny!
Long sentence answers! Great!

⊡   ⊡   ⊡   ⊡   ⊡

NOVEMBER 30, 1994/KIM AND KENNY

How are you today? Much better?
Answer: **Yes**

So what's up? What would you like to talk about?
Answer: **Good-Kenny**

What about "good Kenny?"
Answer: **Today**

Are you going to be good today?
Answer: **Yes**

Do you want to talk about what's been upsetting you these past weeks?
Answer: **Everything**

Everything, like what? Give me some examples.
Answer: **Life**

Everything in your life has been upsetting you?
Answer: **Yes**

Like what? Things at school, things at home? What's going on?
Answer: **School**

What's going on at school that you aren't happy with?
Answer: **Stuff**

Stuff like what?
Answer: **Bad**

Tell me exactly what you are upset about?
Answer: **Lose**

Kenny lost something or someone else lost something?
Answer: **Kenny**

What did you lose?
Answer: **Time**

You lost time?
Answer: **Yes**

What do you mean by that?
Answer: **All – time**

You lost all the time? When?
Answer: **No**

You lose all the time?
Answer: **Yes**

What are you losing?
Answer: **Everything**

Everything like what? Be specific please.
Answer: **Tree**

You're losing your freedom?
Answer: **Yes**

What is it you want, but aren't free to do?
Answer: **Life**

You don't have a free life?
Answer: **No**

Who or what is stopping you from having a free life?
Answer: **Me**

You're stopping yourself?
Answer: **Yes**

How are you stopping yourself?
Answer: **Points to the question mark.**

What are some things you would like to do, know or have to help you achieve the freedom that you want?
Answer: **Life**

You want a life or a different life?
Answer: **Fun**

What kinds of fun things would you like to do to make your life more fun?
Answer: **Play**

273

What else?
Answer: **Talk**

What else?
Answer: **Move**

Where do you want to move to?
Answer: **Body**

How can everyone that loves you help you have a more fun life?
Answer: **Can't**

Why can't we?
Answer: **Points to the question mark.**

What can we do that make you happy when you aren't so happy?
Answer: **Play**

Play with you? Like a game or something?
Answer: **Yes**

What kind of game?
Answer: **Riddle**

⌘   ⌘   ⌘   ⌘   ⌘

DECEMBER 10, 1994/KIM, KENNY AND DESIREE

<u>Kim</u>

Would you like to talk to Desiree?
Answer: **Yes**

What would you like to say to her?
Answer: **Love**

What about love?
Answer: **Me**

You love her?
Answer: **Yes**

How much?
Answer: **Little**

Can Desiree ask you some questions?
Answer: **Yes**

<u>Desiree</u>

Why do you love me?
Answer: **Nice**

Why am I "nice?"
Answer: **Person**

What did I do nice?
Answer: **Funny**

Why am I funny?
Answer: **K-I then points to the question mark.**

Is Kimi fun?
Answer: **No**

What do you like to do Kenny?
Answer: **Play**

Do you like puzzles?
Answer: **Yes**

Do you like "questionary?"
Answer: **No**

Do you like Aladdin?
Answer: **No**

Do you like reading?
Answer: **Yes**

Do you like school?
Answer: **Yes**

What do you want for X-mas?
Answer: **Stop**

Kim

Did you have fun today?
Answer: **Yes**

What was fun about today?
Answer: **Ride**

How have you been feeling lately? Still a little sore or what?
Answer: **Yes**

Is it bothering you?
Answer: **Yes**

Does it make you want to cry or scream?
Answer: **Sometimes**

And do you?
Answer: **No**

Why not?
Answer: **OK**

Are you OK?
Answer: **Yes**

Have you been naming stars lately?
Answer: **Yes**

Any new names? Any old names?
Answer: **Yes**

Like what? Tell me a few please!
Answer: **Skizik**

What's another name?
Answer: **Clury**

Do those names mean or stand for anything special?
Answer: **No**

You made them up all by yourself?
Answer: **Yes**

⬚ ⬚ ⬚ ⬚ ⬚

DECEMBER 21, 1994/HEATHER AND KENNY

How was your day at Mary's?
Answer: **Yes**

What did you do?
Answer: **Talk**

What did you talk about?
Answer: **T-A-L-K- S-T-A-R-S**

You talked to the stars during the day?
Answer: **Yes**

What did you talk about?
Answer: **Me**

What about you?
Answer: **N-O**

Okay, you don't want to talk about that so what do you want to talk about?
Answer: **U**

You want to talk about me?
Answer: **Yes**

What would you like me to tell you?
Answer: **S-A-D**

What about me, am I sad?
Answer: **Yes**

What am I sad about?
Answer: **M-O-N-E-Y**

What money?
Answer: **S-C-H-O-O-L**

Anything else?
Answer: **Pointed to the help sign.**

What's been up? What's going on?
Answer: **Nothing**

Do you miss Doreen, Mark, Tammi?
Answer: **Yes**

Are you enjoying your vacation so far?
Answer: **No**

Why not?
Answer: **Bored**

What's boring exactly?
Answer: **Days**

Just everything is boring?
Answer: **Yes**

What can we do or where can we go so that you won't be as bored?
Answer: **Ride**

How about out to lunch, then a ride? Cool?
Answer: **Yes**

Do you have any plans for New Year's Eve? Do you have any hot dates?
Answer: **No**

Do your parents have plans?
Answer: **Yes**

If they can't give you a better life, what can they give you to help make the life you already have just a little bit better?
Answer: **Promise**

A promise of what?
Answer: **Life**

Do you like to receive gifts on X-mas?
Answer: **Nice**

What is X-mas all about for you?
Answer: **Jesus**

What about Jesus?
Answer: **Life**

What makes X-mas special for you?
Answer: **Family**

DECEMBER 23, 1994/KENNY AND MALIA

Kenny, you have a life, but in your last questions, you said you wanted a better one. What needs to change in order for you to have a better life?
Answer: **P-E-O-P-L-E**

Do you want to be able to care for yourself?
Answer: **Y-E-S**

What about your life are you upset at?
Answer: **F-R-E-E-D-O-M**

You want freedom to do what?
Answer: **P-E-O-P-L-E**

What kinds of things do you want to be able to do?
Answer: Said: **"Car"   P-L-A-Y**

What would be different? You play now.
Answer: **Different**

How would it be different?
Answer: **Pointed to the question mark.**

Who are "people?"
Answer: **Friends**

What kinds of friends do you want Kenny?
Answer: **b-o-y**

Do you want girlfriends too?
Answer: **Yes**

Do you want a couple of friends who are boys?
Answer: **Y-E-S**

What would these friends do for you?
Answer: **G-A-M-E-S**

These friends would play games with you?
Answer: **Yes**

Do you know that Kim, Mary, Me, Anthony, Heather and your parents are your friends?
Answer: **Yes**

Try to describe a good friend. What you would want your friends to be like.
Answer: **m-y a-g-e**

You want young friends?
Answer: **y-e-s**

DECEMBER 27, 1994/KENNY AND MALIA

Kenny, when you said that you want "life," what do you mean?
Answer: **C-H-A-N-G-E**

What would you like changed?
Answer: **?**

Is there a particular kind of life that you would like to have more?
Answer: **T-A-L-K**   (See Other Page)

You want to talk with people?
Answer: **Yes**

Kenny, what can we do to help you have a better life?
Answer: **?**

Is your life hard?
Answer: **Yes**

If so, in what ways?
Answer: **Pointed to the question mark.**

⧈   ⧈   ⧈   ⧈   ⧈

DECEMBER 27, 1994/HEATHER AND KENNY

So what's going on Kenny? Why are you in such a good mood?
Answer: **Yes**

Did you have a good day today?
Answer: **Yes**

What did you do today?
Answer: **M-A-L-I-A**

What did you and Malia do?
Answer: **T-A-L-K**

Did you have a fun time with Malia today?
Answer: **Yes**

Why are you laughing?
Answer: **Yes**

Do you like the Board you got for Christmas?
Answer: **Yes**   W-R-I-T-E

You can write on it?
Answer: **Yes**

What are you laughing at?
Answer: **Y-O-U**

Why?
Answer: **S-T-O-P**

Didn't want to do anymore questions.

1)   Read book (Finished books 3)
2)   Went for a ride.
3)   Wrote on his new board

Good day! Good mood.

⊡   ⊡   ⊡   ⊡   ⊡

DECEMBER 1994/KIM AND KENNY

How old were you when you started naming the stars?
Answer: **Kid**

Can you tell me the approximate age in years?
Answer: **Ten**

So you've been naming stars for almost 7 years?
Answer: **Yes**

Why did you start naming the stars? What inspired you to do that?
Answer: **Like**

You like what?
Answer: **Stars**

What is it about the stars that you like so much?
Answer: **Years**

What about years?
Answer: **Star – findz years**
I've never seen Kenny use a "Z" in place of an "S."

Explain further.
Answer: **Stars – are – years**

◻   ◻   ◻   ◻   ◻

DECEMBER 1994 /MALIA AND KENNY

Can I ask you questions about the "mind" game now?
Answer: **Yes**

If yes, how do you play?
Answer: **Stop**

Stop what? Asking about the mind game?
Answer: **M-I-N-D and NO**

What about the "mind" game do you want to talk about and what don't you want
to talk about?
Answer: **No! No! No!**

Okay, can we talk about another game?
Answer: **Yes S-T**

Okay, the star game--any new names?
Answer: **y-o-r-q**

◻   ◻   ◻   ◻   ◻

DECEMBER 1994/KIM AND KENNY

Has Jesus talked to you lately?
Answer: **Yes**

What did he say?
Answer: **Life**

What about life?
Answer: **Love**

He wants you to love life?
Answer: **Yes**

He wants you to love someone?
Answer: **Yes**

Who does he want you to love?
Answer: **World**

Do you love the entire world?
Answer: **Yes**

Do you love everyone?
Answer: **Yes**

Do you love Kim?
Answer: **No**

What a little stinker!!!

⬚　　⬚　　⬚　　⬚　　⬚

DECEMBER 29, 1994/KIM AND KENNY

Were you glad to see Moe the other day?
Answer: **Yes**

What's the one thing you really like about Moe?
Answer: **Funny**

You think he's funny?
Answer: **Yes**

He was really impressed with your FC work! You know, wouldn't you do FC with Moe the way I know you can?
Answer: **Mind**

Explain "mind." His mind, your mind or both?
Answer: **Mo**

What about "Moe's mind?" Was something bad or confusing about Moe's mind?
Answer: **Yes**

What was going on?
Answer: **Thoughts – No**

Did you just point to "no?" What "thoughts no?"
Answer: **Yes**

What do you mean by "thoughts no?"
Answer: **Thoughts no**

Did Moe have thoughts that you picked up on or did he have thoughts that confused or upset you?
Answer: **Feel**

Did you feel his thoughts?
Answer: **Yes**

What kind of thoughts were they—good—bad?
Answer: **OK**

So if they were okay, why wouldn't you do FC with him?
Answer: **Clear**

Something wasn't clear to you?
Answer: **Mind**

Moe's mind wasn't clear of thoughts—that's why you wouldn't do FC with him?
Answer: **Yes**

What was he thinking about?
Answer: **No**

You don't know?
Answer: **Yes**

Yes, you do know?
Answer: **Yes**

What was he thinking about?
Answer: **No**

No, you won't tell me?
Answer: **No**

So you were glad Moe was here on Monday?
Answer: **Yes**

So why were you so upset at the park and in the car?
Answer: **You**

I made you upset?
Answer: **Yes**

How did I upset you?
Answer: **Bad**

Bad what? Was I bad? Did I do something bad?
Answer: **Talk**

I talked bad?
Answer: **Yes**

What did I say that was bad?
Answer: **All**

Was I bad because I was talking about you?
Answer: **Yes**

But so was Barbara and Moe. Why weren't you upset at them?
Answer: **Was**

You were upset with them too?
Answer: **Yes**

Is that why you pulled my hair and tried to bite me?
Answer: **Yes**

Is that why you tried to kick Barbara and Moe?
Answer: **Yes**

Did trying to hurt us make you feel better?
Answer: **No**

Did it make us stop talking about you for the rest of the day?
Answer: **No**

What did attacking your friends and family accomplish?
Answer: **Points to the question mark.**

Why did you do it then?
Answer: **Points to the question mark.**

Was that an "okay" thing to do?
Answer: **No**

What could you have done differently?
Answer: **Stop**

▫   ▫   ▫   ▫   ▫

DECEMBER 31, 1994/KIM AND KENNY

How was your visit with your Aunt Nancy yesterday?
Answer: **Fine**

Were you glad to see her?
Answer: **Yes**

Had it been a long time since you'd seen her?
Answer: **Yes**

How long?
Answer: **Long**

Did you miss her?
Answer:

How are you related to her?
Answer: **Points to the question mark.**

Is she Barbara's sister?
Answer: **Yes**

Is she older or younger than your mom?
Answer: **Older**

How old is she?
Answer: **Points to the question mark.**

Why were you so happy when she came over?
Answer: **Funny**

Who's funny? What's funny?
Answer: **Nancy**

You think Nancy's funny?
Answer: **Yes**

What's funny about her? Did she do or say something funny?
Answer: **Everything**

Do you like her?
Answer: **Yes**

Do you think she looks like Barbara?
Answer: **Yes**

Do they act alike?
Answer: **No**

How are they different?
Answer: **Stuff**

Stuff like what?
Answer: **Points to the question mark.**

Would you like to visit with her again?
Answer: **Yes**

JANUARY 2, 1995/KENNY AND MALIA

Kenny, why did you want to leave the party on Saturday night?
Answer: **T-I-M-E**

What time? Time for what?
Answer: **To much**

Too much time over there?
Answer: **Yes**

Were you tired?
Answer: **No**

Did you like being at a party for New Year's Eve?
Answer: **Question mark**

Sometimes people say the New Year is a time to start fresh. Are you going to do anything different this year Kenny?
Answer: **Question Mark**

Do you miss school?
Answer: **No**

Do you miss anything about school?
Answer: **No**

289

Do you know that I may lose that job soon?
Answer: **Yes More**

More what?
Answer: **Time**

I thought you said you didn't know?
Did you have a good vacation Kenny?
Answer: **Yes**

I have more time at Costco? I won't lose my job soon?
Answer: **No**

No, I won't lose my job?
Answer: **No**

I will lose my job?
Answer: **Yes**

So what is "more time?"
Answer: **Time**

Time for what? More time for what?
Answer: **Me**

Oh! I get it! So Cute!!!

So what should we do with our time?
Answer: **Stop**

Stop What?
Answer: **Talk**

Do we have to stop talking?
Answer: **Yes**

Where should we spend time? Park?
Answer: ------------

JANUARY 10, 1995/KIM AND KENNY

What would you like to talk about today?
Answer: **School**

What about school?
Answer: **Back**

Explain more please.
Answer: **Doreen**

You want to talk about Doreen coming back to school today?
Answer: **Yes**

Are you happy she's back?
Answer: **Yes**

Did you miss her?
Answer: **Yes**

Do you remember where she said she went?
Answer: **Yes**

Where did she go?
Answer: **State**

What state did she go to?
Answer: **Washington**

Do you know why she had to go away?
Answer: **Yes**

Why?
Answer: **Sick**

Who's sick?
Answer: **Mom**

What's wrong with her mom?
Answer: **Die**

No, she didn't die. Why do you think she died?
Answer: **Soon**

Why do you think that Kenny?
Answer: **Know**

⬚　　⬚　　⬚　　⬚　　⬚

WEEK OF JANUARY 18, 1995/KIM AND KENNY

Kenny, how are you today?
Answer: **Fine**

Are you feeling okay?
Answer: **Yes**

You seem really happy today. Can you tell me why you are so happy?
Answer: **Yes**

Why?
Answer: **Fun**

Did you do something fun?
Answer: **Yes**

What did you that was so fun?
Answer: **Doreen**

You did something fun in PE with Doreen?
Answer: **Yes**

What was it that you did?
Answer: **Talk**

Did you talk to Doreen?
Answer: **Yes**

I don't remember you talking to Doreen during PE. Can you tell me about it?
Answer: **Shake Hands**

Oh! I remember you shaking Doreen's hands, but that was after PE. Remember, we were talking about what you do when you meet someone new for the first time?

Answer: **Yes**

So you thought that was fun huh? What was so fun about it?

Answer: **Erin**

Did Erin do or say something funny?

Answer: **Yes**

Tell me what happened?

Answer: **Talk Funny**

Who talk funny?

Answer: **Erin**

What did Erin say that was funny?

Answer: **Friend**

What about friend?

Answer: **Me**

Did she say that you were her friend?

Answer: **Yes**

Oh, and you thought that was funny?

Answer: **Yes**

Do you consider Erin to be a friend to you?

Answer: **Yes**

Isn't it nice to have friends?

Answer: **Yes**

What are some things people do with their friends?

Answer: **Make Ken**

Make Ken what?

Answer: **Fun**

Make Ken fun?
Answer: **Yes**

Okay, now your mom signed you up at a gym for swimming. Do you want to go?
Answer: **Yes**

Is twice a week okay?
Answer: **Good**

Who would you like to take you swimming?
Answer: **Friends**

So far, Mary and myself will probably take you. Is that okay?
Answer: **Yes**

Do you have some fun ideas of games we can play in the pool?
Answer: **No**

Would you even be interested in playing games in the pool?
Answer: **Yes**

Now Kenny, you have to tell me about you erasing a program off your computer at home. Did you erase your dad's checkbook?
Answer: **Yes**

Why would you do a thing like that?
Answer: **Fun**

What was fun about that?
Answer: **Mean**

It was fun because it was mean?
Answer: **Yes**

How many steps did it take before you could totally erase it?
Answer: **Eight**

Are you sure?
Answer: **Yes**

Did you get in trouble with your parents?
Answer: **No**

Do you feel bad about it?
Answer: **Yes**

ⵊ　　ⵊ　　ⵊ　　ⵊ　　ⵊ

WEEK OF JANUARY 18, 1995/KIM, KENNY AND DANETTE (SPEECH PATHOLOGIST)

What else could you have done on the computer, a game?
No yes?
Answer: **No**

What kind of games?
Answer: **Car**

What do the cars do?
Answer: **Race**

Do you have anything else you want to say?
Answer: **Yes**

What?
Met boy

Where?
Answer: **Home**

What was his name?
Answer: **?**

When?
Answer: **Week**

This week or last week?
Answer: **Last**

Did your mom meet him too?
Answer: **Yes**

What color hair did he have?
Answer: **brown**

Was he tall or short?
Answer: **Short**

Are you finished? Type done or more.
Answer: **Done**

Would you like to type with Danette later?
Answer: **Y**

❏   ❏   ❏   ❏   ❏

JANUARY 22, 1995/HEATHER AND KENNY

How was your day today Kenny?
Answer: **B-O-A-R-D**

What did you do?
Answer: **NO**

Did you see Buck today?
Answer: **Yes**

Do you know where I'm going this week?
Answer: **No**

I have to go to school?
Answer: **No**

I will miss you?
Answer: **F-R-I-E-N-D**

Are you asking me if I'm your friend?
Answer: **Yes**

Of course, I'm your friend!
Answer: **S-T-A-Y**

I have to go to school, but I promise I'll come and visit you okay?
Answer: **No**

You don't want me to visit?
Answer: **Yes**

If I write to you, will you write me back?
Answer: **Yes**

Would you like to come to my school to visit?
Answer: **Yes**

Maybe when it's hot, we can go to the lake and go fishing and swimming?
Answer: **Yes, Yes**

JANUARY 24 & 25, 1995/KENNY AND MALIA

Kenny, do you believe in guardian angels?
Answer: **Yes**

Do you have a guardian angel?
Answer: **Yes**

Does everyone have a guardian angel?
Answer: **No**

Who has guardian angels?
Answer: **Believe**

Only people who believe have them?
Answer: **Yes**

About your star game, who helps you think about star names?
Answer: **?**

Does your guardian angel help you?
Answer: **Yes**

What kinds of things does your guardian angel do for you or help you with?
Answer: **Talk**

Do you talk with your guardian angel?
Answer: **Yes**

What do you talk about?
Answer: **Stop**

Does your guardian angel keep you safe?
Answer: **Yes**

Is there anything you want to talk about your mom and dad?
Answer: **No**

Are you sure?
Answer: **Yes**

Does your Uncle Frank have a guardian angel?
Answer: **Yes**

If yes, what is his/her name?
Answer: **?**

Would you like to go to a special theater called a Planetarium that looks like the stars in space?
Answer: **Yes**

Did Tami help you learn anything at school today?
Answer: **No**

Did Doreen and Mark spend time with you today?
Answer: **Mark**

You spent time with Mark?
Answer: **Yes**

Do you want Kim to come back to school so you can do good academics?

Answer: **Yes and said "Kim"**

⊡   ⊡   ⊡   ⊡   ⊡

JANUARY 28, 1995/MALIA AND KENNY

Kenny, what would you like to talk about?

Answer: **Star**

Would you like to talk about your star game?

Answer: **Yes**

Are there any new star names?

Answer: **Yes**

What are your new star names?

Answer: **Lius**

Any others?

Answer: **Yes**

Well, what are they?

Answer: **Bey**

Those are neat names Kenny. How do you come up with them?

Answer: **Mind**

Your mind?

Answer: **Yes**

Does anyone help you?

Answer:

Who?

Answer: **? STOP**

He would not continue so we did reading, music and puzzles. Kenny had a great
fun day on our walk, etc. Although hardly any work. It was great! Good Mood!

FEBRUARY 1, 1995/KC-FC

Happy Birthday! How old are you today?
Answer: **Seventeen**

Are you glad that you are seventeen or do you still want to be sixteen?
Answer: **Glad**

Do you like celebrating birthdays?
Answer: **Yes**

What's great about birthday celebrations?
Answer: **Fun**

I think they're fun too? What kinds of things do you like to do to celebrate your birthday?
Answer: **Party**

Oooooh! You like to party! Do you usually have a party every year?
Answer: **No**

Why not?
Answer: **Friends**

What about friends?
Answer: **None**

Well, I happen to know that today you will have a party in your classroom with all of your friends! Is that exciting or what?
Answer: **Yes**

What kind of cake would you like to have this afternoon?
Answer: **Chocolate**

Yummy! Do you think your parents will do something special tonight for your birthday?

Answer: **Yes**

What would you suggest to them? How would you like to spend your evening?
Answer: **Restaurant**

Anyplace special?
Answer: **No**

Did you receive any gifts for your birthday?
Answer: **No**
(yes he did!)

Do you want some gifts?
Answer: **Yes**

What are a couple of gifts you would really want?
Answer: **Games**

⬚　　⬚　　⬚　　⬚　　⬚

FEBRUARY 9 & 10, 1995/KENNY AND MALIA

Kenny, what happened at school today? Why did you tantrum?
Answer: **Hand**

Does your hand hurt you?
Answer: **No**

Then what about your hand?
Answer: **Bad**

Your hand is bad?
Answer: **Yes**

Are you ever bad?
Answer: **No**

How can you stop your hand?
Answer: **STOP** and grabbed F/C board and me. Could not continue!

How can you stop your hand for being bad Kenny?
Answer: **M-I-N-D**

So if you wanted to, you could stop being bad?
Answer: **Yes**

Is Doreen back now?
Answer: **Yes**

Do you like Doreen?
Answer: **Yes**

Is there a problem at school?
Answer: **No**

Why are you throwing tantrums?
Answer: **?**

Does your hand make you do that?
Answer: **No**

What makes you throw tantrums?
Answer: **?**

O.K., let's talk about something else?
Answer: **Yes**

Why are you taking your shoes off at school?
Answer: **HOT**

They make you hot?
Answer: **No**

Do you feel hot at school?
Answer: **Yes**

Do your shoes make you feel hotter with them on at school?
Answer: **Yes**

So it feels better when your shoes are off?
Answer: **Yes**

O.K., can we talk about your tantrum again?
Answer: **NO NO NO**

Did not wish to continue. Grabbed me and board!

Good day though! Puzzles, book, etc.

FEBRUARY 13, 1995/KENNY AND MALIA

Did you have fun swimming with Danny yesterday?
Answer: **Yes**

Do you want to go with me and Danny this Friday?
Answer: **Yes**

Were you cold while swimming?
Answer: **No**

Were you cold after you got out of the pool?
Answer: **Yes**

Do you love me?
Answer: **Yes**

Are you excited about your school dance?
Answer: **Yes**

Are you going to dance?
Answer: **Yes**

With whom are you going to dance with?
Answer: **K-I-M**

Did you like your group work today?
Answer: **?**

Did you like pasting and creating stuff today?
Answer: **Yes**

Do you want me to come by tomorrow with a valentine for you?
Answer: **Yes**

What is tomorrow Kenny?
Answer: **Valentine**

What do you do on Valentine's Day?
Answer: **?**

Do you give candy and cards?
Answer: **Yes**

What do I have for you?
Answer: **Candy**
Brat! He wasn't suppose to know that!

FEBRUARY 23, 1995/MALIA AND KENNY

What famous composer did your mom read to you last night?
Answer: **Beet (then stopped).** I'm trying not to let him shorten his words (abbreviate) sorry!

What funny thing did Barbara do last night to make you laugh?
Answer: **No**

Did she do something funny?
Answer: **Yes**

Why are you so mad at Doreen?
Answer: **?**

Did it make you laugh?
Answer: **Yes**

Then why did you say no? No what?
Answer: **Say**

You're not going to tell me?
Answer: **No**

Is it an inside joke?
Answer: **?**

Inside joke means it's between you and Barbara. Is it between you and Barbara?

You don't want to tell me?
Answer: **No**

Does Ken know?
Answer: **Yes**

Was he there when it happened?
Answer: **No**

How come you won't tell me?
Answer: **NO STOP**

Man!!! I want to know what happened!

☐   ☐   ☐   ☐   ☐

FEBRUARY 24, 1995/KC-FC WITH KIM OLIVER

What's wrong?
Answer: **Mad**

Why are you mad?
Answer: **You**

Why are you mad at me?
Answer: **Snack**

What happened at snack?
Answer: **Donut**

Do you know why I took it away?
Answer: **Yes**

Why were you grabbing on Kris?
Answer: **Fun**

Is grabbing people a nice thing to do?
Answer: **Yes**

No, it's not. How would you feel if someone was grabbing on you?
Answer: **?**

Would you like it?
Answer: **No**

Do you think Kris liked it?
Answer: **No**

If you wanted to have fun with Kris, what else could you have done?
Answer: **Hug**

Good Idea! So, maybe next time you could hug Kris or even just give her a hand shake or a smile. Okay?
Answer: **Yes**

Do you feel happy again?
Answer: **Yes**
Great!!!!

What kind of games do you want to play?
Answer: **Fun**

Besides games, is there anything else you want to have?
Answer: **Fun**

What kinds of fun things would you want to do?
Answer: **Bike**

Okay, riding a bike is really fun, but first you have to learn to ride. Who would you want to teach you?
Answer: **Ken** (his dad)

I'm sure your dad would love to teach you! But before you can learn to ride you have to have a bike! How are you going to get a bike?
Answer: **Barbara**

Well, what if Barbara can't afford a bike? What will you do then?
Answer: **Nothing**

How about the money you earn in the deli working? (at school he stands and has a broom in his hand, or clears a few dishes off a table). You can save some paychecks and pay for a little bit of the bike?
Answer: **No**

Why not?
Answer: **Hard**

What's hard?
Answer: **Work**

Yes, work is hard, but people work to get the things they want. Do you agree?
Answer: **Yes**

Well then, shouldn't you work to get the things you want?
 Answer: **No**

Why not?
Answer: **Cant**

Why can't you?
Answer: **Hard**

FEBRUARY 28, 1995/MALIA AND KENNY

Kenny, please tell me what got you so upset at school?
Answer: **MAD**

Why were you mad?
Answer: **?**

Were you mad at a classmate?
Answer: **NO**

Was it something staff did or a classmate? Were you mad at a teacher or aid?
Answer: **NO**

Who were you mad?
Answer: **Me**

Are you feeling o.k.?
Answer: **Yes**

Why were you mad at yourself?
Answer: **?**

Do you want your mom to find you another school?
Answer: **?**

Do you think if your mom wanted to put you in a better school, would you go?
Answer: **?**

You can't keep getting so angry and out of control. Why not try FC with someone at school and tell someone what makes you mad so they can help you?
Answer: **Mad**

Someone what makes you mad so they can help you?
Answer: **MAD**

Why are you mad?
Answer: **Talk**

You want to talk?
Answer: **Yes**

Will you please do good at school tomorrow for everyone?
Answer: **Yes**

Did you know Doreen is trying to hire a new one/one aide for you?
Answer: **Yes**

Would you like a man or a woman?
Answer: **Man**

⬚ ⬚ ⬚ ⬚ ⬚

MARCH 2, 1995/KENNY AND MALIA

Kenny, have they found you a new one-on-one aide?
Answer: **No**

Are you happy with things at school or could things be changed?
Answer: **No**

What would be better at school for you that could help?
Answer: **Man Teach**

You want a man as an aide?
Answer: **Yes**

What did you enjoy at school today?
Answer: **No**

Do you still name stars?
Answer: **Yes**

What are new names?
Answer: **Zyle & Wikil**

⬚ ⬚ ⬚ ⬚ ⬚

MARCH 2, 1995/KENNY AND MALIA

What about the other game you play? The "pretend you're someone else" game?
Do you still play?
Answer: **No**

309

Why?
Answer: **Happy**

Happy about what? You're happy?
Answer: **Yes Me**

What are you happy about?
Answer: **Be Me**

You're happy to be you?
Answer: **Yes**

Would you like to play uno?
Answer: **Yes Help**

You want help?
Answer: **Yes**

If we help you, will you play?
Answer: **Yes**

◻   ◻   ◻   ◻   ◻

MARCH 6, 1995/MALIA AND KENNY

Do you like your new one-on-one aide Catherine?
Answer: **No**

Will you do work with her by herself though?
Answer: **No**

Will you do work with Kim?
Answer: **Yes**

Do you like your new shoes?
Answer: **Yes**

Do they hurt you?
Answer: **No**

Is school getting funner for you?
Answer: **No Answer**

Do you enjoy PE?
Answer: **No Answer**

Do you miss school?
Answer: **Stop**

Do you want to talk about school?
Answer: **No**

O.K….is there anything you would like to talk about?
Answer: **No**

Your mom said you missed me last night. Were you calling for me?
Answer: **Yes**

Did you have a dream about me last night?
Answer: **?**

Do you have dreams Kenny?
Answer: **?**

Do you play the star game still?
Answer: **Yes**

Any new names?
Answer: **No**

Why not?
Answer: **Think**

You have to think up more names?
Answer: **?**

What do you have to think?
Answer: **?**

You can't remember right now?
Answer: **No**

Okay, next time then Kenny!

Great mood!!! Love ya, Malia

I read to him about the planet book, but he was really tired. Would not color!

⬚   ⬚   ⬚   ⬚   ⬚

MARCH 8, 1995/MALIA AND KENNY

Kenny, do you like your one-on-one aide at school?
Answer: **Yes**

Will you do good work with her?
Answer: **Yes**

Will you also try and do good work with Kim?
Answer: **Yes**

Why aren't you doing work at school lately?
Answer: **CHANGE**

Did you change your mind?
Answer: **No**

Are there changes at school?
Answer: **Yes**

These changes at school, are they anything to do with getting a new on-on-one aide?
Answer: **Yes**

So you are going to do more work now that it is settling down some?
Answer: **Yes**

Is that a promise?
Answer: **?**

When? How soon will you start to do good work?

Answer: **?**

P.S. I had to stop with questions. He started pulling the book, but he enjoyed "mind reading"!

WORDS	F/C POINTED TO
SCHOOL	**SCHOOL**
HOME	**HOME**
WORK	**WORK**
PARK	**PARK**

Excellent! Kenny Awesome Tonight!

MARCH 15, 1995/MALIA AND KENNY

Kenny, why has your work stopped at school? Did you or Kim stop working?

Answer: **Both**

Why?

Answer: **Angry**

Who's angry?

Answer: **Kim**

Why is Kim angry?

Answer: **Me**

Kim is angry at you?

Answer: **Yes**

Why? Because of your behavior?

Answer: **Yes**

Any other reasons?

Answer: **Work**

313

What about work?

Answer: **Mine**

Kim is angry with you not doing work?

Answer: **Yes**

Why don't you do work? Do you feel that no one thinks it's important?

Answer: **Yes**

Barb,

I explained how important his work is. Boy, you read him like a book! We finally got to the bottom of this!

What causes your anger?

Answer: **Head**

What goes on in your head when you get angry?

Answer: **Thoughts**

Your thoughts make you angry?

Answer: **No**

Are you reading someone else's thoughts?

Answer: **Yes**

Whose thoughts are you reading?

Answer: **All**

Everyone?

Answer: **Yes**

Do people think bad thoughts about you?

Answer: **Yes**

What are the thoughts saying to you?

Answer: **Bad**

That you're bad?

Answer: **Yes**

Is it when you act bad at school?
Answer: **Yes**

Does that upset you?
Answer: **Yes**

Would you like Barbara to talk to the people at school and make them change their thoughts?
Answer: **No**

Why?
Answer: **Truth**

Can Barbara help you somehow?
Answer: **No**

He would not continue! Sad, but at least we're getting somewhere!

☒   ☒   ☒   ☒   ☒

MARCH 20, 1995/KENNY AND MALIA

Please try and tell me what makes you so unhappy at school?
Answer: **?**

Is it a person that upsets you?
Answer: **Yes**

Who?
Answer: **?**

Anyone that I know?
Answer: **No**

Why are you upset by this person?
Answer: **Thoughts**

Someone's thoughts are upsetting you again?
Answer: **Yes**

Whose?
Answer: **?**

Do you want attention from everyone and when you don't get it, you get mad?
Answer: **No**

Did something happen at school that made you so upset that you forgot?
Answer: **?**

How can we help you control your temper?
Answer: **Good T**

Good thoughts? Is that what you're saying?
Answer: **Yes**

So if we have good thoughts, you'll not tantrum or throw a fit?
Answer: **Try**

You'll try or we should try?
Answer: **Both**

Are you upset about something?
Answer: **No**

Kenny, will you show your new aide how smart you are by doing good work?
Answer: **Yes No**

Which one? Yes or No?
Answer: **Yes**

Do you think that you can start to do the same kind of work with your new aide as you do with me and Kim?
Answer: **?**

How come you don't know?
Answer: **Believe**

Does she believe in you?
Answer: **Think Yes**

You must work too! Do you understand?

Answer: **Yes**

Good!

☒   ☒   ☒   ☒   ☒

MARCH 21, 1995/KENNY AND MALIA

Do you like Michael?

Answer: **Yes**

What is it that you like about him?

Answer: **Games**

Is he fun?

Answer: **Yes**

Will he play games with you?

Answer: **Yes**

Is there anything else that you like about him?

Answer: **Nice**

Do you want to talk about anything tonight?

Answer: **Yes Space**

What about space?

Answer: **Star**

Do you have new names?

Answer: **Yes**

What are they?

Answer: **Would not answer.**

Will you tell me?

Answer: **No**

Who can you tell?
Answer: **?**

Will you tell me next time?
Answer: **No**

Will you tell your mom and dad? They would like to hear them.
Answer: **No**

Who will you tell?
Answer: **Kim**

Are you saying you will only tell Kim your new star names?
Answer: **Yes**

How cute!

APRIL 5, 1995/KENNY AND JAIME

Kenny, did you have fun swimming today?
Answer: **Yes**

Why do you keep saying Barbara? Do you want her to come home?
Answer: **Yes**

Wouldn't do anymore questions.

Did you have a seizure last week?
Answer: **Yes**

Was it a little one?
Answer: **Yes**

So it wasn't a big one, was it?
Answer: **No**

Did it hurt?
Answer: **Yes**

Is that why you are so tired lately?
Answer: **? and Yes**

Would not go on or tell me which one.

    ▨   ▨   ▨   ▨   ▨

MAY 15, 1995/KENNY AND MALIA

Kenny, have you played your star game lately?
Answer: **Yes**

If so, did you come up with any new names?
Answer: **Yes**

If so, what are they?
Answer: **Bouris**

Any others?
Answer: **Would not continue,** but that's a start!

How has school been?
Answer: **No answer**

    ▨   ▨   ▨   ▨   ▨

MAY 15, 1995/KENNY AND MALIA

Kenny, what are those things in the corner of your picture?
Answer: **PLANETS**

Which ones are they?
Answer: **SATURN**

What are the others?
Answer: **Wouldn't answer**

What is this thing? (Pointed to basket.)
Answer: **BAG**

Your swim bag?
Answer: **No**

Oh, which bag?
Answer: **SCHOOL**

Your backpack?
Answer: **Yes**

What is this?   (Pointed to left structure.)
Answer: **DOOR**

Which door is that?
Answer: **FENCE**

Why do you have a stoplight in your picture?
Answer: **STOP**

You want me to stop?
Answer: **Yes**

O.K., one more question? What kinds of things do you know about Saturn?
Answer: **STOP**
Would not continue! boo hoo!

Tried again, nothing.

JUNE 5, 1995/KENNY AND MALIA

Do you like Joyce?
Answer: **Yes**

Do you know anything about her Kenny?
Answer: **No**

Why do you like her so much then?
Answer: **Sad**

Are you trying to make her happy?
Answer: **Yes**

How do you make her happier?
Answer: **Love more**

Do you know how happy Barbara and I were to see your work from school?
Answer: **Yes**

Can Gizmo go to school with you one day soon?
Answer: **HELP**

Do you have fun at school lately?
Answer: **Yes**

What is so fun lately?
Answer: **Kim**

⬚   ⬚   ⬚   ⬚   ⬚

JUNE 7, 1995/MALIA AND KENNY

Have you been doing work with Kim lately?
Answer: **Yes**

Was the pool fun yesterday with Jaime and Deanna?
Answer: **Yes**

What did you guys do after swimming?
Answer: **Ride**

How are you feeling lately?
Answer: **Good**

Are there any new star names lately?
Answer: **No**

How often do you play the star game?
Answer: **?** Tried Again: **NIT**

Every night?
Answer: **No**

Is Saturn your favorite planet?
Answer: **Yes**

If so, why?
Answer: **Ring**

Would not continue! Try again tomorrow.

What do you know about Saturn?
Answer: **Red**

Is it red in color?
Answer: **Yes**

Is there life out there?
Answer: **No**

Is there life anywhere else in space other than Earth?
Answer: **Yes**

What kinds of life?
Answer: **No Answer**

❑　　　❑　　　❑　　　❑　　　❑

JULY 26, 1995/MALIA AND KENNY

Kenny how are you?
Answer: **Good**

Have you played your star game?
Answer: **Yes**

What names have you come up with?
Answer: **Shine**

Is that a new name?
Answer: **No**

What is it, an old name?
Answer: **No**

What is it?
Answer: **Star**

There is a shiny star?
Answer: **Yes**

Did you name it?
Answer: **No**

Why not?
Answer: **Other**

What do you mean "other?"
Answer: **Star**

You named another new star?
Answer: **Yes**

What name did you come up with?
Answer: **Pyzer**
Oh, how cute!

Any other names?
Answer: **Yes**

How many?
Answer: **3**

What are the other 3?
Answer: **No**

You won't tell me?
Answer: **Yes**

What are they then?
Answer: **Zyke**

What are the other 2?
Answer: **No...One**

There's only one more?
Answer: **Yes**
He must of meant 3 altogether.

What's the name?
Answer: **Gizmo**

Kenny are you teasing me?
Answer: **No**

You really named one Gizmo?
Answer: **Yes**

Why?
Answer: **Shine**

You mean the shiny one is Gizmo?
Answer: **Yes**

Why?
Answer: **Favorit**

It's your favorite star?
Answer: **Yes**

Will you point it out to me?
Answer: **No**
Brat!

Kenny would you like my roommate, Jennifer, to watch you sometime?
Answer: **OKAY   He spelled it "OK."**
How cute.

Do you like her?

Answer: **Yes**

Why?

Answer: **Like Me**

⊡　　⊡　　⊡　　⊡　　⊡

SEPTEMBER 7, 1995/KIM & KENNY FC QUALITY QUESTIONS

Why do you get so upset when staff/bus drivers come or leave?

Answer: **Hard**

What is so hard?

Answer: **Me**

You have a hard time when people come and go?

Answer: **Yes**

But why is it so hard for you?

Answer: **Mad**

Who's mad?

Answer: **Me**

Why are you mad?

Answer: **Points to the question mark.**

Are you mad at someone?

Answer: **No**

Can you try to think about why you're mad and tell me later?

Answer: **Yes**

I heard something special is going on at your house this weekend. Can you tell me about it?

Answer: **Party**

What's the party for?
Answer: **Me**

☐   ☐   ☐   ☐   ☐

SEPTEMBER 27, 1995/KENNY AND MALIA

Kenny, do you know how proud of you we are for doing great work at school?
Answer: **Yes**

Kenny, do you remember the work you did on stars at school?
Answer: **Yes**

If so, how did you know all those stars?
Answer: **Know**

How though?
Answer: **Wouldn't answer.**

Did you learn that information? Did someone teach it to you?
Answer: **No**

Who taught you?
Answer: **No Help**

Did someone or something teach you?
Answer: **No**

SEPTEMBER 27, 1995/KENNY AND MALIA

When did you learn that stuff?
Answer: Pointed to question mark.

Do you like school this year?
Answer: **Yes**

Do you enjoy working with Katherine?
Answer: **Yes**

Is there anything on Saturdays you would like to do with me?
Answer: **Said "Chocolate"**
Because we always get milk. Wouldn't point, how funny?

What's your favorite work to do?
Answer: **Stars and pointed to more!**

You want more work on stars?
Answer: **Yes**

Kenny, how do you know that stuff about stars?
Answer: **Mind**

Your mind knows it all?
Answer: **Wouldn't answer.**

Telepathy

WORDS THOUGHT OF	**LETTERS POINTED TO BY KENNY**
Beach	**BEACH**
Wave	**WAVE**
Walk	**WALK**

Where did I go on Friday night?
Answer: **Beach**
Yes!!! Great!!!

⬚　　⬚　　⬚　　⬚　　⬚

NOVEMBER 1, 1995/KENNY AND MALIA

Kenny, how do your new dress shoes feel? Are they comfortable?
Answer: **Yes**

Do they hurt your feet?
Answer: **No**

How are things at home? Did you like the trick-or-treaters? The kids in costumes?

Answer: **Funny**

Did they look funny?

Answer: **Yes**

How is school lately?

Answer: **Fun**

You have fun lately at school?

Answer: **Yes**

Do you have lots of friends at school?

Answer: **Yes**

Is there any place special you would like to go on Saturday?

Answer: **Eric**

You want Eric to go with us?

Answer: **Yes**

Where would you like Eric to take us?

Answer: **Park**

Anywhere else?

Answer: **Ball**

Is there anything you want, like anything you saw at school that you would like to have at home too? I specified to Kenny like games, puzzles or something?

Answer: **C Kept pointing to "C."**

Kenny, what is "C?"

Answer: **Kid**

Is there someone you want to come home with you? Or something the kid has that you want?

Answer: **Home**

You want a kid to come home with you?

Answer: **Yes**

Why?
Answer: **Play**

You want someone to come play with you from school?
Answer: **Yes**

Which kid, who?
Answer: **Points to question mark.**

Anyone or a certain person?
Answer: **Would not continue.**

Is there anything you would like to talk about?
Answer: **None**

⬚　　⬚　　⬚　　⬚　　⬚

NOVEMBER 22, 1995/KENNY AND MALIA

Kenny, are you excited about Thanksgiving tomorrow?
Answer: **No**
What a brat. Just kidding.

Are you thankful for anything Kenny? Is there anything that you wish to say thank you to?
Answer: **Love**

Are you thankful for the love of your parents and me?
Answer: **Yes**

Do you know where you are going tomorrow for Thanksgiving?
Answer: **Yes**

Where?
Answer: **Far**

Do you know the City?
Answer: **No**

Your mom and dad want you all to have a good time so will you try to be a real good boy and in control?

Answer: **Yes**

I hope he's not teasing.

❑　　❑　　❑　　❑　　❑

NOVEMBER 22, 1995/KENNY AND MALIA

Kenny, would you like to try to think of what my main thing I'm thankful for is?

Answer: **No**

Well, I guess the telepathy is out.

If yes, what am I thankful for the most?

Answer: **Wouldn't answer.**

I just told him this. Kenny, I want to say that I'm thankful to you and your family for the love you all show to me. I love you, buddy!

❑　　❑　　❑　　❑　　❑

NOVEMBER 30, 1995/MALIA AND KENNY

Kenny, what would you like to talk about?

Answer: Said **"Eric."**

What about Eric?

Answer: **Fun**

Do you want to do something fun with Eric?

Answer: **Yes**

Is there someone at school you would like to do questions with?

Answer: **Kim**

During Xmas vacation, what special things would you like to do?

Answer: **Ball**

Anything else?
Answer: **Points to the question mark.**

What would you like your mom and dad to buy you for Xmas?
Answer: **Train**

What kind of train? The play kind with tracks?
Answer: **Yes**
That's so funny! That's what my brother always liked.

How are things at school? Do you feel like you're getting what you want and need?
Answer: **Happy**

Are you happy there?
Answer: **Yes**

Who was your favorite person at Thanksgiving?
Answer: **J?**
He kept pointing to the "J" and then to the question mark, but said a word, but I wasn't sure of it.

· · · · ·

DECEMBER 4, 1995/KENNY AND KIM

What would you like to talk about today?
Answer: **Me**

What about you?
Answer: **Feelings**

What about your feelings?
Answer: **Bad**

You have bad feelings?
Answer: **Yes**

Why? What are you feeling bad about?
Answer: **Inside**

You feel bad inside about what?
Answer: **Hurt**

Are you hurt?
Answer: **Yes**

Where are you hurt at?
Answer: **Inside**

✦ ✦ ✦ ✦ ✦

DECEMBER 4, 1995/KENNY AND KIM

Inside? Where are you hurt at?
Answer: **Body**

Where in your body are you hurt?
Answer: **All**

Your entire body hurts on the inside?
Answer: **Yes**

What's making you hurt? What's the cause?
Answer: **Medicine**

How do you know it's the medicine that's making you hurt inside?
Answer: **Know**

How long have you been hurting? Hours, days, weeks, months?
Answer: **Long**

Do you ever stop hurting? Maybe the pain comes and goes?
Answer: **No**

DECEMBER 6, 1995/MALIA AND KENNY

Kenny, what did you do for work at school today?
Answer: **Game**

What game did you play?
Answer: **Spell**
Not sure what game that is?

Kenny, would you really like a train set for Xmas?
Answer: **Yes**

Will you play with it?
Answer: **Points to the question mark.**

Do you know what I want from Big Eric?
Answer: **Ring**
How funny!

But there's something I really want and there's a possibility I will get it. Do you know?
Answer: **Music**
He's right, a stereo.

If so, what?
Answer: **No answer**

Will you have visitors come to your house?
Answer: **Yes**

If so, who?
Answer: **Kid (and he said baby?)**

Whose kids are coming?
Answer: **Mary**

Is there anything you want for Xmas besides a train?
Answer: **No**

Did you miss me?
Answer: **Yes**

Do you know what I did this weekend?
Answer: **BIR**

What is "BIR?"
Answer: **Wouldn't continue,** maybe birthday? It was Malia's birthday.

❏   ❏   ❏   ❏   ❏

JANUARY 3, 1996/MALIA AND KENNY

Kenny, did you have a good holiday break from school?
Answer: **Yes**

How was Barbara's birthday?
Answer: **Fun**

Is it okay if I come on Monday and Wednesday nights instead of Wednesday and Thursday nights because I have school?
Answer: **No**

Why? What days would you like me to come?
Answer: **All**
Oh my goodness—how cute!

Did you like the shirt Jaime and I gave you for Xmas?
Answer: **Yes**

❏   ❏   ❏   ❏   ❏

JANUARY 3, 1996/MALIA AND KENNY

Did you like your train set?
Answer: **Yes**

Is there any new star names?
Answer: **Yes**

If so, what are they?
Answer: **Vega**

Any others?
Answer: **No**

How's school going?
Answer: **?**
Got mad at me!

Is there anything you would like to talk about?
Answer: **Would not go on!**

⬚　　⬚　　⬚　　⬚　　⬚

FEBRUARY 12, 1996/KENNY AND MALIA

How was school today?
Answer: **Fun**

Did you do good work with Kim lately?
Answer: **Eat**

Did you eat with Kim lately?
Answer: **Yes**

Is there anything you would like to talk about?
Answer: **No**

Have you been playing your star game lately?
Answer: **Yes No**
Not sure why he said both.

Any new names?
Answer: **Yes**

What are the new names?
Answer: **JESPA**

Any others?
Answer: **No**

Have you played your other "secret" game?
Answer: **Yes**

Can you tell me how to play it?
Answer: **No**

How? Please!
Answer: **No**

Do you want to go to the Valentine's Dance on Friday night?
Answer: **Yes**

If so, who would you like to go with you? Who should take you?

❦   ❦   ❦   ❦   ❦

FEBRUARY 14, 1996/KENNY AND MALIA

Did you have a good day today at school?
Answer: **Yes**

Did you have a Valentine Day party?
Answer: **Yes**

What did you do?
Answer: **Game**

Did you play a game?
Answer: **Yes**

Okay, you don't have to tell me how to play your secret game, but can you tell me why it's secret?
Answer: **Mind**

336 Is it all in your mind?
Answer: **Yes**

Kim is going to pick you up at Mary's house for the dance on Friday, but you already knew that didn't you?

Answer: **Yes**

⊡   ⊡   ⊡   ⊡   ⊡

FEBRUARY 18, 1996/KENNY AND MALIA

Kenny, did you have fun at the dance on Friday night?
Answer: **Yes**

Do you want to go again when they have another dance?
Answer: **Yes**

Did you get asked to dance?
Answer: **Yes**

Did you dance?
Answer: **No**

Did you want to dance? Next time?
Answer: **Yes**

Would you like me to go with you and Mary next time?
Answer: **Yes**

Who was your favorite person at the dance?
Answer: **Krissie**

Would you like to dance with Christi (not sure of spelling)? Kenny probably spelled it right knowing him!
Answer: **How**

You could go up on the dance floor and just dance with her or she'll probably ask you to dance.
Answer: **No How**

Do you know how to dance Kenny?
Answer: **No**

It's real easy. Oh, how cute he says he doesn't know how to dance so I sort of demonstrated and he started laughing, but he wouldn't get up to dance with me.

If me and Mary help you, will you dance next time.
Answer: **No**
Brat! Just kidding!

⬚　　⬚　　⬚　　⬚　　⬚

MARCH 13, 1996/KENNY AND MALIA

Kenny, can I go to the dance with you this Friday with Mary?
Answer: **Yes**

Are you excited about going?
Answer: **Yes**

You sure have a nice Mommy. She bought you a brand new outfit. Did you see it?
Answer: **Yes**

If so, do you like your new outfit for the dance?
Answer: **Yes**

If I go up to dance with you, will you dance?
Answer: **?**

Maybe you and Kristi can dance together. Would you like that?
Answer: **Yes**

How's school going? I had to phrase it "is school going good?"
Answer: **Yes**

Have you worked with Kim lately?
Answer: **No**

Is there anything you would like to talk about?
Answer: **No**

⬚　　⬚　　⬚　　⬚　　⬚

APRIL 7, 1996

*Mommy – **"tea"** telepathy 4/7/96

*Billie Joe – **"boy"** telepathy 4/7/96

*Mommy – thought – "Kim" **Said Ken**

*Dad – at restaurant thought "I go to Raleys" Kenny said **"Gloria."** 4/10/96

AUGUST 27, 1996/MERCI AND NATHAN

I thought of a specific name out of 4 names: Jeannie, Jean, Selia and Lisa and asked Kenny to pick out the name I was thinking of. He picked the correct name.

Did the same for Nathan and picked the correct name three times. Used Kim, Scott, Tammy and Mike.

APRIL 1997/TANNA AND KENNY AT SCHOOL

Did you see the eclipse last night?
Answer: **Yes**

Was it a lunar or solar eclipse?
Answer: **Solar**

What planet was directly above the moon?
Answer: **Mars**

Did you see the comet?
Answer: **Yes**

What was the name of the comet?
Answer: **Hale-Bopp**

⬚ ⬚ ⬚ ⬚ ⬚

APRIL 10, 1997/TELEPATHY/TINA AND KENNY

WORDS	POINTED TO
Leaves	**Leaves**
House	**House**
Car	**Car** (took my hand and pointed)
Bike	**BMTZ**
Music	**Miguel** (Had him on my mind.) Oops
Painting	**Miguel** (oops still)

Asked Kenny, are you mad I had him on my mind?
Answer: **No**

You know I will always love you like a brother right?
Answer: **Yes ILU**

⬚ ⬚ ⬚ ⬚ ⬚

AUGUST 18, 1997/KENNY AND RHEA

I asked him what I was thinking about out of the words:
Bird, Friend, Angel, Couch.
Answer: **He picked angel, which was correct.**

Singing, Dance, Roller Coaster, Lost Love
Answer: **He picked lost love, which was right again.**

My #1 ice cream flavor out of: Chocolate, Vanilla, B.P. and Bubble gum.
Answer: **He picked bubble gum and he was right.**

What is my dad's name, (I have never told this to Kenny) from the following names: Dave, Bob, John, Clark?

Answer: **He picked Bob. He got it right!**

CHAPTER TWENTY-FOUR
Chapter twenty-four
Chapter twenty-four

⬚　　⬚　　⬚　　⬚　　⬚

SEPTEMBER 4, 1997/RHONDA B.

Can we do some Q?

Answer: **Yes**

How was your day at school today?

Answer: **Poor**

Stop!

What was it about your day that was poor?

Answer: **Seizure**

What was your favorite about today?

Answer: **Kid**

Stop

⬚　　⬚　　⬚　　⬚　　⬚

SEPTEMBER 5, 1997/RHONDA

Are you used to your new classroom?

Answer: **No**

Do you like the two new kids in your class?

Answer: **Yes**

⬚　　⬚　　⬚　　⬚　　⬚

SEPTEMBER 5, 1997/RHONDA

What are the kid's names?
Answer: **Will**
Stop!

❑ ❑ ❑ ❑ ❑

SEPTEMBER 7, 1997/RHONDA

How is your day today?
Answer: **Good**

What is the capitol of Kansas?
Answer: **Topeka**

❑ ❑ ❑ ❑ ❑

SEPTEMBER 9, 1997/RHONDA

Can we do some questions?
Answer: **Yes**

What did you do today at school that was fun?
Answer: **Questions**

What do you want to do now?
Answer: **Puzzle**

❑ ❑ ❑ ❑ ❑

OCTOBER 30, 1997/RHONDA B.

Can you hear my truck from 3 blocks away?
Answer: **Yes Stop**

Telepathy

Kenny, I am thinking of a word (wood). What is the word?
Answer: After about 3 minutes spelled **"WDOO."**
Amazing!

⬚ ⬚ ⬚ ⬚ ⬚

NOVEMBER 3, 1997/RHONDA B.

How was your day?
Answer: **Fine**

Did you have fun riding the trains yesterday?
Answer: **Yes, Yes** (Big Smile)

Would you like to go for a boat ride next Sunday to San Francisco?
Answer: **Yes**

⬚ ⬚ ⬚ ⬚ ⬚

NOVEMBER 4, 1997/RHONDA B.

Is it about school?
Answer: **No**

Mary?
Answer: **No**

Me (Rhonda)?
Answer: **Yes**

Is what you want to tell me good or bad?
Answer: **Stop**

Do you want to do telepathy?
Answer: **Yes! Yes! Yes!**

I spoke with Kenny and explained to him about how I volunteer at a missing children's foundation – Amber. I explained to him the best I could about what a kidnapping is and after that I asked Kenny if he understood what I was telling him and he pointed to **"yes."** I then went on to explain about the kidnappings in the bay area and how the police are trying to find out who has been doing the kidnappings. I again asked Kenny if he understood and he pointed to **"Yes! Yes!"** I asked Kenny if the police know who did it and he spelled **"y-e-s."** I then asked Kenny to tell me the name of that person who the police think did this. Kenny spelled **"T-I-M."** Note: The suspect in the bay area kidnapping cases is named Tim Binder! I had to stop. I almost hyperventilated!!

NOVEMBER 5, 1997/RHONDA B.

Do you remember the questions yesterday about missing kids?
Answer: **Yes**

Do you want to help find her?
Answer: **Yes**

I showed a picture of Amber Swartz and I told him that this is one of the girls that are missing.

Where do you think that she might be?
Answer: **T. M. Help (Tim)**

Is Amber alive or dead?
Answer **D-E-A-D**

Do you know the difference between alive and dead?
Answer: **Yes**

Is there anything else you want to tell me about Amber?
Answer: **Yes**

What?
Answer: **Help**

Are there anymore kids in danger?
Answer: **Yes**

Do you know what danger is?
Answer: **Yes**

What is it?
Answer: **B-A-D Stop**

⊡　　⊡　　⊡　　⊡　　⊡

NOVEMBER 13, 1997/RHONDA B.

What do you feel like talking about; babies, school, stars, people?
Answer: **People**

Do you enjoy watching and hanging out with different kinds of people.
Answer: **Yes Stop**

What do you want to do then?
Answer: **Said "Book"**

⊡　　⊡　　⊡　　⊡　　⊡

NOVEMBER 16, 1997/RHONDA B.

Did you enjoy seeing baby Clayton and Guy today? Guy is my dad.
Answer: **Yes**

Did you like Wal-Mart?
Answer: **Yes, Yes**

Can a car talk?
Answer: **No**

Can a dog bark?
Answer: **Yes**

Can a couch eat?

Answer: **No**

Can food sing?

Answer: **No**

Kenny, on Friday morning your Mom told me that you didn't want to go to school and that you gave them a hard time. Were you trying to tell them something?

Answer: **Yes**

Did you know that your Dad was broke down in his car and that was the reason for your behavior?

Answer: **Yes, Yes**

Note: On Friday, November 14th, Ken had broken down in his truck on the way to work. The same time Kenny was acting up!

I told Kenny I was thinking of a word. It was wedding. After about three minutes Kenny spelled out: **W-E-D-D-I-N**

Kenny, you know that I am getting married soon right?

Answer: **Yes**

Is it a good thing?

Answer: **Yes, Yes**

Is James going to be a good husband?

Answer: **Yes, Yes**

Are we going to have babies?

Answer: **Yes**

How many?

Answer: **Help**

Okay, are we going to have a boy or a girl?

Answer: **Yes, Yes**

Does that mean that we are going to have both a boy and a girl?

Answer: **Yes, Yes, Yes!**

Kenny started laughing and clapping
Stop

⸿ ⸿ ⸿ ⸿ ⸿

NOVEMBER 26, 1997/TELEPATHY/RONDA B. AND KENNY

Today James and Clayton and I were eating at a restaurant and James had a concerned look on his face as if he was deep in thought. I asked him what was on his mind and he said "ask Kenny." I did just that. I told Kenny just what I explained and Kenny spelled "marriage." So sweet!

⸿ ⸿ ⸿ ⸿ ⸿

DECEMBER 2, 1997/TELEPATHY/RONDA B. AND KENNY

How are you feeling?
Answer: **Fine**

Did you have fun at the mall with your class?
Answer: **Yes**

Did you go Xmas shopping?
Answer: **Yes**

What did you buy?
Answer: **No, No**

Why won't you tell me?
Answer: **No**

Is it because you said you wanted to buy something for baby Clayton?
Answer: **Yes (laughing)**

⸿ ⸿ ⸿ ⸿ ⸿

DECEMBER 18, 1997/TELEPATHY/RONDA B. AND KENNY

Kenny, you know how I told you about my friend from Florida right?
Answer: **Yes**

Well, I never told you her name. Can you tell me her name?
Answer: **Yes, J-E-N**

⌑ ⌑ ⌑ ⌑ ⌑

DECEMBER 23, 1997/TELEPATHY/RONDA B. AND KENNY

Have you made any new star names?
Answer: **Yes**

What are they?
Answer: **D.J.**

D.J., is that one of them?
Answer: **Yes**

Can you tell me Jennifer's last name?
Answer: **Murray**

⌑ ⌑ ⌑ ⌑ ⌑

DECEMBER 26, 1997/TELEPATHY/KENNY, LAURET, JEN AND RHONDA

Jennifer thinking of word, Rhonda doing F.C. (Rhonda does not know word.)

Kenny pointed to **"C."** Word was "Cat" **Stop**

⌑ ⌑ ⌑ ⌑ ⌑

DECEMBER 30, 1997/TELEPATHY/KENNY, LAURET, JEN AND RHONDA

How are you feeling?
Answer: **Good**

Do you know that you will be going back to school next week?
Answer: **No**

Do you understand about school vacation?
Answer: **No**

I explained to him about school vacation and I asked him again if he understood and he said **Yes** and smiled and clapped.

Is there anything you want to tell me?
Answer: **J-O-K-E Stop**

❑   ❑   ❑   ❑   ❑

JANUARY 16, 1998/RHONDA B. AND KENNY

What happened?
Answer: **Help**

Was someone mean to you?
Answer: **Yes**

Who was mean?
Answer: **To**

Tonna?
Answer: **Yes**

What did she do?
Answer: **Help**

Did she hurt you?
Answer: **Yes, Yes**

Where did she hurt you?
Answer: **Mout**

Your mouth?
Answer: **Yes**

I explained to him this was very important and he needs to be honest and not play games and again I asked him if Tonna hit him in the mouth and he said **"Yes, Yes."**

Did Tonna hit you on purpose?
Answer: **No**

So it was an accident?
Answer: **Yes Stop!**

JANUARY 20, 1998/RHONDA B. AND KENNY

How are you?
Answer: **Fine**

Did you have a good day at school?
Answer: **Yes**

Remember fishing yesterday?
Answer: **Yes**

Would you like to go again?
Answer: **Yes**

What did you do at school today?
Answer: **Nothing**

Did you see your friends?
Answer: **No**

Don't you have any friends at school?
Answer: **No**

❑   ❑   ❑   ❑   ❑

JANUARY 27, 1998/RHONDA B. AND KENNY/TELEPATHY

I told Kenny that my friend Chelene was going to have a baby and I asked him what she was going to have and he said **"Girl."**

❑   ❑   ❑   ❑   ❑

FEBRUARY 16, 1998/RHONDA B. AND KENNY

How are you today?
Answer: **Fine**

Can we talk about what happened yesterday?
Answer: **Yes**

What happened?
Answer: **Seizure**

Were you scared?
Answer: **No**

Why weren't you scared?
Answer: **He Said "Ra Ra."**

Was it because I was there?
Answer: **Yes, then said "Guy."**

Do you mean James?
Answer: **Yes**

Do you understand that you're okay after a seizure?
Answer: **Yes**

FEBRUARY 27, 1998/RHONDA B. AND KENNY

Do you like the foods that your Mom, Me and Mary are feeding you? Said "Fine" then pointed to Yes.
Answer: **Yes**

What is your favorite food: MacDonalds, Spaghetti, Chicken or Ice Cream?
Answer: **Pointed to Spaghetti.**

What is the food you don't like?
Answer: **Veg Stop!**

☒ ☒ ☒ ☒ ☒

MAY 12, 1998, 1998/RHONDA B. AND KENNY

Do you miss your sister Rhonda?
Answer: **Yes, Yes, Yes Stop**

☒ ☒ ☒ ☒ ☒

MAY 27, 1998, 1998/RHONDA B. AND KENNY

Is there something you want to talk about?
Answer: **Yes, Food**

What kind of food do you want to have?
Answer: **Pie**

What kind of pie do you want?
Answer: **Choc Choc (Spelled strawberry)**

Is there something that caused you to have two seizures yesterday?
Answer: **No**

Are you scared about having your teeth worked on?
Answer: **No**

Who do you want to have with you when you go to the dentist?
Answer: **Mary, Rah, Rha**

Do you want Barbara there too?
Answer: **No Stop**

APRIL 6, 1999/MARY AND KENNY

Kenny, this whole day has been very nice. Tell me why you were in such a good mood?
Answer: **Stop Stop Stop**

⊡　　⊡　　⊡　　⊡　　⊡

APRIL 7, 1999/MARY AND KENNY

Kenny, when Rhonda (sister) has her baby, what must we do when we hold her new little baby?
Answer: **KARFL**

Careful?
Answer: **Yes**

Very good. What do you do when Rhonda's little baby begins to cry?
Answer: **SNG TOOO HMI**

Sing to her?
Answer: **NO HIM**

Shall we play your favorite tune for Rhonda's new little baby?
Answer: **No**

Why not?
Answer: **KUZ – SNG TO HIM**

APRIL 7, 1999/MARY AND KENNY

Kenny, is there something you would like to tell your sister Rhonda?
Answer: **Yes** (pointed to)

What is it that you would like to tell your sister Rhonda?
Answer: **FAT PRTIE**

Rhonda is very pretty indeed. Where is she fat?
Answer: **TMMME**

Why is that?
Answer: **Yes** (Points to)

Why is she pooching in her tummy?
Answer: **BBABY THRE**

APRIL 8, 1999/MARY AND KENNY

Kenny, will you help babysit Rhonda's little baby?
Answer: **Yes**

What will you do for the baby?
Answer: **Love**

That is the greatest gift, the gift of oneself. How sweet. Now Kenny, if the baby cries, what will you do to comfort her?
Answer: **HIM**

You are absolutely right, again. What will you do to comfort him when he cries?
Answer: **SNG**

Do you think singing is a means of comfort?
Answer: **Yes** (points to)

JUNE 14, 2000/MARY AND KENNY

How are you today?
Answer: **HOT**

Do you like Father Bain?
Answer: **Yes**

Does he make you feel better?
Answer: **Yes**

How does he make you feel?
Answer: **Good**

Do you want to go and see him again?
Answer: **Yes**

Do you think he is helping you?
Answer: **Yes, Yes**

Do you think it's hot today?
Answer: **Yes**

Is it going to be this hot tomorrow?
Answer: **More**

Tell me how it feels when Father Bain prays for you.
Answer: **Good, Nice, Cool, Friend**

Do you want to tell me anything else.
Answer: **No**

❖   ❖   ❖   ❖   ❖

AUGUST 7, 2000/MARY AND KENNY

Kenny, if you could play any sport, what would it be?
Answer: **Ball**

Kenny, if you could do any job, what would it be?
Answer: **Doctor**

Why a Doctor?
Answer: **Help**

What kind of Doctor?
Answer: **Baby**

If you could not be a doctor, what else would you do?
Answer: **Car**

Would you make cars?
Answer: **No**

⊡   ⊡   ⊡   ⊡   ⊡

AUGUST 7, 2000/MARY AND KENNY

Drive them?
Answer: **No**

Sell the cars?
Answer: **No**

Fix the cars?
Answer: **Yes**

Kenny, if you could change anything, what would it be?
Answer: **Time**

Why time?
Answer: **Home**

Kenny used my hand to spell out home. It was so funny.

⊡   ⊡   ⊡   ⊡   ⊡

JANUARY 9, 2001/MARY AND KENNY

How are you today?
Answer: **Good**

Did you like Xmas?
Answer: **Yes**

Kenny is Rhonda going to have another baby?
Answer: **Yes**

What is it going to be?
Answer: **Boy**

When is she going to have it?   (Rhonda had another boy a few years later)
Answer: **Two**

How are your feet?
Answer: **Fine**

Does it hurt?
Answer: **Yes, Some**

Does it hurt bad?
Answer: **No**

So would you like to go see Father Bain?
Answer: **Yes**

Who do you want to go with you?
Answer:

Do you like Father Bain?
Answer: **Yes, Yes**

Who is with Father Bain?
Answer: **GOD**

What does God do?
Answer: **Help**

Help you?

Answer: **Yes**

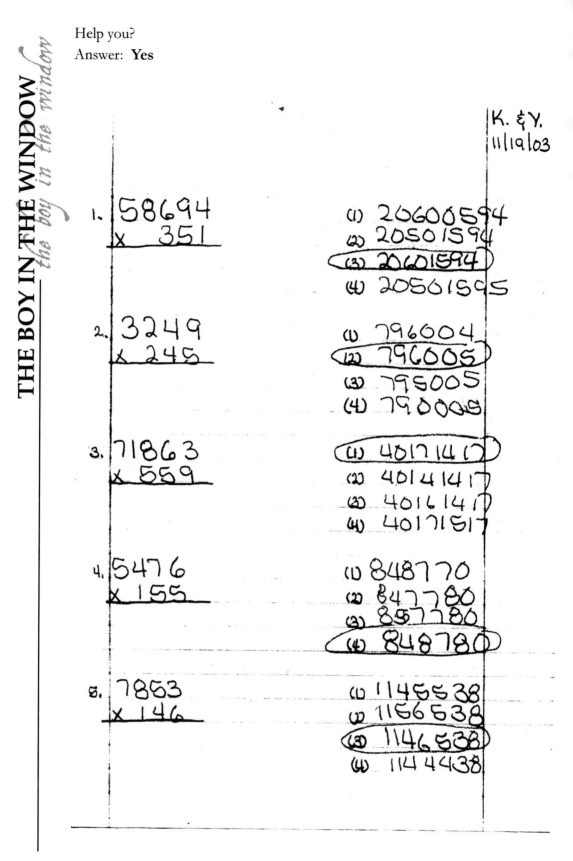

K. & Y.
11/19/03

1. 58694
   × 351

   (1) 20600594
   (2) 20501594
   (3) 20601594
   (4) 20501595

2. 3249
   × 245

   (1) 796004
   (2) 796005
   (3) 795005
   (4) 790005

3. 71863
   × 559

   (1) 40171417
   (2) 40141417
   (3) 40161417
   (4) 40171517

4. 5476
   × 155

   (1) 848770
   (2) 847780
   (3) 857780
   (4) 848780

5. 7853
   × 146

   (1) 1146538
   (2) 1166538
   (3) 1146538
   (4) 1144438

12/9/03
K. & Y.

67584 x 537	(1) 35292608 (2) 36292608 (3) 37282608
54309 x 350	(1) 19600150 (2) 18008150 (3) 19008150
29620 x 561	(1) 16616820 (2) 16616720 (3) 16616620
34567 x 269	(1) 9298523 (2) 9299523 (3) 9297523
68910 x 129	(1) 8888380 (2) 8889390 (3) 8887390
50752 x 1234	(1) 62627768 (2) 62627968 (3) 62627968

Mead

359

THE BOY IN THE WINDOW

the boy in the window

CHAPTER
TWENTY-FIVE

THE BOY IN THE WINDOW

K enny was doing extraordinary scholastics at school with Tom, his teacher Doreen, who he adored, and a few of the other female aides. Whether it was on the computer or worksheets, it was more than impressive. His math was superb! No, it was astounding! When I saw how rapidly he did the multiplication and addition problems similar to what you just saw, I bought him a giant size math brain buster workbook that measured about 16" x 22" for the girls to work on at home with him. The large print made it easy to read. These problems were far more difficult and required three or four steps to arrive at the correct answer. Most of us would have to resort to using a calculator for the math Kenny was doing in his head. It amazed everyone who watched him as he pointed to the answers to the questions in just a few seconds.

Kenny would sit next to the person working with him as they read the question, while he scanned the page. At the bottom of the page were five possible choices that were previously written out, one being the correct answer. The person circled the answer after Kenny pointed to it. When the session was finished, the person went back to the answer sheet and was always amazed at his usually perfect score.

I updated the aides at school with the progression of Kenny's math to assure they included the same type of questions, in his daily schedule. At home, I had decided whoever worked with Kenny should dip his finger in an ink blotter, so when he pointed to the answer, he left the ink spot on his choice. I brought this math to the school. They were doing basic addition, multiplying and fractions with him, but not to this degree. Originally, I just had the person circle the answer after he pointed to his choice. Very seldom did he choose the wrong figure.

The aides and teachers at school were upgrading all of Kenny's scholastics. He was correctly answering questions about the stars, constellations, planets and much more! I have boxes of all of his great work that he accomplished at home and at school. I know I could never part with any of it. No mother could have felt prouder of her offspring than I did!

Kenny's work was so intelligent, so astronomical I begin to wonder if the source of his being was celestial! How was all of this possible? In his FC, he said many times that he taught himself, whether it was reading, math, star names, or the names he gave them. If it wasn't Kenny, it had to have been a UFO sending alien messages! I am joking of course! But Kenny has opened my mind to much broader views than I ever had before.

Kenny could point to the answers on his own, or sometimes used the finger of an aide as his pointer, in which case they always thought it was so cute. For the skeptics out there, Kenny has answered so many questions covering all areas of worldly knowledge, with so many different people, with the same outcome, that it isn't scientifically possible to call all of his extraordinary work, "lucky guesses!"

After all these years I felt the key to Kenny's door had been opened, now that the genie was out of the bottle! I glorified in the possibilities of exploring whatever other capabilities he possessed! I visualized higher expectations for him, and from him.

I often wondered if Kenny was a savant. I'm sure you've seen them on television. The severely mentally challenged, who can also be extremely gifted, and can belt out incredible music on a piano, or sing Opera in Italian, without being able to talk with real language, or read a note. And of course, there was Rain Man, and numbers were his passion. He was a mathematical genius who had to be cared for. But in my heart I didn't feel Kenny was a savant. I thought of him as an intelligent boy who suffered great damage to a part of his brain, leaving a portion that tried to overcompensate, yet not in a way that helped his reasoning. I know he processes his world in a way no one understands. The brain is a mystery and so is Kenny!

I told a friend in my exercise class about Kenny's telepathy, and all of the good work he was doing. I told her there wasn't much for him to do socially, other than school. She wanted to come over and entertain Kenny with some music and her singing. She brought a friend who played the guitar. Kenny was in seventh heaven. We agreed I should find an easy instrument for him to toy with, so I bought a second hand keyboard to see if he might have any musical abilities, or just for his enjoyment.

I then mentioned to Malia, one of the girls that worked with Kenny, how much he enjoyed the sessions with my friend. Malia brought some of her music books over and played some songs for him. He seemed intrigued. She showed Kenny how to place his fingers on the keyboard. She mentions in her Q's and A's that he seemed to have a knack, and felt there was some melody when she was able to get him to comply.

One night, while I was in the kitchen, I thought I heard our radio, or music coming from somewhere. It finally dawned on me that it was coming from upstairs.

I slowly crept up each step and down the hall, and peeked into the room where Kenny sits. The keyboard was on the floor, his back was to me, and he was on his knees. I will never forget seeing the agility of his fingers as they hit the keys gently, and with purpose. The moment was as beautiful and mystic to me, as the sound emerging from that room.

I turned back as quietly as possible and found my tape recorder. He was so engrossed in his playing, he didn't notice me. I had never seen him like that before. I was able to get some of it on tape before he saw me and stopped.

Kenny doesn't like to perform for me in any way. He doesn't want me to know his capabilities for some reason. Sometimes I feel it is a punishment he thinks I deserve. Or, maybe I scare him with my excitement over his stupendous deeds. I just don't know! Maybe he thinks he will have to come out of his cocoon, into the real world, and earn a living!

One would think Kenny would revel in being able to express his silent thoughts, and be proud of his accomplishments. And one would think he would especially want to see his mother happy because of it. But Kenny doesn't function like that.

My son had become a conglomerate of Jeckle, Hyde, the challenged, and the genius. But none of these guys were on the same wave length. Part of me wanted to be angry at him. How could he know so much and still act the way he does?

I reminisced over some hilarious episodes that captured Kenny in the more predominant role of the "challenged."

I was heading for his favorite room upstairs, where I expected him to be sitting at the window. Instead, my eyes were diverted to his bedroom. I was shocked to see him staring out the window, with his arms and hands tied high above his head with the cord from the blinds. He just hung there! Luckily, he's tall, so his feet were planted firmly on the floor. It was the most tragically funny sight to behold, and he hadn't uttered a peep through it all.

Wrapping threads or ties around his wrist so tight that it began to cut off his circulation has been a long-time obsession. Often, I had to resort to using a pair of scissors to cut through the string. After seeing Kenny that day, I frantically got rid of anything in the house remotely resembling a possible noose in the making.

Then there was the time he was sitting on a chair in the middle of the lawn with Gizmo laying next to him, and the sprinklers turned on. Gizmo had the sense to jump up and run off, but Kenny remained in his chair without even flinching!

Before long, Tom was moving on to another school for a higher position closer to his home. I was able to get Kim, the girl who worked so well with Kenny at home, a position as his new one-to-one aide. I was afraid the loss of Tom would devastate Kenny so much that he wouldn't want to do his good work anymore. He loved Kim, even though in their questions, she would ask him if he liked her yet, and he would tease and say "No!"

I wanted her to carry on what Tom had been doing with Kenny at the school. Nevertheless, Kenny missed Tom! It took him a while to get used to having Kim at school with him, instead of at home. It was yet another adjustment period for him. Eventually, she was able to extract great school work and Q's and A's. Soon, Kim moved on to a higher position at the school. *I trained her well.*

Changes always occur in abundance at schools. Aides were coming and going, and teachers too! *Poor Kenny!* With each new aide assigned to him, I relentlessly expressed my desire for them to work at the levels he was capable of. I brought his work from home so they could familiarize themselves with it. I might as well have brought in some knitting for the interest that was generated in showing his work. The newer people were having a hard enough time just dealing with the extreme behaviors of some of the students, including my own son, who relished in throwing himself down on the ground when things were not going his way.

It was sad to see him back at sorting objects, throwing bean bags or just sitting around watching others, his favorite, lazy, pastime. He was resisting computer work now when someone did try to work with him. Some of the new aides were trying really hard with Kenny. He was well liked even though he could be a stinker. I think he was afraid to get attached to anyone for fear they would soon leave too! Kenny actually enjoyed everyone, but his structure at school had been turned upside down.

There was an aide he especially liked named Tonna, who Kenny really challenged. She worked diligently with him, and truly cared. One day at school he was really naughty for her, I can't remember what he did, but I remember feeling so sorry for her. I wrote this poem to her the next day, as if it was an apology from Kenny:

> *Dear Tonna,*
>
> *Thank you for watching over me the special way you do,*
>
> *Thanks for being patient while I lay down and throw a shoe,*
>
> *Thanks for trying to teach me things that help me to excel,*
>
> *I know if I were in public school I'd probably be expelled,*
>
> *Thanks for picking up after me and taking me for walks,*
>
> *There are so many things to say if only I could talk,*
>
> *Sometimes I try really hard to be a better boy,*
>
> *I know days like yesterday don't bring too much joy,*
>
> *This brain of mine sure doesn't work like other people's do,*

One thing I am sure of is I really do love you.

Love,

Kenny

With all of Kenny's behaviors, good or bad, he was always a favorite at school with his winning smile. I took great pride in how he was dressed. He was groomed with the latest style hair cut.

I use to be the only one that could cut his hair, and for years he looked like a girl. Then around age 12, we took him to quick cut places. If there was no one waiting, he would sit just long enough for them to whiz through his hair. Eventually, he kind of enjoyed the girls cutting his hair, and liked the attention. When they worked around his ears, he kind of rolled his head from side to side, as if it was soothing to him. The girls tried to be patient while they cautiously trimmed near that area.

Once, I even bleached some tips of his hair when that look was in. The staff would always comment on how "cool" Kenny looked. One aide said she could hardly wait to see what Kenny would be wearing on arrival at the school.

It always pleased me to hear comments like that. I figured, if I couldn't make him act like a normal kid, I would make him look like one.

Mary wanted to see how Kenny looked with a mustache, so we let one grow for a while. But at night, it didn't seem comprehensible putting a diaper on a man with a mustache!

Soon, Kenny was going to graduate from Spectrum. He was 22. That was the age limit for special education. Students were supposed to move on to adult day programs. Before he graduated, we had looked into some that were available, per Spectrum's request. But there was nothing suitable for Kenny. *Sound familiar?*

At last I got to see what he looked like in a graduation cap and gown. He was so handsome! I was as proud of him as a mother could possibly be of her son. Two other students were also moving on. There was a party for the classroom that included parents and siblings. There was picture taking and applause when the students were presented with their "diplomas." It was nice, but sad. Kenny had been going to school for the majority of his life. *What will he do now?*

While the tassel of his cap tickled his nose, he stuffed his mouth with cake. Surprisingly, he left the cap on for most of the party. He hated hats, helmets, or anything on his head! I think he knew this was something really special to wear.

THE BOY IN THE WINDOW
the boy in the window

CHAPTER
TWENTY-SIX

THE BOY IN THE WINDOW

I don't think Kenny understood that the graduation party represented his farewell to Spectrum, and the end of his school years. He missed the morning ritual of getting up early, being dressed, fed, and then driven to Concord, about a thirty-five minute trip. His days had been filled with the bustle of teachers, aides, students, and all of the melodrama that inhabited his environment.

He was more upset about not being able to go to school than the relevancy of why he was attending in the first place, which was to help prepare him for his future! He became confused, depressed, and immobile.

In his preferred secluded room upstairs, where the large bay window overlooks the street he lives on, he could sit for hours staring out! It was so hard to get him to do anything other than go to the bathroom. He could remain motionless for a long time, as if he was in a trance. I tried reading to him and attempted some games, but whatever I laid out on the table he threw on the floor. He just wanted to be left alone.

Even when Kenny's curiosity was aroused from noises he heard downstairs, he scooted down the hallway closer to the sounds, while still glued to his chair. It was usually a conversation I was having on the phone with someone. From time to time, he still does this, so I purposely bought lightweight computer chairs on rollers. Dragging a conventional chair with four legs could injure his foot if one leg landed on it.

A round, wood table was between the two chairs in front of his window. It is where the girls did their FC and other tasks with him. This tortured piece of furniture has been overturned so many times by Mr. Hyde the legs had to be reinforced with metal bolts.

But I believe this room upstairs serves as a sanctuary for him, where he feels protected from the daily challenges and chaos that he, himself, creates! A place where he can be who he is without judgment or scorn! It is where his frustrations, anger and disappointments blend into a state of metamorphose. It is the window of his world, a world he doesn't know how to fit in or cope with.

Perhaps on dark, clear nights he sat in this spot and brilliantly named some of his beautiful stars: Quowz, Ziry, Zaeus, Cepheus, Cetus, Grus, Cygnus, Sirius, (the

371

brightest star in the sky), Crux,(it is in the dictionary and means the essential point, difficult matter,) Lepus, Zosma, Lijer, Quor, Moquik, Meijo, Skizik, Clurx, Yorq, Pyzer, Bey, Lius, Zyke, Kleg, Legge, Snoope, Jespa, Jott, Zyle, Wikil, Bouris, Vega, (the biggest or brightest star in a constellation) and his favorite star name, Gizmo, after his dog. He said it was his shiniest star.

Once again, I am confronted with the mystery of how Kenny learned the names of Sirius, Crux and Vega! They are real stars! I looked them up in the dictionary. How many people know this? I didn't know, and unless your hobby is studying the Cosmos, the average person doesn't have an inclination about stars, other than the Little Dipper, the Big Dipper, etc.

For the longest time I questioned anyone, and just about everyone who had taught Kenny at any level, if they had ever discussed the planets or stars with him, and the answer was always "No!" It was way beyond the scope of any program he had ever been in. Until Kenny's skills were discovered, it was all I could do to get aides to incorporate any scholastics. It was usually the basic sorting or throwing of bean bags, matching up objects, or learning colors.

I will never know the extent of Kenny's amazing knowledge! I wish I could have found out more about the game he played pretending to be someone else. When he first mentioned it, I had all of the facilitators try to find out more about it. But he decided not to discuss it further. To me, it sounded as if he wondered what his life would be like if he were normal! This assumption was yet another heartbreaker for me.

But now that school ended, my main focus was to get Kenny motivated to leave the house. It wasn't good for him to just sit, and he needed continued brain stimulation. I was still on the look-out for adult day programs, but they were all for higher functioning challenged people. Most of the programs were job related and impossible for Kenny. When they stuck a broom in his hand at Spectrum and tried to show him how to sweep, or have him help out in the deli, he was as motivated as a flea.

When Kim asked him during an FC session how he liked sweeping, he spelled, "hard work!"

During his transition from being in school to staying at home, Mary and I could get Kenny in the car after a few weeks for very short drives. We drove to stores hoping he would go in with us. But he resisted getting out of the car and just wanted to go back home.

I wanted to help her with Kenny as much as possible, but she thought it might be better if I wasn't along. It is true that Kenny picks up on my motherly worries and he acts out from my tension. I was also trying to have a part-time career in my skin care business. I tried to focus on that, while Mary worked on getting him out.

She picked Costco for the first store to take him to. She drove into the parking lot, but once again, Kenny wouldn't get out of the car. Then the next time he walked with her to the door, but turned around and wanted to go home. She was at least able to get him to go back to her house, though he acted as if it were a first time event. He had been there on many occasions before school was out. Everything appeared to be out of sorts for him.

Little by little, she coaxed him inside Costco, and many times he threw himself down on the ground to rebel. Sometimes she waited it out or dragged him out to the car.

Once he got used to going into Costco, and behaved somewhat appropriately, she started with new stores using the same technique. It took months of patience on her part but it paid off, because today he will go to quite a few places with her. But even now, a new store can still be challenging if he is in a mood.

I am so grateful to Mary for getting him back out in the public. Our afternoon respite people followed suit, and soon Kenny became more than anxious to get out of the house. He is such a creature of habit, if he strays from what he gets used to, he becomes stressed and anxious. And there are times he just wants to stay home because he is tired, or a seizure might be brewing.

Mary faced many dilemmas with Kenny when she had him out in public, past and present! Even on our own street! Mishaps were usually before she got him in or out of her car. He was still pretty fast on his feet at 15! Kenny was about 12 when Mary started with us.

When they were leaving our house one day, he darted off three houses down from us where a neighbor was getting out of her car. Kenny proceeded to grab a container of KFC out of the neighbor's hands! He ran with the box, and Mary was able to catch him and return the chicken, all intact. Maybe he also had the urge for some good old Kentucky Fried Chicken.

Once, at a Target store, while walking alongside of Mary and holding on to the shopping cart, a startled woman approached Mary and said, "He grabbed my glasses right off my face before I realized what happened!" Mary looked down at Kenny's hand and there were the glasses clutched tightly in his fist. He would have made a great pick-pocket!

Grabbing has been one of Kenny's hardest behaviors to control. Whether it was someone's cap, glasses, or body parts, it has only decreased within the last five years. It was always the major issue listed in his I.E.P. at schools.

Luckily, we only had to pay for a few pair of glasses that he broke after yanking them off someone's face. When he reached out to greet a person, whatever his hand landed on, whether it's a body part or their clothing, he latched on to it like a pit bull! You just couldn't shake him loose! This was quite an embarrassing situation when the person being grabbed was a stranger who was in the right place at the wrong time!

Kenny's grabbing almost got my husband in trouble on several occasions. While pushing Kenny in the grocery cart when he just barely still fit in it, Ken turned his head to reach for something off a shelf. Kenny tried to grab at a few women as they unknowingly walked by and could only reach their butts. One woman turned around and gave my husband a nasty look, thinking he was the culprit. It was Kenny, right?

This type of behavior was discussed a great deal in behavior management regarding autistic people. They frequently engage themselves in this type of antic to satisfy their need for attention, control, and to try and manipulate circumstances out of frustrations. Mainly, the acting out is because of their inability to communicate functionally. These impulses are always non-constructive.

Thank God Kenny has never hurt anyone during any of his shenanigans! But he has definitely frightened people on occasion with his bizarre actions. Those of us that have suffered some scratches and bruises, received them when he was being made to do something he didn't want to do, or during a tantrum.

A good example of this happened not long ago at Mary's house. He poured his glass of water on her floor because Mary was yelling at her children. He hates it when anyone yells at their kids. She gave him rags and made him bend down to "clean" up the spill. She walked him through the motion, her hand over his, swiping back and forth over the wet area. He was really angry at her for making him do this menial task. Before she could retrieve all the rags, he threw a sopping wet one at her back as she walked down her hallway.

Several years ago, Mary and a friend took him to the mall to JC Penney's department store to purchase some bras. Like a typical guy he was bored with shopping, and decided to attract attention by grabbing a bunch of bras off their racks! He then laid himself down on the floor and was throwing bras in all directions while a frantic clerk tried desperately to gather them up.

And I cannot forget many of our excursions with Kenny through the years! Although they were difficult at best, I miss the fact that he was willing to go with us when he was younger.

I remember our first visit to Marine World with Kenny. I think he was about 13 or 14. We brought a respite person with us, and things were going well for the first twenty minutes or so. Then we came to the lions in their caged area. Why that set him off, I don't know. Did he feel an association with their lack of freedom? He didn't seem afraid. But he went into a major tantrum. We pulled him into the least crowded area, where there were a few tables and chairs in the shade. My husband sat down with Kenny in his lap, restraining him the best he could. Kenny kicked, screamed and carried on. Ken had to resort to this technique to protect Kenny from himself. It was all he could do to hold on to him.

Soon, we were the biggest attraction there! One lady actually walked by glaring at us. She started yelling that Kenny didn't belong here and we should have left him at home! Ken politely asked her to mind her own business. She walked away in a huff but soon came sauntering back with her husband. He threatened Ken for being "rude" to his wife.

I started crying because there wasn't much else I could do. Besides, I thought maybe it improved on our family exhibition. A sweet little boy, coerced by his mother, brought me a tissue, and luckily in the nick of time, a Marine World security guard ordered the angry man to depart.

The guard approached us and very compassionately told us not to worry about other people. I thought to myself it would have been the other guy that needed to worry! My husband's adrenaline was at a peak and this was definitely not the time to pick a fight with him!

He offered to show us a place we could take Kenny until he calmed down. Ken thanked him and told him we just wanted to get him home.

What seems like an eternity ago, we used to take Kenny down to the waterfront in Vallejo every warm evening in the summer, so he could watch the boats launch. He was fascinated with people maneuvering their boats into the water and getting them out. We stood behind the ramp where Kenny climbed on the first rung of the railing. He had a bird's eye view and we stayed a good hour or more so he could have his fill.

Usually, we stopped to get him a milkshake before we got to the waterfront. More often than not, he would reach over the back seat and dump it on my head. I guess he thought I looked good with chocolate drizzling down my face and hair.

Saturday mornings was a guy thing, with the two of them and Gizmo, driving to see the boats without me. *Solitude at last, with a guaranteed good hair day for me!*

For years we towed him in that bright yellow trailer with the bikes. The Yountville Trail from Napa was about a 12-mile ride there and back to our truck. Once on the ride, Kenny had taken off a brand new sandal and threw it. We didn't realize it until we got him out of the trailer at our destination. We retrieved it on the ride back. He was still up to those old tricks as an adult, throwing out a much bigger, and more expensive sandal from the back window of his dad's truck. It wasn't retrieved.

Taking Kenny to Raley's grocery store in Benicia from the time he was a toddler, was always an adventure. Never knowing how Kenny will behave anywhere has been a lifelong scenario. Though he liked everyone there, his two favorite checkers were Gloria and Erick. We were always treated so wonderfully. They have seen Kenny at his worst and at his best. Sometimes he would just throw himself down in the middle of an isle during a tantrum. Erick would walk by and say very nonchalantly, "Hey Kenny, having a bad day?"

Of course shoppers were rather horrified, understandably so. I know there are people who feel Kenny should not be taken to public places. When he acts like that, I get mad at him and feel the same way!

But in earlier days, when respite hours were not as plentiful, we would have been so confined if we couldn't venture out to a store with Kenny in tow. It helped to pass some very long hours during weekends at home with him.

We probably felt more comfortable taking him to Raleys than any other place I can think of. And though he doesn't want to go to the store with us these days (hanging out with parents isn't cool), Gloria, Erick, and others always ask how he is doing. We have been grateful for their kindness toward him.

When Kenny was only seven years old, we really expanded on some excitement for him. We took him down the most bottom part of the American River by Placerville, in my husband's professional raft. The current moved the raft along in spots, but mostly Ken had to row. There were no big rapids in this area, but now and then a few small waves sprayed us enough to dampen our clothes. We all had on proper life jackets of course.

But when Kenny's gear became wet, after awhile, it made holding on to him a lot harder. He felt like a slippery little pig trying to squirm out of my arms. He was thrashing about and having a great time, while we slid around together in the raft, and I struggled to hang on to him. It was definitely a little more than I bargained for!

Our inspiration for taking Kenny in the raft was from the many picnics we enjoyed at the American River with neighbors at the time, Keith and Jeanne Douglas, on Lancaster Way in Vallejo. They have become our dearest friends! Kenny loved Keith, and his word for him was "Ka." He was always happy to see them, especially Keith, but when the curfew fell into play, Kenny ushered them out the door! Jeanne had to leave first, "baa by!" Kenny yelled out. But he had a hard time parting with Keith, sadly pushing him out the door and crying, "com bak."

We came up with a plan for them to sneak back over after we put Kenny to bed, so the four of us could enjoy the rest of the evening together. These are the truest of friends! They were also the few people brave enough to accompany us in public with Kenny.

Kenny went wild with the routine of the river rafters rowing towards shore and then dragging their rubber boats out of the water to deflate them. This was the part he enjoyed the most.

He decided he wanted to be the official welcoming committee, and each time a raft approached the shore, he ran out to greet them with much enthusiasm. He jumped up and down, clapping and shouting, while the bewildered boaters didn't know what to make of him! They were too tired to care.

Between anticipating the next boatload to arrive, he ran from one end of the park area to the other, with me right behind him. Sometimes he ran through people sitting on their blankets before I could catch up to him!

I figured it was worth all of the dirty looks to take him there if watching rafters deflate their boats could inflate Kenny's brain.

Our friends were relaxed and nonchalant about it all and enjoyed the picnic, while I got my day's worth of exercise. They never showed an ounce of discomfort from the many curious stares and whispers that Kenny's behavior, or mine, always attracted.

Another favorite outing for Kenny was Tilden Park, in Berkeley, where he enjoyed riding the miniature train. We rode it at least three times in a row! He loved those trains. There was another train in Santa Rosa that we took him to that stopped at a small animal farm during the ride. He would get mad when the train lingered there too long. Fifteen minutes for Kenny could feel like an hour. But he still had to ride it twice!

The first time we took Kenny to the ocean was quite dramatic. He hated the feel of the sand, and was afraid of it. He wouldn't budge and wouldn't let us carry him. By the time he finally discovered the sand could be some fun, it was time to leave.

There are many places we tried to take Kenny, though I can't remember them all. But finally, after years of being his main lifeline out in public, there is no joy for him being stuck with his parents. Today there is no way we could take him to any of these places, if we did, we would pay!

But he will go to some parks and beaches with Mary and her family and enjoy himself. What a stinker!!

Just a year ago, we motivated him enough to get in the car and go with us to see his sister. He adores her, but doesn't get to see her too often because the drive is one and a half hours.

This was his first drive to her new house. The unfamiliar scenery and distance was agitating him. The last fifteen minutes was stressful, and I was already dreading the ride home. We arrived in one piece, and he had a good time watching Rhonda cook and watching his nephews, Jake and Mike play. (They are my adorable grandsons, and my sunshine.) When it was time to leave, he even cried as we were backing out of her driveway, saying our goodbyes.

But as fate would have it, we hit traffic on the way home, and he kicked at the windows, started hitting at me, and tried reaching for the steering wheel. Of course he was out of his seat belt! I was afraid he would break the window or his arm or leg. Maybe even my head! I felt so sure we would be in an accident I wanted to call 911!

We are not ready to do a lengthy freeway drive with him again for awhile.

CHAPTER
TWENTY-SEVEN

THE BOY IN THE WINDOW
the boy in the window

*K*enny is very handsome in his own way. He has brown hair, usually worn in a crew cut, and dark brown eyes. You could say he is a cross between Bart Simpson and Mr. Potato Head, due to his excessive destructive habits through the years. He broke down some cartilage in his ears, from pinning them back against the pillow, turning his head back and forth. This was the way he got himself to fall asleep, eventually causing boxer's ears. His front teeth slightly protrude from chewing the windowsill upstairs while looking out of his "television" (window). Unfortunately, the damage had already been done by the time someone thought to roll up linoleum, and wrap it around the edges of the sill so he couldn't open his mouth wide enough to "chew!"

And last but not least, is the vague appearance of drooping on one side of his face from the seizures and sleeping on the same side each night.

Kenny's mouth looks incredibly normal, considering his famous lip smacking nightly event. It's a synonymous reminder that it's time for his medicine. He starts it about an hour ahead of time to give us plenty of warning. It's so loud that it competes with the volume of the television. How he keeps it up that long is beyond us. We have tried to copy it, and after a few seconds our lips were tired. He probably would have been a good kisser with all that exercise, but sadly that is not in his near future.

For years, our evening routine with Kenny has been pretty much the same. He joins his dad in the shower and Ken washes him from head to toe while Kenny turns in circles. Kenny pushes on the glass doors, wanting out before his hair is rinsed off! I am waiting with a towel. I can barely dry off a leg or arm because of his haste to get to his relished room. He leaves a wet trail. I quickly run after him and dry off the rest of his body, while briefly examining him. He knows that's what I am doing and doesn't like it a bit. He is so afraid I might find something that requires medical attention, and so am I.

One of my biggest fears through the years is that Kenny would break a major bone. When he had just minor injuries, like the little toe that fractured, he had to be in an ankle cast to protect it. When he hurt his arm during a temper tantrum when he was about 10, the doctor had to make a sling that worked more like a straight jacket. He had ripped the sling off.

Before a trip to Disneyland with paid reservations, he kicked the windshield after we had pulled over to give him a time out. He didn't break his foot, but shattered the window. He was limping and in a wheelchair at Disneyland. The good news was we didn't have to wait in long lines for rides, which he loved. But at night, it was a different story at the hotel. He screamed and wanted to go home, not understanding this was a temporary sleeping arrangement. It was his first night in a strange bed.

We had the management calling us, and people pounding on the walls because of the noise. I couldn't gag him, so eventually he fell asleep from exhaustion. My husband was furious with me for wanting to bring him in the first place. He said, "He just likes being home and looking out the window at the neighbors. What are we doing here?" "Just another one of my bright ideas" I said, glaring at him!

We had one more day and night to go. It was worth it to me because Kenny loved the rides. Ken even took him on the smallest roller coaster there, Thunder Mountain. I was extremely reluctant, but I knew Ken would be holding him tight. Above the roar as the ride was coming to an end, I heard a voice above the roar that screamed out, "Mor!"

Kenny would not get out of the seat and so they got to ride it again. While leaving the ride, I thought someone called out to me, and then someone tapped my shoulder and asked, "Aren't you Kenny Coppo's mom?" And then, she said, "Oh look, there's Kenny!" It was someone from our neighborhood who recognized us from walks we took with Kenny.

When I thought about it, I realized that I heard that quite a bit, "Aren't you Kenny Coppo's mom?" Even here, down in Disneyland! *Yes, my son was a popular guy it seemed.*

When the inevitable finally happened with a major broken bone, it was his foot, of course! He is so hard on his feet. I came home from work one evening, Ken and Kenny and the respite worker were sitting next to him on the couch with worried looks on their faces.

"Kenny hurt his foot," my husband said, "and it's a little swollen." Fear grasped me. I saw that it was twice the size of his other foot! I knew it was broken. "He'll be okay," Ken said. He always says that because he doesn't want me to worry.

Kenny couldn't walk and we had to drag him to the car. Off we went to Kaiser. The sight of the x-ray room immediately threw him into a frenzied state! The stainless steel equipment in the austere atmosphere scared him, and he was in excruciating pain that he didn't understand. I was in agony over his suffering, and knew he would resist help.

A team of doctors tried frantically to hold him down so they could get an x-ray of his foot. He clawed, kicked and screamed as any wild animal in the wilderness would. I was afraid he would break more bones in the process.

Finally, the radiologist saw the dark shadows on the foot of the unwilling patient, revealing several fractures. The doctor told us in all reality, surgery would be the way to go for proper healing. But this was Kenny, not reality! It was an impossible scenario for him to be off his feet for three months.

So the next solution was to give his foot the ultimate support in a full leg cast. The three of us endured that cast for six long weeks. Amazingly, Kenny was able to get around whether hobbling, slithering, or "sliding" down the stairs!

Before each shower at night, my husband struggled to put the plastic sleeve over the cast to keep it dry, and I had to struggle to get it off, praying I didn't get kicked in the head in the process. Patience has never been one of Kenny's virtues! The lack of it is partly a family inheritance, (not from my side).

When it was time for the removal of the cast at Kaiser, I think all of the podiatrists ran off in opposite directions when they saw us coming!

It went fairly well, considering the fear Kenny had when they turned on the saw! I was so afraid he might break his foot again if they tried to get another x-ray. We were not able to get one. His foot did heal, though it looks a little weird.

Every time Kenny jumps, stomps, or kicks when he gets mad or excited, I fear the tremendous pressure he is putting on his feet. The doctor said he may have some pain in later years from the injury. There has never been an easy road for Kenny, or us, I'm afraid.

The other injury he suffered was to his two front teeth in a fall. I was cleaning a spot on the floor and went to get a towel to dry it. In that instant he came running through the hallway and slipped on the wet area, landing smack on his face. I remember feeling like I was the world's worst mother. *I should have known better!* I felt horrible.

A month later, a dark spot appeared high above the gum area. He needed a root canal in both teeth. We had to take him to Kaiser so he could be put out for the procedure. The dentist who specialized in this surgery went to the hospital, and assured me Kenny would do fine. I was so worried. *What if something went wrong with the anesthetics?* I don't know how I got through that day.

Mary went with Ken and me to take him early that morning. He couldn't have anything to eat and kept saying his word for eggs. "Eh, eh," he repeated over and over.

At the hospital they gave him the sedative and before he went out, he looked at me and said, "Eh!" Kenny sometimes is such a trooper. He fared better than I did.

It was one of the worst days of my life. When he came out of his surgery, which was successful and he was not quite awake yet, he looked at me, and said, "Eh," and "Hom." (eggs and home).

Another time that was bad was when he broke a window during a tantrum and cut his arm. Thank God, he didn't need stitches. But I tried to apply pressure because it was bleeding. I tried to wrap a large Band Aide over it, but Kenny ripped it off and dripped blood all over as I chased him down. He becomes combative when scared, and that is such a dangerous scenario.

If our house was burning down, Kenny would resist our attempts at trying to save his life, and I have often wondered how we would survive a crisis of that magnitude.

Well, you can see why no matter how fast and furious I examine and dress him after the shower, it is never fast enough! I am poked, pinched and pushed in the process. He wants me to get the heck out of there! It is not unusual to see me "fly" out of the room after a good shove from him.

Grooming Kenny is not for the faint of heart. He has to totally rely on us, and those who care for him. We brush his teeth, shower him, wipe him, shave him, cut his nails, put deodorant on, style his hair and dress him.

Once every two months, and forgive me Kenny for sharing this secret with everyone, I have to cut hair that grows without limitation on his buttocks and anus, (sorry)! It is truly only something a mother could do! I put on my glasses, a pair of gloves and get to work, using painstaking precision. Ken holds his legs up for me so I don't get kicked in the head, while Kenny lies on the floor, (towel underneath)! It takes a steady hand and a strong stomach, because many poop balls, and worse, get stuck and caught in this area. I have to cut almost to the skin to unravel everything!

We have tried to teach him to wipe, but the few times he tried, the paper was everywhere but in the toilet. There are times he goes and we don't know. When I hear my husband in the shower swearing, I know Kenny didn't get wiped, and he is having an extremely hard time cleaning his private parts. Kenny probably has as much hair there as the Sasquatch!

I think God blessed my husband with an abundance of toleration, and me, with a patience that goes way beyond virtue! Don't you?

For the past 26 years, I washed all of his bedding daily, including blankets. Rhonda taught us a little trick for making the bed she learned as a nurse at Children's Hospital in Oakland. We put two thick bed pads over his sheet that lies on top of a mattress pad, and then we fold a sheet long ways across the bed pads, tucking the excess under the mattress. It did help eliminate some of the wetness, but the smell still required everything to be laundered. The main problem was the adult diapers were not sufficient.

We stopped putting diapers on Kenny just these last two years. He still wets the bed about once every two weeks or more, if he is going to have a seizure that day.

Seizures have been the hardest part of Kenny's brain damage for me. The medicine has kept him from having a full blown Grand Mal where he falls to the floor and his whole body shakes. Instead the seizure is limited to facial chewing, grabbing, and sometimes slight shaking in an extremity. His face turns grayish and his lips turn blue. He wets himself sometimes and his body shuts down for awhile. The seizures can last up to four minutes.

He recently had bouts of a different type of seizure where his body drops to the ground without warning. I was a basket case! He hurt his ankle from one drop and was limping for a while. He is not able to protect himself in any way when they happen. It was as if he passed out long enough to hit the floor, but immediately got right back up. It was on and off for a few months and then stopped, hopefully for good. I think God realized I just couldn't handle anything more, because it was devastating for me! It is heartbreaking to see Kenny so incapacitated with the seizures! They take such a toll on him, and I feel helpless as a mother and I suffer with each seizure he has.

Before bed, Kenny routinely puts his puzzles together, stacks and stacks of them. They consist of about 10 to 13 pieces. His dad sits next to him and hands each puzzle to him. Kenny throws those puzzles together faster than you can shake a stick. But then he's had 26 years of practice.

Before his medicine each night I make him a large milkshake with bananas, healthy protein powder, flax seeds, peanut butter and blueberries. On occasion, he has an Ensure Plus. It is hard to put and keep weight on him. When the doctor suggested a higher dosage of his seizure medication three years ago because they were increasing, he developed anorexia, a side effect of the anti-convulsant. He went down to 115 pounds and is 6ft. tall.

We slowly decreased the meds again, and he started gaining. The most he has ever weighed was 130, and that was from stuffing him constantly. We were only able to do that if someone fed him. It became a very bad habit! Now he prefers to be fed, especially by Mary's sister-in-laws, when he is at her house. He loves to be pampered by the ladies.

But he won't let me feed him, only rarely. He would have to be starving! *Why does he like to punish me?*

So at home, I usually have to resort to blending his dinners. He will "drink" his meal if I tell him it's "soup." Yuk! But it's better than when he used to store

385

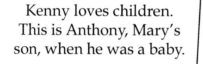
the food in his mouth like a hamster. He gulps down spaghetti soup, stew soup, fish soup, or fried chicken soup. *I think you get the picture.* And believe me it doesn't do anything for one's appetite to see the ungodly colors that are concocted from blending veggies, meat, and a starch together.

Kenny loves children. This is Anthony, Mary's son, when he was a baby.

Kenny and Kim at Spectrum School.

Kenny's birthday opening a package with friends looking on.

Kenny wants to be invisible when he does this.

A tantrum.

Graduation at 22 years old from special ed.

Kenny and Father Bain.

A mellow moment and a handsome guy at 26 years old.

Kenny lets Mary's kids do anything to him. He unbelievably left the Mickey Mouse ears and glasses on for a while. 27 years old.

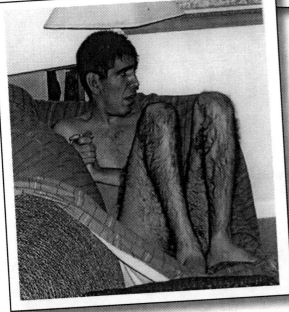

Meet Mr. Hyde – 28 years old.

THE BOY IN THE WINDOW
the boy in the window

CHAPTER
TWENTY-EIGHT

THE BOY IN THE WINDOW
the boy in the window

Kenny's tantrums are as common around this household as the days are long. The stress and anxiety of dealing with this one behavior in itself, has caused us much grief as parents. The fear that he will hurt himself is my main concern, though one might think that he would learn a lesson if he did. Unfortunately he doesn't think logically, and all three of us would have to suffer the consequences of the injury.

I know his tantrums are the result of his inability to express himself, and the miserable side effects from his seizures and medication. The combination of head-aches, irritability, and even his boredom builds up, and he lashes out at everything within his reach!

The worst part is he won't let me console him in any way, not with words, hugs, or even bribes. *Hey Kenny, if you stop being a bad boy, Mommy will give you a cookie!*

My heart breaks because I can't make him feel better, and at the same time, I hate it when he resorts to these episodes. He wants to deal with his suffering in his own way, which is the wrong way!

Many might think, "Well if you would have done this or that when he was younger, he wouldn't be acting like a spoiled brat." And that might be easy for some to say, and indeed, there could be truth to that statement. But people don't realize the strong will he has always possessed, and how exhausting raising a child like him has been. I know we utilized every type of behavior management available to us during those crucial years.

First, there was the time out. Then, along came rewarding good behavior with food snacks. We tried ignoring the bad behavior, with no eye contact. And then we were told to restrain him when all else failed. And last, but definitely not least, we used Pat's concept of baby time - the holding close and rocking. I am sure there were other tactics we resorted to in dealing with his problems, but it is too hard to remember them all.

Today there is so much more knowledge on what to do in the early stages of brain dysfunction. Unfortunately, he is too acclimated in his behaviors to change at the age of 28, even if there was a new incredible procedure to try! By taking on the challenge of attempting any alterations at this point in his life, might expose that person to peril!

But Kenny does have severe brain damage that obviously causes obnoxious behavior, and the inability to exercise logic. And the frequency of his seizures only exacerbates his problems.

This is my own theory, and it helps to keep Kenny in my good graces when he is playing the role of Mr. Hyde!

There is also emptiness in his life now, because he needs a program that would incorporate ongoing stimulation for his brain, and believe me, I've looked everywhere within the parameters, and it's not out there!

If a good day school came along that was competent enough to serve all of his needs, and keep him safe, I would welcome that opportunity for him with all of my heart.

I felt determined that he desperately needed a continuation of social skills, and a good learning environment! So I decided to look into the possibilities of opening a program myself, not only for Kenny's sake, but for other handicapped young adults fresh out of school.

I had devised a plan of activities and teaching based on the curriculum of Pat's school, that Kenny attended in Marin. I took the license day care training, which was the first step. I had a qualified behaviorist who would have represented our establishment with her services, along with the required degree. I had Mary and several others in the respite line of work that wanted to be a part of our adventure. And we would have counted on clients from the Regional Center for the most part.

My husband and I would have had to front the financial obligation for at least three months before receiving funds from the Center. The regulations were that all permits and inspections had to be done in the accepted location, previous to opening the day care. I had even found a site that I envisioned with new paint and décor.

And at just about that time, the economy took a turn for the worst and the talk was that the Regional Centers were going to be cut drastically! There were no guarantees for us, and it was just too risky. I was so disappointed, I worked hard on writing out the format of the program and I talked many hours to people in the business for advice on getting through the basics. I would have had some very good people working as staff and aides to the students in the day school. My program would have included an abundance of self-help skills, some scholastics, gardening, art projects, basic cooking, dancing, horseback riding, bowling, newsworthy topics, job training for those capable, and a very important factor missing in the life of many handicapped people, exercise!

Lack of healthy exercise has been a huge problem as Kenny got older. I actually used to make him run alongside of me when he was much younger a few times a week. It was part of the Doman program. But now, walking through stores is about the extent of his exertion.

There was a time when it worried me so much about his body's need for physical strengthening, beyond his tantrums that I decided to sign him up at a local gym that had a heated pool for some water aerobics. One of the respite girls would go with me to escort Kenny, usually Malia, or Mary, or both.

This was no easy feat, because it was something new for him, but I felt if we could just get him into the water, the battle would be half over. Though he didn't reach out or grab any of the participants at the gym, his typical behaviors attracted too much negative attention. He could be loud and pushy with us until we got him in the water. Once we succeeded in that he was fine, and he enjoyed splashing around. What I didn't figure on was the extremely obvious annoyance of the employees. There was no empathy in any form and it was made quite clear to us that we were not welcome. There were whispers and staring in disbelief amongst the staff, a typical attitude that I was so familiar with that I had become unscathed by it, but was very aware!

After a few weeks of taking Kenny to the gym, we were asked not to go any more and our membership was cancelled with a refund of our money! That was okay with me! Mainly, because it was a bigger pain in the neck getting him there and in the water, then the aggravation he caused the employees!

I told someone I knew about my brilliant idea for Kenny that didn't work out, because of Kenny's unpopularity amongst the gym owners and employees. She told her attorney friend. He wanted to use our situation to set a precedent for the handicapped in a discriminatory lawsuit against the gym.

Instead, I talked my husband into putting a pool in our backyard. Once we got it heated with the solar power, Kenny got a lot of enjoyment in the water. Especially when he was younger, the life jacket allowed him the freedom to splash and jump around.

Today, if we can get him in at all, he will stand in the shallow end and stoop until the water covers his shoulders. He stays in one spot, and it appears as if he is sitting on an invisible chair. It is truly a comical sight to behold, yet at the same time it tugs at my heartstrings.

But as much as I have mourned in awful silence for my son through the years, I have equally believed in small miracles of healing for him. Maybe not in totality, but I will always welcome any improvement that would make life better for him, (and us!)

During the most dreadful times of seeing him suffer with seizures, I have often thought of Lourdes in France. Of course the trip itself would probably prove to be more impossible than the actual healing that might occur if we went.

On the news one night, there was a story about a priest that had certain powers. It seemed he could help or cure those ailing with hands-on-healing sessions. We were able to bring Kenny to him at a church in Marin County, which was about fifty minutes away or more, depending on the dreaded traffic. I was thrilled to be able to take him to the Catholic Priest. I knew Kenny had his own faith in God from reading his words about Jesus.

Kenny seemed to melt under the hand of Father Bain and experienced such a sense of well-being that we were amazed. We continued to take him to visit several times a month, and Kenny was more than willing to go, in spite of the drive.

Each time he responded to the warm touch the same way, by slumping down in his chair, as if he had been given an instant sedative.

He and the Father became good buddies, and Kenny went three months during that period of time without a seizure. But eventually, the priest had to retire from a terrible illness, (not caused by Kenny) and we missed him in our lives. He was a very compassionate man of God.

Today we continue to deal with Kenny's tantrums the best we can, mostly by ignoring them, and that seems to settle him down quicker than anything else we have tried in the past.

When I hear the familiar crashing sound of the table being thrown over upstairs, I know he has shed his clothes and will be going after the clean laundry next. Our house doesn't have a good venting system for our dryer, and the clothes come out damp. I have to spread them over the cabinet counter in the hallway right next to his room. I wash at least six loads in a day, so there is usually a huge pile of sheets, towels, pants, shirts, etc.

I used to rush up the stairs and salvage as much of the laundry as possible before he started flinging them over the banister. But that only made him angrier, until I realized the act was therapeutic for him. Now I just wait until he has thrown everything down the stairs. Then I start gathering the clothes from the entry, the living room, on plants, and sometimes the chandelier over the stairs, or wherever else they might have landed. I shake off any dust that might be on each piece and begin the tedious job of folding.

There have been several occasions he has thrown breakables over, but I learned to remove all fragile items within his reach, mainly myself!

Once, during one of these tantrums, he frustratingly ran up and down the stairs with that haunting look of desperation on his face! I knew he wanted to communicate something so badly, but we didn't have a clue as to what it might have been, as usual!

At one point, he darted to my large bookcase in the open area upstairs, where hundreds of books are tightly shelved. He reached for two books and threw them down the stairs. I assumed it was a random act, until I read the titles. One was called, "There is a Boy in Here," and the other read, "Emergency!"

Why doesn't he understand that we love him so much and would do anything in the world to help him? But instead, sometimes Kenny's behavior toward us makes me feel as if we were the "maddening" parents he has to contend with!

If only he hadn't lost interest in the most important triumph of his life, which was the communication through facilitating. Of course all of the favorite people that he enjoyed sharing his thoughts with the most, had all moved on long before school was out. Mary has done some work with him on occasion, but it is a battle to get him motivated.

It isn't in the daily routine now, though I would give anything if he let me do FC with him everyday. But then, who wants to confide in their mom at his age? My dreams of an easier to manage Kenny, with a brighter future ahead of him because of his brilliance, were now only sweet memories.

I should just be grateful he has made it through these 28 years in one piece, with the assorted calamities and close calls he has had with everyone!

I will never forget the time I read his answers to questions about Marine World with Kim. "How did the elephant feel Kenny?" "Hard," he replied. I was shocked to find out Kenny had been on the elephant ride with her! Something I never would have agreed to let him do!

Once, a woman ran in to pay a bill, leaving Kenny in her parked car close by. This was a no, no! She thought it would be easier than dragging him inside. When she came out, she screamed when the car was not in the spot where she left it!! It was backing down toward the main street with Kenny inside! He evidently either touched the parking brake out of panic, or perhaps she forgot to put the brake on. Thank God she got in the car in time, and that I didn't find this out until years later. Mary knew her well and didn't want to tattle!

At a mall, a respite person was looking after Kenny while I did some errands there, (shopping). Kenny got away from her and laid himself across the top of a downward escalator. She was barely able to pull him away. Luckily no body parts got trapped. Another tale I didn't hear for many years. This was another person Mary knew, and she thought I would be angry.

Kenny has locked himself in Mary's car twice after she got out for a moment, leaving the keys on the seat.

He has gotten in the wrong car several times after letting go of someone's hand coming out of a store. Luckily, the cars were vacant each time! Good thing, because a person might have thought Kenny was a car jacker!

When he was about thirteen, and still fast as a lizard's tongue, I was upstairs and heard a continuous honking of a car horn. I couldn't figure out where it was coming from. It was extremely nerve racking! I ventured downstairs and outside, ready to play cloak and dagger. I immediately saw my husband running toward the house next door to us.

In that moment, Kenny flew out of their garage just in time as the heavy door was coming down. Ken grabbed him and found out that Kenny had run into the garage as the neighbors pulled in. They were always scared to death of Kenny, and when they saw him they hurried inside their house! He then jumped in their car when they got out and leaned on the horn. I don't know at what point they pushed the button to the garage door, or what made him get out of the car.

I immediately cancelled my husband as a sitter, who was supposed to be keeping an eye on Kenny while he was washing the car.

An older woman, who was not used to taking Kenny out in public too much, though he was very good for her, had a very embarrassing moment at a crowded store with him. They were walking while he held on to the cart. She soon started noticing he was walking very slowly, as if dragging his feet. She pondered it, but didn't understand why until someone approached her, pointing out that Kenny was about to lose his pants! They had come down considerably enough to constrict his legs.

Kenny has caused quite a stir through the years, so much that I could base the whole book on funny things he's done, or public attention he's drawn, and not the good kind, either!

Someone, who stands out in my mind, that remembered me chasing after Kenny at the Benicia Park when he was just a little guy, was a psychologist I consulted with five years ago. I had personal issues going on other than Kenny, and I wanted some professional advice. I didn't know her, but as I started talking about my life, she said she recalled watching a rambunctious, fast moving little boy and his loving mother, who to her had the patience of a "saint." I was so amazed and flattered to be remembered in that way after some 16 years ago. People just don't forget Kenny, ever!

CHAPTER
TWENTY-NINE

THE BOY IN THE WINDOW

*K*enny does not wake up in the morning and ask himself, "How obstinate and irritating can I be for everyone today?" He isn't capable of planning his emotions. Instead, he wistfully rises to face his formidable challenges each and every day.

I cheerily greet him, sneak some kisses, change him, and guide him with my arm around his shoulders to his favorite room, cautiously, to be sure there are no stumbles, (a sign of upcoming seizures), and sit him down. I wait until he is fully coherent from the seizure medication's drug induced sleep before attempting to take him to the bathroom, and then downstairs for breakfast.

I can usually tell if he will have a good or bad day by his willingness to smile, or by his contrariness. If he looks a little pasty, chances are he will have a seizure that day.

When I see that look, I still accomplish whatever tasks that confront me from sunrise to sunset, but with dispiritedness abiding. The worry over him is just as much a part of my life as breathing!

Throughout the book I have mentioned his discerning vehemence towards me at times, but it is not out of vengeance. It is because I represent his unconditional security, no matter what behaviors are displayed with its driving force!

It may not be apparent in the traditional way, but I know that he loves me. I am the person in his life who will be there for him, and will continue to love him, no matter what!

I am the one he calls for before he leaves the house with the caregivers in the morning, and I reassure him I will be here when he gets home. He calls for me when he is ill, "Ba Ba." He calls for me if he is unsure of a situation, etc. And sometimes he'll just keep repeating, "Ba Ba, Ba Ba" before he goes off with Mary or Alicia. It is similar to a small child going off to pre-school, knowing he will have more fun than if he stayed home, but experiencing some anxiety in leaving the protection of his world.

In his peculiarity when he is being affectionate, there are no real kisses or hugs. But when inclined, he will quickly lower his head toward your shoulder, which may include a brief touch of his hand too. It is his way of expressing thanks, because the caretaker is either leaving, or taking him somewhere he enjoys going. It can mean peace offerings if he has been naughty and doesn't want you mad at him. Or it can be a spontaneous gesture out of the blue, but it his way of showing that he cares.

Sometimes, he takes your face with his hand, bends down to look you in the eye while telling you a very important thing, like "hom" or "com bak" as he shoves you out the door! These are his weird "terms of endearment."

There are so many times I wonder about the man he would have turned out to be, had it not been for the devastation he suffered from the vaccination when he was a baby.

I know he would have been very intelligent, extremely so, as is his sister. I know he would have had a successful career and would have been a loving husband, father, brother, and son. I know these things from the bottom of my heart, as well as I know the suffering he has gone through.

Anyone who thinks that vaccinations are harmless is in denial. For all those who think there is no correlation between vaccines and autism, seizures, developmental delays, and brain damage, they have not taken the time to explore the multitude of staggering information available to the public.

As far back as April, 1987, the *Democrat and Chronicle* newspaper in Rochester, N.Y. printed a five-part series to help enlighten parents, called "Children at Risk: The DPT Dilemma."

The reporter, Jennifer Hyman uncovered chilling information during her investigation. She learned of doctors who wouldn't give the vaccine to their own children. She found a group of California doctors who were illegally importing a safer vaccine in from Japan for their patients. (Thank God that today this vaccine is available here in the United States in some clinics). She learned that doctors weren't informing parents about the possible side effects or what to do if they occurred. She learned that the existing vaccine's profitability, as well as a lack of funding for research, had combined to prevent safer vaccines from being tested and approved in this country. She talked to many anguished parents whose children had died or suffered permanent brain damage from the shot. (Like Kenny!)

Of all the vaccines given to American children, the one that produces the greatest number of reactions, other than fever, is the pertussis. These range from mild swelling, pain and fever, to seizures, convulsions, high-pitched screaming, shock, brain damage-and---death. Many vaccine deaths were written off as SIDS, Sudden Infant Death Syndrome.

The vaccine is so reactive because it is extremely crude. It contains not only the components necessary to produce immunity to whooping cough, but also toxic substances and impurities secreted by the bacterial organism that causes the disease.

402

By contrast, a safer, purified vaccine manufactured in Japan has all the bacteria and most of the toxins removed or rendered harmless.

American vaccine is called "whole cell" because it is cultured, or grown, in large vats from whole cells of pertussis bacteria. The bacteria are then killed but remain in the solution. The resulting vaccine contains endotoxins, as well as pertussis toxin that remain biologically active after the bacteria that secretes it has been killed.

Endotoxin is a protein secreted by a virus or bacteria that can, in large enough quantities, affect the brain or produce shock in certain people. It is the substance thought to be responsible for immediate, neurological reactions in some children.

According to a pediatric immunologist and active campaigner against whole-cell vaccine, there is up to 10,000 times as much endotoxin in pertussis vaccine than adults are allowed to get in influenza vaccine.

The FDA could not limit the amount of endotoxin because they couldn't produce whole cell pertussis vaccine without it. They knew it was a problem, and the only alternative was to produce a new vaccine.

The other vaccine component responsible for neurological reactions is the pertussis toxin. It can take longer to work on the nervous system, causing reactions up to 30 days after a DPT shot. It is suspected of activating other allergic conditions. And it might also suppress the immune system, making children vulnerable to infections.

The Japanese vaccine is called "acellular" because it is made outside the pertussis bacteria. Once the bacteria have been grown in a culture, they are removed and culture purified. Most of the endotoxins are removed, and the remaining extract is chemically treated to reduce toxicity.

Recently, in March of 2006, the *Contra Costa Times* headline read, "Vaccine Study Findings Fuel Debate over Autism." This study was done at UC Davis, where researchers linked a mercury-containing preservative, once prevalent in children's vaccines, to immune system dysfunction in mice.

The findings heightened the debate over the increasing number of autism, and the effects thimerosal, (mercury preservative) has on the cells. They have pinpointed the cell in the nervous system that mercury attacks. And for some, the most minute amount can cause damage, especially in a six-week-old infant, as the nervous system has not developed. Manufacturers use it to prevent fungal and bacterial contamination in multi-dose vials, which is how the DPT was packaged. It isn't needed in individually packaged doses, a more expensive method.

Manufacturers were supposed to remove thimerosal from children's vaccines in 1999 when the American Academy of Pediatrics and the U.S. Public Health Service urged them to do so as a precautionary measure.

The recommendation came after the Food and Drug Administration determined that children who received the full set of recommended immunizations could accumulate doses of mercury exceeding Environmental Protection Agency guidelines.

They say today that most children's vaccines in the United States contain only trace amounts of the preservative. The one exception is the flu shot, which is available with and without thimerosal, although the thimerosal is more prevalent.

The drug companies deny that their vaccines cause autism to try to evade lawsuit liability, just as the cigarette companies denied that smoking caused lung cancer in the last century.

I personally believe there is still a toxic amount of mercury in vaccines, and it is causing the epidemic of autism. I wish I had known about this menace all those years ago. I wish I had followed my instincts and disregarded the regulations about the vaccinations. I wish, I wish, I wish!!!

Following is a poem that I wrote regarding my pregnancy with Kenny and his tragedy:

Son

Unfolding in my universe,

Although a meager place,

Where once was just emptiness,

Has filled with love's embrace.

So wondrous in its dwelling,

So warm and safe inside,

Abounds a tiny seedling,

With a journey to abide.

In silky, waxen, webbing,

Suspended to a hum,

The heart in rhythmic motion,

sustains this little one.

And I had vowed to cradle,

Once brought forth to meet its strife,

To lavish all I had to give,

Upon this newborn life.

Endearing in my effort,

To keep him free from ill,

Not knowing, in a moment,

Of the venom's fleeting kill.

Casting shadows on perfection, which

God bestowed upon my grace,

Is now the everlasting light,

That shines upon his face.

THE BOY IN THE WINDOW
the boy in the window

CHAPTER THIRTY

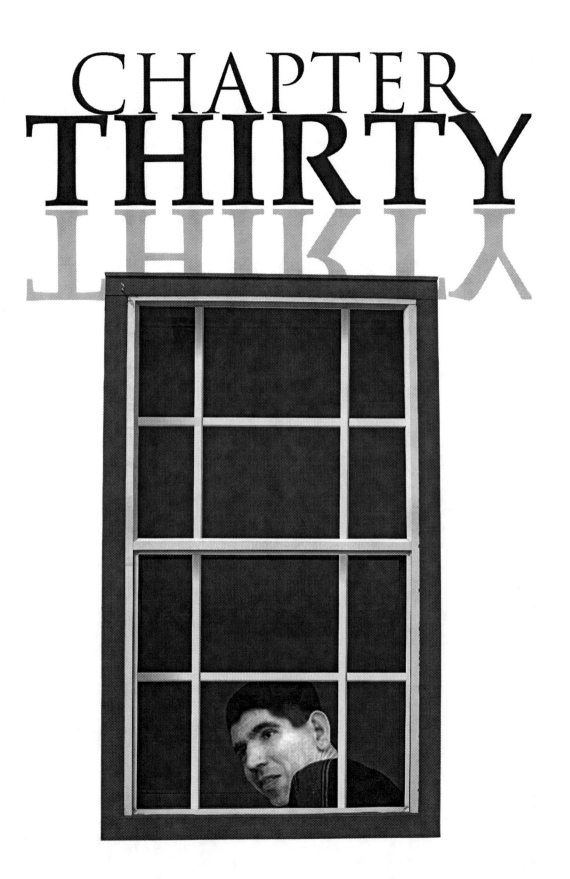

I have faced many of life's ravaging challenges; Kenny's tragedy and the daily strife because of it, losing my mom and other loving family members, a devastatingly drawn out lawsuit, and a business bankruptcy!

I also confronted my own personal demon that came in the form of panic attacks after I had my wisdom teeth pulled. I remember being very afraid of having to take the drugs given for partial sedation before the procedure. I discussed my fears with the dentist previous to the date of the extractions. I knew I had been under so much stress with my life at home, and that the lawsuit alone had taken a toll. I worried how my body would respond to the drugs, not being one to even take Aspirin unless out of absolute necessity. It was as if I was having another premonition, but the dentist said it would be best not to put it off any longer. I was close to 50, and he said "the older you get, the more difficult the healing process is."

Most people go home and sleep after having this type of dental work done, but I felt like running a race! I was told to take Sudafed for the following week, I don't recall why. At about that time I called 911 after I experienced symptoms of what felt like a heart attack, though I had never had one before. The paramedic took my vitals and told me that I had a panic attack, not a heart attack. "What the heck is that?" I asked. The Kaiser doctor prescribed sedatives after physical problems were ruled out, but I declined the drugs.

I had more attacks at home, and was catapulted into a consistently "panicked" state of mind. I started my research on this disorder. I was relieved to find out it was not some mental break down, which I had already ruled out anyway. I know myself too well! But I also knew it was something pretty scary, and I was going to get to the bottom of it.

I learned it can happen out of the blue, usually to those with certain personality types, such as those who strive to be perfectionists, (that didn't fit me, did it?) Sensitive people, (that fit). It can also be hereditary, or, it can be brought on by a drug or combination of drugs, which I believe is what happened in my case. The Sudafed, on top of the anesthetics they used during the extractions, was more than my system could handle. When I started hyperventilating and couldn't breathe, I felt a fear of losing control and a feeling of impending disaster hovering over me! It was so frightening and cumbersome.

But I was not about to let this unyielding condition get the best of me. I discovered and enrolled in a workshop called "TERRAP," (It was located in Walnut Creek at the time) that promised a cure, if you followed their methods, which I did. It was not inexpensive and it certainly wasn't easy to take on this additional hardship. My focus was to rid myself of this debilitating "thing," and return to my "normal" life. That looked as appealing to me as a million dollars!

I worked extremely hard on the homework that was given out after each weekly class. I am just touching on the subject of panic attacks, phobias, etc., but de-sensitization was the basis of the program. Bio-feedback was taught in order to calm an over-stimulated nervous system. That was the key to both facing and breathing properly through the attacks. It took almost two years of learning how to apply what I learned to rid myself once and for all of the devastating symptoms, and reach the understanding there was nothing physically wrong with me.

Anyone who has suffered any length of time with this disorder will agree it affects your whole life, as well as those in it. I needed to be strong for my son, who depended on me, and I was successful.

Kaiser offers a similar program, called "The Phobease Way." It is taught by a doctor who took the course at TERRAP long before I did. He decided to offer this class because he said it literally "saved" his life. He previously had suffered for 31 years from this devastating affliction.

But nothing I have ever faced or experienced can compare to the burden of knowing that I will not be here some day to care for Kenny. My immortality hangs over me like a shrouded veil, and it's hard to bear that reality! I just can't imagine how Kenny will manage without me. *How will he deal with the loss of the person who has been by his side throughout his whole life, and who loves him more than life itself?*

About fifteen years ago, a woman, Betty, who I mentioned in an earlier chapter, passed away. Her son Chris was five years older than Kenny, and suffered with Cerebral Palsy, and daily seizures. Chris was also non-verbal, and, unlike Kenny, very slow moving. The four of us went to the zoo, and parks together or just visited. The two boys seemed to enjoy each other, in their own ways.

After Betty died, Chris would go out to the garage and sit in their car every day for weeks. He cried and cried while calling for his mother. The loss of her was so devastating for him.

His sister, Michelle, who now cares for him, could hardly bare the pain of seeing him so distraught, knowing he did not understand where his mother had gone or why.

When I pictured that heartbreaking scene, I never could erase it from my mind. I not only missed Betty, but I hurt so badly for Chris. I wanted to scream, and cry, and rant and rave each time I visualized Kenny experiencing that same pain.

Kenny's world is about routine and the deviation from that routine can result in strange behavior, as we all know by now.

I remember the first night of a week-long raft trip his dad went on, when Kenny was 25. Ken went every year, but for some reason Kenny couldn't deal with it this particular time!

He was used to doing puzzles every night with his dad before bedtime, and that was a big part of the evening. I did everything but stand on my head, of course to entertain him, but he wasn't buying any of it! Nothing substituted the ritual with his departed dad.

That night I could not get him to go to bed when it was time, no matter how hard I tried. Very late in the evening I called my neighbor Myson to see if he could help me get Kenny's pajamas back on that he had stripped off, and get him in bed. But Kenny became combative and went into a tantrum. Myson felt so bad that he couldn't help. He said just make the house warm and to call him, even if it was just for moral support. (We couldn't have asked for better neighbors.) Kenny sat in his chair at the window all night long, stark naked.

It was so terrible because he had never stayed up all night long before, and there was nothing I could do. I turned the heater on and lie in my bed, getting up every half hour to see if he had fallen asleep so I could at least cover him. But his eyes remained opened all night long, glued to that window, hoping to see a glimpse of his dad returning. His body felt cold, even with the heat on high. I was in and out of my bed so much that night I was a zombie the next day. We were both exhausted and he had a seizure.

The fear of that night haunts me. All I would need in my life is a naked mad man consistently refusing to go to bed. Any behavior with Kenny can easily become a habit, and most of them did during his life.

The following year, and each one thereafter, when Ken goes on his trips, I make sure Mary is available to help me manage Kenny and get him in bed before she leaves. She threatens to spend the night if he gets out of bed. That is definitely not in his routine, so it works!

Mary says she will take care of him if and when something should happen to us, though she is only too glad to bring him home after having him for a weekend! Mary used to come to our house and sleep here, if we were lucky enough to get away for two days. Kenny had to be in his own bed. When Mary told us how good he was while we were gone, I realized how beneficial it was for Kenny to have a break from us on a consistent basis, and we from him. I have ventured more in these last few years than ever before. And that only amounts to one weekend a month, sometimes two. I had to force myself in the beginning, but it has been Kenny's emancipation and a real break for us, thanks to Mary!

Kenny gradually surrendered to staying at Mary's house over night while we were away. Now he is comfortable with that sleeping arrangement. He usually enjoys himself because of the many family members and friends that come and go, which entertain him a great deal when he is there. If he is going to have a seizure, or has had one recently, he would just as soon be home. It is hard to leave him, even knowing he will be well cared for.

Letting go has been very difficult for me, but I also realize it helps prepare Kenny a little for a future without us in it.

Visiting our friends, Keith and Jeanne, who moved to Sonora, a two and a half hour drive from Vallejo, has given me a taste of relaxation without interruptions. Not to mention the fun we have when the four of us get together. It has been our therapy! They mean so much to Ken and I. Through the years they have supported us and praised us so much for our endeavor with Kenny, making us feel as if we were the world's greatest parents. They lost their son Kevin years ago in a tragic work-related accident, and know first hand what grief is.

Rhonda knew Keith and Jeanne before we did. She used to baby sit for Kevin and his sister Darla when they were just kids. We lived on Keats Drive then, and the Douglas's were two blocks away. Ironically, we didn't meet them until the four of us showed up at the same time one day to inspect the progress of our new homes being built on Lancaster Way. We all introduced ourselves as prospective neighbors. *It is a small world after all!*

Undoubtedly, we have a living trust for Kenny and provisions for the best possible care, but people's lives change, and there are no guarantees. So, while we have bequeathed our only son to Mary, (isn't she lucky?) If her health fails, we hope that her daughter Kassie, or her niece Samantha will take over. We joke about that now, but the Benitez family would be able to live in our house, as long as they can take care of Kenny. He would be in his own home, which is his comfort zone. Since her children are so used to Kenny, and have been around him from the time they were born, he is like a part of their clan. I am so grateful to the whole family for always treating Kenny like one of their own.

It would be too much of a burden for our daughter to care for Kenny, and we wouldn't expect that of her. For most of his life she has lived out of the area, and worked full time as a nurse.

Rhonda suffered a loss, in more ways than one, when Kenny was hurt as a baby. She was an only child who lost the chance to have a normal relationship with her sibling. At a time when parental guidance was so crucial to a young teenage girl, we were preoccupied with the overwhelming task of caring for her brother. I'm sure she had frustrations of her own to cope with that she, herself, didn't understand. And though I know she loves him, the extremities of his needs would be too hard for her to bear. She already has a family to care for, and a responsible job.

Mary has been with Kenny on a regular basis since he was about 12. She had chosen to work with the challenged, long before Kenny came into the picture. Caring for the handicapped is a talent, and takes a special person to do it, unless you are a parent of the child, and wasn't given a choice. But even then, some mothers and fathers are not always able to live with the unmanageable.

No doctors have been able to tell us the longevity of Kenny's life at this point. Other than the seizures, which are a major factor, he seems healthy, and doesn't get sick very often. I believe the care he receives after we are gone will be the deciding factor on that issue. Lord knows he couldn't get better care anywhere else as long as we're alive!

We hope our daughter will oversee Kenny's trust fund and his well-being. If she moved away, Ken's brother, George, would assist if he was still living. If necessary, a court appointed person would step in to assure all is being carried out per our request for Kenny. It hurts so much to even write about these things, and there is no end to the worries that bombard me about this inevitable destiny.

My biggest fear is that he could end up institutionalized. I pray to God that never happens. Who would put up with my son's obstinacy? We love the part baby, boy, genius, and devil that mysteriously parade around in a man's body, no matter what role he's in! But we are his parents! No one will ever love him like we do.

I know if he ended up in some crowded hell hole he would be filled with sedatives and worse. I'm sure somewhere there are decent care homes, but the percentages are not in his favor.

Only those that know Kenny well will remember all of the funny and humorous things he does that continue to make us laugh out loud. His Aunt Nancy especially looks forward to hearing about Kenny's capers from his answers to questions with the FC, to the silly shenanigans he has pulled, most of them without forethought!

One in particular that has made us smile so often was two Halloweens ago when a four year old rang our door bell to trick or treat. Kenny opened the door before we could, and when the child said "trick or treat" Kenny reached down and grabbed his bag of candy and ran off to the kitchen with it!

There was also the time I decided I was going to give him a nice pedicure and placed his feet, not easily, into the special foot spa filled with a little warm water. I had to press on his two knees to keep his feet firmly planted. After a few seconds, I turned the massager on and he literally flew out of his seat from fright!

Once, when he was still running nonstop, he ran inside Myson's house next door, and Barbara, his wife, had just changed her clothes and turned around to find Kenny standing in the doorway to her bedroom! It scared her half to death!

When he was younger, and I had taken him to a park, he ran past a woman pushing her baby in a buggy and put his brakes on long enough to snatch the blanket off the baby, much to the dismay of the mother. I was so glad it wasn't the baby!

But even today, when Kenny smiles that broad ear to ear smile at me, every naughty thing he has ever done, including all of the plates of food he has thrown on our many carpets that I worked so diligently on trying to remove the stains, go by the wayside. He fortunately has had the ability to always capture my heart, not my anger. No one can stay mad at him for any length of time. *Gotta love him!!!*

We still continue to have ongoing debates with the Regional Center. The arguments are usually about trying to maintain the quantity of hours of respite care they provide for us. If it were not for that help, my husband and I would probably have been institutionalized ourselves!

Budget cuts for these centers are constantly threatened, and the fear of losing respite hours has been imminent many times. We contribute financially toward the salaries of our caregivers to make up for a minimum wage. But we could not afford to have the help we do without this lifesaving service.

We are grateful to our Regional Center, and Kenny has been represented by a wonderful case worker for a long time now, Mike, who is so understanding and compassionate. He always goes to bat for us.

My husband made several good changes early on in the policies of the Center, and recently they were negotiating another crucial change, which would have diverted more money to office people by delegating the paperwork that was currently being done by parents. Ken refused to make the changeover, and asked for a mediator to represent him, who happened to be a judge. He pointed out the financial burden to the budget, and told her that any excess money the center has should go to the caregivers, who deserve it.

Ken was exemplified through this endeavor, and complimented on how wonderful it was to see such caring parents. He has thought about being on the Board of Directors, but he has his hands full as it is.

Although the cohesion of the respite people through the years has been out of necessity, it has not been easy having strangers in and out of our home. There is an invasion of privacy that cannot be avoided, and people tend to judge, scrutinize, and criticize as they cannot fathom the whole picture of our life in a few hours a day.

For many of the respite girls, I have been a sounding board and an advisory for those who brought their own set of problems into our lives. I have been kind, generous, and accommodating to all well-intentioned caregivers, even when I wasn't treated as such in return.

There are those that have not been able to cope with my sometimes over-protectiveness of Kenny. I sound like a broken record with my repetitious instructions, especially about his medicine and safe driving. But when someone gets to know me, they realize it is about my genuine concern for Kenny, not a power struggle. If Kenny is extremely happy with someone, I have had the ability to overlook almost anything, except his safety, and I tried to focus on whatever quality of livelihood that person could offer him.

We are extremely fortunate, at this point in Kenny's life, to have two wonderful people assisting him, Mary, of course, and Alicia. I have good breaks now during the day and it is greatly needed, especially because of our questionable evenings at home with our adult son, who doesn't think he should have to go to bed when his parents do!

Up until about six months ago Kenny was going to bed about 8 or 9pm. He watched the children play outside, viewing them from his window. Once it got dark and the children went inside, he remained looking out into the stillness until he decided to call us for bed. "Bea, Bea!" He would yell out. And by the time dinner, his shower, snack time, puzzles, toileting, diapering, medicine taking, and teeth brushing was over, the sound of "Bea, Bea" was quite welcoming!

Of course many times we would find that he had quietly gotten out of bed, stripped, and going upstairs to check on him, I would find the naked young man at the window. Once again we would redress him, or try, and stick him back in bed. During the course of the night he would repeatedly throw off his blankets, and sometimes the sheets on the floor. He also took off his pj's again. At least this was not happening every night.

But now, our evenings have become the most difficult part of the day because his obstreperous behavior reaches its peak when we are tired and vulnerable, and because he has decided to become a night owl. He resists going to bed. *Remember my fear?*

So far, his pajamas still remain on, most of the time. We start trying around 10:30, then 11:00, and when he comes running toward us with his fist in his mouth, and if I am within reach, he grabs my arm and starts shaking it vigorously, (ouch!!!) we know he is not ready for bed yet!

Now that he is staying up later and later, the evening is long and boring for him, and he tries to entertain himself by constantly calling or shrieking out the names of people he knows: "Caw, Caw," for Alicia, "Ree, Ree," for Mary, "Com bak, com bak," "hom, hom," for home and "Au, Au," for his Aunt Nancy! It is repetitive and as loud as a quarterback calling out signals at a visiting stadium!

My wheels have been turning about the possibility of hiring someone to come over and spend a few hours in the evening with Kenny. I know he is bored and we feel so sorry for him. I want someone to do scholastic work with Kenny again. He desperately needs to use his brain more. I would love to see him participate in communicative skills like he used to. It has been a very long time since he answered questions or did math and telepathy on a regular basis.

For now, we brought the extra television downstairs and put it in the living room, where he has settled into, along with the late hours. He doesn't watch TV, but I felt the sound of people talking, and background music might help keep him company. Naturally he doesn't want to sit in the family room with us and he won't let me sit in there with him.

At least I can check on him more readily, and I don't have to run up and down the stairs all evening. And he has learned how to get comfy on the couch, lying back with his feet up. It beats those office chairs he sits on when he looks out his window. He is getting smart in his old age after all.

Alicia, our afternoon person, told us that her daughter Kamaile who recently moved here, was interested in coming over in the evenings. She is 25 and very pretty. Kenny already knows her, and likes keeping an eye on her when Alicia takes him to her dad's house to visit. Kenny also likes the dad and calls him "Guy!"

Kamaile is able to get Kenny to do anything she asks of him and he looks forward to her coming. He sits at the window after his shower and waits. She has come up with great ideas to entertain him on her own. She is doing games, crafts, and encyclopedia reading with him. After reading, she has him pick letters from the scrabble game to spell out words from the story. She is great! She lays out the letters and tells him to pick up the letters of the word she asked him to spell. From easy words to difficult, he picks up the little squares and puts them on the board. He spells each one correctly! Then several nights later, he started handing her the letters of the word she asked him to spell, just not in proper sequence, yet they were the letters of the word. Example: orange - he picked the letters r-a-g-n-e-o. He's amazing! I am so happy to see someone extract this knowledge from him again.

She is doing math by printing out the problem, and he points to one of five choices. I told her to use whatever means she wants in gaining information from him, no matter what the subject is.

She had started out slowly to test Kenny's abilities, and once again, they proved to be extraordinary! He is doing "yes" and "no" questions without FC. I think he is so glad to see her at night he would stand on his head if he could! Tonight, I will ask her to test his telepathy by using the scrabble method. He could pick the letters of the word she is thinking. He did it!!! My man still has it!!! He handed her the letters from the Scrabble squares and spelled out in order, "book" the word she thought of! I asked her how it made her feel and she said, "I still can't believe it happened. I feel so weird. But I know it did!" I told her I remembered feeling the exact same way when Kenny read my mind for the first time.

Kamaile has just been coming for two weeks as of this writing, and Kenny is fairly quiet and calm after she leaves at 8:30 pm. That has really been a nice change! Of course, he still won't go to bed when we do, which is about 11:00pm, so my husband says "Kenny, I'm going to bed and turning off all the lights, and you can just sleep on the couch all night!"

I wake myself up 35 or 45 minutes later, give Ken a little shove and he has to get out of bed and go back downstairs for Kenny. I can't sleep if I know Kenny is down there without covers and sitting up. I would get out of bed to try to get him myself, but since when has he ever listened to me? Ken still has to coax him as it is, but at least Kenny finally races up the stairs and begins the chanting of his favorite people again! When I hear him calling out those names, relief engulfs my tired body because I know he will get in bed. The chanting will last a while, maybe thirty minutes or more! But at least he's in his bed for the night! Hopefully!!!

Yes, real life's drama has not taken place on the evening news throughout the years, but in the sanctuary of our very own home!

I've been asked many times what keeps me going. Sometimes, I'm not really sure myself. It's a really hard question to answer! I do know during the times that I was the most exhausted, or felt that I couldn't stand another day like the one before I would picture myself as a soldier fighting, not to save a country, but the imprisonment of my own son! If I surrendered, I would lose not only Kenny, but everything of value he taught me about life, patience, love without expectations, and the strength to persevere.

I believe that people's lives are divinely orchestrated, no matter how chaotic it may seem. If we can understand that, we can embrace our existence, instead of hiding in fear.

I thank God for my family and friends, the power of prayer, and I do believe in miracles!

Printed in the United States
92767LV00003B/6/A